Screwed!

Screwed!

*How Foreign Countries Are
Ripping America Off and
Plundering Our Economy—
and How Our Leaders
Help Them Do It*

Dick Morris and Eileen McGann

An Imprint of HarperCollinsPublishers

HarperCollins books may be purchased for educational, business, or sales promotional use. For information please write: Special Markets Department, HarperCollins Publishers, 10 East 53rd Street, New York, NY 10022.

FIRST HARPERLUXE EDITION

HarperLuxe™ is a trademark of HarperCollins Publishers

Library of Congress Cataloging-in-Publication Data is available upon request.

ISBN: 978-0-06-220142-3

12 13 14 ID/RRD 10 9 8 7 6 5 4 3 2 1

To Eugene J. Morris (1910–2010),
an inspiration to us both . . . still

Contents

Screwed!

Introduction

"Just before the Chinese President was to
arrive in the U.S., a radio show host asked me
what I would say to him if I were President. I said
I would have told him to stay home. Don't come
here until you stop screwing us."
                                        Donald Trump, January 2011

America is being ripped off.

And our own leaders are not just complicit, they're actively assisting in the process.

A newly fashionable dogma of globalism—enthusiastic support for an economic and cultural view of "the world as one"—has supplanted a fundamental concern for the interests and needs of American citizens in the priorities of our national government. Instead, more and more, we are encouraged by the political and corporate power elite to view ourselves as citizens of the world, where international committees, not individual nations, make the rules that we must follow.

As if pride in our own country and a desire to maintain our democratic institutions is just some kind of knee-jerk nationalism by out of touch, embittered, old-fashioned, and cranky people.

This planetary imperative, inculcated in top schools and advocated by the bureaucratic elite, routinely supersedes our own domestic needs and led to one economic catastrophe after another, and, unfortunately, more are coming.

The fact is that we are increasingly ruled by an incestuous and institutionalized worldwide liberal bureaucracy. These so-called experts, who have led us off the cliff in the first decade of the twenty-first century, continue to command our obedience. And our elected officials won't defy them or even think for themselves.

In the globalist community, democracy is utterly unfashionable. These elites see voters as annoying masses who are simply too stupid to know what is really good for the world. Their contempt extends to our leaders: They view legitimately elected officials as dangerous demagogues exploiting their voters' credulity. They believe, instead, that career experts like themselves, trained at the top academies, weaned on Wall Street, and institutionalized in the bowels of government bureaus, are destined to rule the new world, telling us what to do, how to live, and dictating what we earn.

Everywhere we see the wreckage of their decisions. We see it in the rusting hulks of their favored banks and companies, the metastasizing cancer of personal bankruptcies filed by ordinary American families, and the flawed consequences of their misbegotten policies. As Talleyrand once said to the Bourbon kings of France, they "learn nothing and forget nothing" and constantly proffer the same discredited solutions.

And our own leaders won't stand up for our interests. Hypnotized by the beat of globalism, they throw away our prosperity, drive our own companies into insolvency, and strangle us with regulations and taxes to our competitive disadvantage.

Meanwhile, other nations focus only on their own self-interest. They laugh as our environmental regulations and labor laws put our own companies out of business and yield the playing field to them. They chant anti-American slogans and fund terrorists while raking in our foreign aid.

What's wrong with this picture?

Global institutions encroach on our national sovereignty, usurping decisions about our own economy, energy, environment, land, and businesses. When Cuba, Venezuela, and Russia drill off Florida shores while our own government won't grant US companies permits, we see a microcosm of what afflicts us.

It's time to stop this and reclaim our democracy, own sovereignty, and our common sense.

Because foreign countries and companies are exploiting us, right on our own soil. Many foreign countries want—and get—something concrete from us. In order to get what they want, more and more foreign governments are hiring influential lobbyists, usually former top bureaucrats or members of Congress, to shape American policy and American aid in their own particular interest. In 2009 and 2010, for example, foreign entities spent $487 and $460 million, respectively, on trying to influence Congress and the Obama administration and use the media to propagandize their point of view![1]

Even the late Muammar Gaddafi had a seat at the table, hiring a former Congressional leader to do his bidding.

It's no wonder that our foreign policies are so dysfunctional. In many cases, they are developed with the input of our enemies!

It's time to change the way things are done in Washington.

For at least the last sixty years, elite technocrats have determined our national and international policies.

They shuttle between government and academia, reveling in their shared assumptions and priorities, but never consulting us or caring much about what we think. Their elitist self-absorption has created a vast disconnect between the agenda of those who determine and administer our foreign policy and our collective national values.

This disconnect has led a majority of American voters into the grip of pessimism and despair, animated by a conviction that our nation has passed its peak.

A July 2011 poll conducted for *The Hill* found that 37 percent of likely voters believe America's best days are over and 62 percent think that we are being overtaken by other countries in important ways.[2]

This pessimistic view was prevalent in the views of a majority of voters in both major parties, as well as independent voters:

PERCENTAGE OF LIKELY VOTERS BY PARTY IDENTIFICATION THAT BELIEVE OTHER COUNTRIES ARE OVERTAKING THE US:

Republicans	70%
Independents	63%
Democrats	52%[3]

And America is no longer universally considered the strongest economy in the world. A February 2011 Gallup poll found that, for the first time, 52 percent of Americans identified China, not the United States, as the leading economic power in the world today.[4]

The lingering recession and economic uncertainty have contributed to a widespread and growing crisis of confidence in the American government. All across the United States, people in different walks of life no longer now believe that the federal government is developing and enacting national policies in their interest. In fact, in a July 28, 2011, poll conducted for *The Hill,* a majority of the respondents indicated that they believed that political decisions on the federal level actually have a negative effect on their lives.[5] Even more stunning is the finding in the Rasmussen poll during the same period that only 17 percent of Americans believe that "our government is governing with the consent of the governed."[6] This is a startling repudiation of the traditional long-standing covenant between the voters and the government and underscores the need for radical change.

This book will examine the ways in which nations and international organizations take advantage of us, expose the cost it imposes on us, and probe how our own leaders are complicit in the process. The book will identify many of the bureaucratic villains who have led us into the economic mess that we now face. It will recommend commonsense solutions to rectify the situation, end foreign exploitation, and make America's leaders put our needs first once more.

It's time to take back America.

Because, after all, it belongs to us.

PART ONE

A World Without Democracy; America Without Sovereignty

Government of the people, by the people, and for the people is on the verge of perishing from this earth. It is succumbing not to fascism or communism. It vanquished both of those formidable foes. Nor is it in danger of falling to Islamist extremism. Our increasing energy independence precludes that scenario.

Nor are we mortally threatened by dictatorships around the world. The tyrants who rule other countries are sitting, ultimately, on volcanoes that are ready to erupt at any minute. As Mubarak, Gaddafi, Milosevic, Hussein, and so many others have learned, the volcano remains quiescent for only so long. The current rulers in China, Russia, Iran, Venezuela, and Saudi Arabia should take note.

However, democracy is, still, under siege from its real enemy, bureaucracy: government by so-called experts. In each important sector of our lives, these experts are taking over, removing power from the hands of the governed, and always acting in what they perceive as our own best interest. But always without asking our permission.

As C. S. Lewis (quoted by Mark R. Levin in *Liberty and Tyranny*) pointed out, "regulation by do-gooders can be the most frightening of all tyrannies, a tyranny exercised for the good of its victims may be the most oppressive. It may be better to live under robber barons than under omnipotent moral busybodies. The robber baron's cruelty may sometimes sleep, his cupidity may at some point be satiated; but those who torment us for our own good will torment us without end, for they do so with the approval of their own conscience." Levin describes how the moral busybodies seek to oppress us with "soft tyranny," telling us what to do for our own good. And, as Lewis noted, they will "torment us without end" if we give them the chance.[1]

Look how far soft tyranny has advanced already!

We no longer control our nation's economy. The Federal Reserve Board does that.

And we no longer control the Federal Reserve Board. The International Monetary Fund (IMF), working through the G-20 group of nations, sets the policies that the Fed is obliged to follow.

We can't decide whether to go to war. The United Nations does that with its Russian and Chinese vetoes hanging over our head. Globalists are even trying to make the waging of a war without UN approval an international crime of aggression, and hold our leaders individually and criminally responsible if they commit it.

We don't control our trade policies. The World Trade Organization (WTO) does that, decreeing that we must have zero tariffs and let in every import, while China rigs its currency to undercut our prices.

We don't set our own manufacturing and energy policies. The climatologists and their green allies do that. They decree how much carbon we can emit, from what sources, and when we can do it. Meanwhile, India and China have increased their greenhouse-gas emissions by 10 percent a year in each of the last three years without sanction or consequence.

We don't control what our Congress does. The lobbyists and special interests do that, financing the campaigns of incumbents who do their work out of view, in committee, inserting clauses in fine print to serve their clients.

We don't control land use policies in our own communities. The global environmentalists do that, using UN treaties to structure decisions about what we can build and where our cities can grow.

We don't control our social policies. The courts do that, legislating from their lifetime appointments on the federal and state bench, unelected and unaccountable.

We don't control our borders. Nobody does that, and more than 12 million people live here illegally.

Meanwhile, internationally, bureaucrats of Western nations have coalesced into a major new drive for power, using international institutions to control the actions of nation-states. Not only do they now try to dominate decision making in their own countries, they want to erect a superstructure of control over all elected national leaders to supersede their authority.

Economists, diplomats, academics, sociologists, demographers, climatologists, international bankers and lawyers, and other elites feel they know what is best for us and are determined to override the decisions of our elected democracies to impose their visions on us.

The international bureaucrats, both American and European have one aim: to cripple the power of we the people of the United States. Ever since the end of the Cold War, they have come to see the unipolar world, dominated by the American democracy, as a dangerous thing. Unwilling to trust the American people with the tremendous power of global leadership, they are trying to marginalize the United States and subsume it within a superstructure of global governance.

To them, the prospect of depending on the wisdom of any democratic electorate is problematic. They see the US electorate as embracing cowboy capitalism, jingoist nationalism, and self-satisfied isolationism. Domestic bureaucrats and supposed international experts seek to ensnare us in a web of laws, regulations, and treaties—using what they call *soft power* to control us. We are like Gulliver being tied down by the Lilliputians.

Implicit in their entire global construct is the notion that these experts know best and that democracy is a poor substitute for their collective wisdom.

And we are cursed with a president who sees things their way. As Marion Smith of the conservative Heritage Foundation wrote: "The Obama Administration's direction on human rights and global engagement is consistent with the prevailing international mood. Pooled sovereignty is all the rage among governance experts and practitioners throughout Europe and elsewhere."[2]

"Pooled sovereignty?" What a ridiculous phrase. It is an oxymoron! Sovereignty means the power and control that a nation exercises over its own territory. By definition, it can't be pooled. And, even if it could be, we don't want to be!

Liberals are pressing for ratification of the Law of the Sea Treaty so that we won't run our coastline. The international community will do that, stripping us of the right to use the oceans at our borders as we wish.

They also want us to become part of the International Court of Justice so we won't run our own criminal justice system. The court will do that. Americans won't have the right to trial by jury in this court. Increasingly, international legal precedents find their way into US Supreme Court opinions.

BUREAUCRATS AND BANKERS TRIUMPHANT: HOW THE FED TOOK OVER THE ECONOMY

The erosion of our democratic control over our lives and our institutions starts at home, with the Federal Reserve Board. Nowhere is the ceding of democratic control to the elites more evident than in the charter, operations, and imperious unaccountability of the Fed.

The Federal Reserve's powers over the economy clearly exceed those of the president or Congress. It can raise or lower short-term interest rates at will. It determines the size of the money supply. As a regulator, it controls the vast majority of our nation's banks and, through the provisions of the newly enacted Dodd-Frank legislation, exercises formidable power over the banks and even the nonfinancial institutions it does not regulate.

The supremacy of the Federal Reserve, cemented in the wake of the current economic and fiscal crisis, reflects the victory of our domestic elites over popular government. The Fed is run by a fifteen-member board. Seven of them come from a self-perpetuating group of bankers, chosen by their fellow bankers, with no popular or political involvement. Eight members, including the chairman, are appointed by the president for fixed terms and subject to Senate confirmation. The insulation fixed terms gives the chairman of the Fed makes political control very tenuous and indirect.

The president's power of appointing the chairman of the Federal Reserve Board is more apparent than real. Whenever the chairman's term comes up, Wall Street clamors for his reappointment to shore up business confidence. They wonder, aloud, whether the president will throw Western civilization into chaos by naming his own man. Since 1953, we have had eleven presidents of the United States, but only five chairmen of the Federal Reserve (not counting G. William Miller, who served for only one year). Presidents Eisenhower, Kennedy, Johnson, Ford, Reagan, Bush 41, Clinton, Bush 43, and Obama have all been content to reappoint the chairman who was serving when they took office. These presidents differed with one another radically in their economic policies, but they all bowed to Wall Street when it came to naming the chairman of the Federal Reserve Board—the key economic policy-making position within their control. Presidents change their cabinet frequently and at will, but not the chairmanship of the Federal Reserve Board.

The battle between the experts and the people for control over the economy goes way back in American history.

In 1791, in President George Washington's first term, Treasury Secretary Alexander Hamilton and the ruling Federalist Party created the Bank of the United States largely at the behest of financiers and northeastern industrialists. Hamilton's philosophical and political rival, Thomas Jefferson, viewed the bank with suspicion, distrusting concentrated economic power.

As the bank's power grew, it began to conflict with the interests and needs of America's westward expansion. Pioneers wanted easy credit to buy land and put down stakes, but the bank was committed to high rates and limited credit. The same theme has recurred throughout our history: Those without money want easy credit to amass wealth, while those already financially endowed want tight money policies to protect it.

In the early 1830s, populist President Andrew Jackson from the then-frontier state of Tennessee struck back against the bank and its champion, Massachusetts Senator Daniel Webster. Jackson prevailed, warning that if one institution had control over the currency, credit, and the money supply, it would become an oligarchy strangling the economy and corrupting the government.

However, it soon became evident that Jackson had gone too far in killing the bank entirely, because there was nothing to take its place. Each state chartered its own banks, which fueled rampant speculation and currency instability. A disastrous depression followed in the late 1830s, and the economy hobbled along without a stable currency.

Pressed by the financial demands of the Civil War, Lincoln and Treasury Secretary Salmon Chase printed *greenbacks*, paper currency not backed by gold but by bonds sold to the public. Amid the exigency and urgency of the Civil War, the northern public accepted the greenbacks and bought the bonds that underpinned them.

But, as the Civil War ended, tight money policies returned. In 1863, Lincoln created federally chartered banks and, after Appomattox, Wall Street called upon the government to stop printing paper currency and return to a gold-only money supply.

These tight money policies, coupled with the high protective tariffs business demanded, enraged the farmers. They had to borrow money to buy feed, seed, fertilizer, and land, and then had to pay back these loans with ever-scarcer dollars, as the value of the currency increased. And, compounding their anger, they had to purchase household goods that were more and more expensive because of the high tariffs.

In 1896, their discontent erupted into a political war, a key turning point in our history. The Democrats, largely from the South and the West, were led by presidential nominee William Jennings Bryan, who demanded that tight money policies end. His core idea was to let silver, which was more plentiful than gold, circulate as an additional form of currency. He called it bimetalism. He stirred farmers into a crusade crying, "You shall not crucify mankind upon a cross of gold." The Wall Street-dominated Republicans nominated William McKinley, as they recoiled in horror at the idea of a cheap currency and insisted on a gold-only, tight-credit money supply.

McKinley won and gold reigned supreme. Tight money had triumphed. American capitalism boomed on a foundation of sound money behind high protective tariff walls.

However, the tight credit policies kept dragging down the farmers, who still dominated the American economy. Financial panics dogged McKinley's successor President Theodore Roosevelt. But the private sector regulated, and righted, itself. When Roosevelt faced a massive economic panic in 1905, he summoned J. P. Morgan (not the bank, the man) to the White House and asked him to intervene to stop financial collapse. *Forbes* describes how Morgan rallied Wall Street's bankers and "sent the vice president of the Stock Exchange down on to the floor with their money to buy significant positions in blue-chip American stocks at some 300% of their market value. That action staved off complete collapse of the banking system . . ."[3]

However, the panics kept coming, and nobody could stop the one that seared through the country in 1907 from dragging down prosperity. The economy and the banking system had become too large for any one man, or bank, to regulate it and prevent panic from leading to collapse.

So, on December 23, 1913, President Woodrow Wilson signed legislation, part of his New Freedom agenda, creating the Federal Reserve Board.

And, with the ascension of the Fed to power, our economy came to be managed by an elite of economists, bankers, and financiers, without much reference to the power of democratically elected officials.

Initially, the Fed's mandate was to promote banking stability, protect the currency, and hold down inflation.

Throughout the 1920s, the Federal Reserve Board permitted relatively easy credit policies and fueled the stock market boom of the roaring decade. Investors were allowed to buy stocks on credit (margin) with only a minimal down payment, and a giant speculative bubble began to form.

And a devastating bust followed when the stock market crashed in 1929 and the economy reeled into the Great Depression. But the Federal Reserve made the depression far worse. The Fed did not see its job as fighting unemployment or mitigating the effects of the depression, but rather focused on fighting inflation and protecting the currency. When the Fed's leaders saw first Hoover, then FDR, spending more and more to fight the depression, they worried that the resulting budget deficits would undermine the currency and trigger inflation so they raised interest rates, which tightened credit and deepened the depression. This huge mistake denied the economy badly needed stimulus after the 1929 crash. Then, the Fed repeated its mistake, raising rates again in the mid-1930s, helping to trigger the depression of 1937 to 1939.

The board's fear of inflation in the '30s was completely fanciful. Inflation? Hardly. Prices were in free fall as consumer demand fell apart. But the Fed persisted in its policies.

The liberals who controlled Congress were so angry at the Fed's tight credit policies that, as soon as World War II ended, they retaliated by passing laws in 1946 and again in 1978, under liberal Democratic presidents Truman and Carter, expanding the mandate of the Fed to include moving toward full-employment policies as well as fighting inflation.

This new mission for the Fed set up an inherent conflict between fighting inflation and promoting full employment.

Economists realized that to hold down prices, the Fed needed to lower demand for goods and services to stop the economy from overheating and too much spending power from accumulating. If demand were allowed to rise unchecked, too much money would end up chasing too few products or services, causing prices to rise. Thus, the Fed would respond to fears of an overheated economy by raising interest rates and reducing the money supply. William McChesney

Martin, chairman of the Federal Reserve from 1951 to 1970, famously described the process as "taking away the punch bowl just as the party got going."[4]

But the Fed's other mission, fighting unemployment, required the opposite policy. To create jobs, demand had to rise, stoked by low interest rates and easy credit. Lean too far one way, with easy credit and low interest rates, and inflation threatened. Lean too far the other way, with tight credit and high rates, and joblessness rose as the economy sagged.

Back then, in the 1960s, the subject of Fed policies was still in play as a political issue. Voters still had a choice. The ensuing debate broke largely along partisan lines with Republicans fearing inflation and favoring tight credit, and most Democrats worrying more about unemployment and wanting an expansive monetary policy.

Crusty Texas Congressman Wright Patman, chairman of the House Banking and Finance Committee from 1965 to 1975, constantly railed against high interest rates imposed by the Fed, echoing the historic demands of his agrarian constituents for easier credit. Patman snarled at Fed Chairman Arthur Burns as he testified before Patman's committee: "Can you give me any reason why you should not be in the penitentiary?"[5]

The battle over Fed policies, between tight money and easy credit, had raged through the first two hundred years of our country's history. Hamilton faced Jefferson over the establishment of the Bank of the United States. Webster battled Jackson over killing the bank. McKinley ran against Bryan over maintaining the gold standard. And liberals expanded the mission of the Fed to fight unemployment after its way too restrictive policies during the depression. Each battle was but a continuation of the same conflict between tight and easy credit, Wall Street and the populists, urban versus rural America, manufacturers against farmers, big banks fighting to absorb smaller community banks, Wall Street competing against Main Street small businesses.

Eventually, a political consensus developed among the nation's leaders to leave these matters to the Federal Reserve Board and take them out of our politics. Around the time of the Kennedy administration, Keynesian economics was the rage and the idea became fashionable that the economy could be scientifically managed to avoid the extremes of the business cycle. A little increase in interest rates here, a bit of a cut there, and the economy would purr along with low inflation and minimal unemployment. Increasingly, politicians were reluctant to interfere with the Fed and politicize its deliberations. A huge issue in American politics was shifted out of democratic politics and delegated to the supposed experts at the Fed.

But then came the Vietnam War. Reluctant to give up his dreams of a Great Society even as war costs soared, President Lyndon Johnson refused to cut domestic spending or raise taxes. Deficits rose. Nixon continued the irresponsible course and double-digit inflation set in by the end of the '70s.

The Fed saved the day. Under the leadership of Chairman Paul Volcker, it raised interest rates high, triggering massive unemployment, and bringing inflation to a sudden halt. When things returned to normal and inflation was tamed, the Fed loosened up on the controls and the economy boomed during the '80s.

From then on, America learned to trust the Fed. At a time when it had to stand up against the entire country and, literally, cause a recession, it had done so without flinching. We all came to trust the Fed, which had cured the economic problems more than the elected officials who had caused them.

During Dick's time at the Clinton White House, criticism of the Fed was forbidden. While President Clinton overtly avoided clashing with Federal Reserve Chairman Alan Greenspan, he privately believed that structural factors, like the higher productivity (triggered by computers and the Internet) and the flow of low-priced foreign imports, would hold down inflation and, thus, that the Fed could and should loosen up a little. When the president gave voice to these ideas in public, suggesting that the Fed should loosen credit and permit a higher level of economic growth to solve the budget deficit, the establishment arose in howls of alarm and indignation.

But, eventually, Clinton had his way and the Fed came around to agree with his assessment of the economy. The Fed cut the short-term interest rates, which it directly controls, and the bond market, heartened by the balanced budget, cut-long term rates as well. A decade of prosperity followed.

Then, on 9/11, bin Laden attacked and the Clinton prosperity came to a sudden halt as commercial activity slowed down and the travel industry tanked. The Fed, basking in the glow of public praise after the prosperity of the '90s, tried to prolong the good times by cutting rates and encouraging lending. The first decade of this century saw a concerted effort by the Fed to feed demand. Nobody worried about inflation. The Fed forgot to take away the punch bowl. The easy credit led to speculative bubbles—savings and loan real estate investments, Internet stocks, and, finally, subprime mortgages—with consequences that were disastrous.

After the economy fell apart in 2008, the Fed just accelerated the policies that it had pursued in the 2000s. It was as if the lunatics had taken over the asylum. The Fed, historically the guardian of the currency, suddenly behaved like the ultimate populist, printing money like a madman, almost tripling the money supply in only two years (likely another huge mistake for which we will pay with hyperinflation). Deficits didn't matter. Feeding the economy was all that counted.

However, in the process, a new political reality had taken hold. No longer was the Fed bound at the hip with the Republican Party, committed to fighting inflation and protecting the currency. Now, it was more joined with Democrats, who wanted an expansionary fiscal policy and were willing to accept the attendant risks of inflation. Wall Street, too, switched sides, no longer standing for sound money but increasingly operating like a casino, taking bets and riding hunches.

The lunatics have truly taken over the asylum.

But, despite its misjudgments, the Fed still reigns supreme, arrogating to itself decisions about credit, money supply, inflation, and unemployment. Elected officials are loath to challenge it. Senators and congressmen can only sit back and watch as these demented decisions are made. Voters don't count. No democracy permitted here. Compared to the Federal Reserve, the Vatican is democratic!

HOW FRANCE AND GERMANY ARE TRYING TO TAKE CONTROL OF OUR ECONOMY

Now this phenomenon of government by expert-elites has moved even further away from government of the people. The international community is empowering the International Monetary Fund (IMF) to be the *capo di tutti capi* (boss of all bosses), the superagency to control and coordinate the policies of all the central banks, Fed included, making it even more remote from popular, or even national, sovereignty.

The IMF wants total control over the economy of the world and, through this ultimate form of mission creep, advances toward its objective.

Originally founded in 1944, as a result of the Bretton Woods Conference to stabilize and protect the global banking system, the IMF became something of a fire department, putting out currency conflagrations throughout the world. As one emerging economy after another went through the trauma of speculators attacking its currency, the IMF always came to the rescue. Mexico, Malaysia, Thailand, Argentina, South Korea, Russia, and others leaned on IMF funding for survival.

When speculators like George Soros spotted a weak currency lagging behind the herd, they would pounce, anticipating an easy kill and the profits that would come from selling the targeted nation's currency short, at which point the IMF would swoop down to defend the currency and back it up with massive global resources.

From there, the IMF proceeded to its own version of fire prevention, intervening earlier in the process to steer countries away from lax fiscal policies and big deficits before they reached a mass critical enough to make them a target for greedy speculators on the prowl.

Its prescription for righting the financial ships of the various countries was always the same: austerity. Like an international bad news bear, the IMF demanded higher taxes and less spending. Never mind that its policies slowed economic growth, spread poverty, and promoted social unrest: they lowered budget deficits and made the nation's currency less vulnerable.

The mission of global nanny led increasingly to what Third World leaders called a *new colonialism*. As currency predators hovered nearby, the IMF brought more and more countries under its protective wing, demanding less spending and higher taxes in return.

(Greece, Italy, Spain, and Portugal—the European miscreants—were immune from IMF supervision because they had adopted the euro, a currency regarded as too big and too stable to fail.)

This new colonialism did not sit well with the less-developed nations of the world. While the fire department was welcome when the flames closed in, the IMF increasingly became a hated institution in the capitals of the world.

Not content with ruling the developing world, the IMF began to expand its mandate to try to take over the other economies of the world, including ours. It set itself up as the staffing for the G-7 group of nations (now expanded to the G-20) to set goals for each nation's economic and fiscal policies. It started to issue quarterly reports on their compliance with the policies it had decreed.

The G-20 group of nations grew out of the original G-7, a body set up to coordinate global economic policies. The original seven members were the United States, the United Kingdom, France, Germany, Japan, Italy, and Canada. The expanded G-20 framework now includes the original G-7 plus Russia, China, South Korea, Australia, Argentina, Brazil, Mexico, South Africa, Saudi Arabia, Turkey, India, Indonesia, and the European Union itself. Together, these nations account for 80 percent of the global Gross Domestic Product (GDP).[6]

The purpose of the G-20 is nominally to bring the rapidly developing economies in China, Brazil, and India into the framework of global economic planning. *Bloomberg Businessweek* notes that "Brazil and other fast-growing developing nations are seeking a greater voice at the Washington-based fund [the IMF], which was set up at the end of World War II to help ensure stability of the global monetary system. Emerging markets, which are growing twice as fast as their developed counterparts, say that their voting power doesn't reflect their weight in the global economy."[7]

However, reaching out to Brazil, China, and India was not the real purpose behind the expansion of the G-8 (Russia joined the G-7 nations in 1997) to the G-20 or the growth of the oversight role of the IMF. The actual, and unstated, goal is to reduce the power of the United States and enhance that of Europe. Even though our GDP is equal to one-fifth of the globe's[8] and one-third of the G-20 nations,[9] we get only one of twenty votes. Our GDP exceeds that of thirteen of the G-20 nations combined and about equals that of the entire European Union put together.

To get an idea as to how the United States is the giant Gulliver being tied up by Lilliputians in the G-20, compare the GDPs of the G-20 nations:

GDPs OF G-20 NATIONS[10]

United States	$14.5 trillion
China	5.9
Japan	5.5
Germany	3.3
France	2.6
United Kingdom	2.3
Brazil	2.1
Italy	2.1
India	1.6
Canada	1.6
Russia	1.5
Australia	1.2
Mexico	1.0
South Korea	1.0
Turkey	.7
Indonesia	.7
Saudi Arabia	.5
Argentina	.4
South Africa	.4

While the emerging markets increased their power when the expanded G-20 came into being, Europe really cleaned up. The Western European nations get five votes on the G-20: Britain, Germany, France, Italy, and the European Union itself. In the guise of expanding the global economic discussion to include emerging economies, Europe has cemented extra votes for itself and extra powers over the American economy.

However, it's not really a European power grab at all. It's a German and a French power grab. Berlin and Paris shape European opinions and policies. Britain has always been something of a lagging, outsider country when it comes to European integration. (It was excluded from the original Common Market for years when France vetoed its inclusion.) Italy has no power. Rome is just hoping somebody will pay its debts.

Ultimately, the European Union itself, and the original Common Market that preceded it, was conceived by French leader Charles de Gaulle and German Chancellor Konrad Adenauer as a way for their nations to regain their prominent place on the world stage. France lost its prestige when it fell to Hitler in World War II, and was cut out of the so-called big three nations that ran the Allied side in the war (the United States, the United Kingdom, and the Soviet Union). And, of course, Germany lost its moral authority and legitimacy as a result of its Nazi policies, which caused the war in the first place. Both nations needed to get well. And each wanted to form a critical mass that could stand up to the United States and serve as a counterweight to its power, all the while cowering behind our nuclear shield against the Soviet menace.

Europe's play for increased power included writing in the IMF as the staffing agency to advise the G-20 countries on global economic policies. At Bretton Woods, the United States and Britain set up the International Monetary Fund and the World Bank as the two agencies of global economic development. The informal agreement was that the United States would name the head of the World Bank and that a European would head the IMF. From the beginning, the IMF was the European entity and the World Bank was American.

So, when the IMF reinvented itself as the staff of experts to advise the G-20 nations and set the policies for their economies, it was really a way for the bureaucrats of the European Union to expand their reach further.

Even the decision to expand the group of nations to twenty countries enhanced the power of the IMF and, therefore, Europe. A group of twenty is far less capable of decisive action and more easily manipulated by the mandarins who staff it than an elite club of eight members. And, while the G-8 was a forum of presidents and prime ministers who were often prima donnas as they pranced and posed for the voters back home, the G-20 was designed for central bankers and economics ministers (in our case, the Treasury secretary), a more easy group to manipulate

In forming the G-20 and becoming its staff, the IMF and its European masters now have a framework to take giant steps toward their goal of global bureaucratic domination. Using its power through the G-20, the IMF tells the United States to cut its deficit, raise its taxes, and to reduce private sector corporate salaries. If the United States doesn't comply, it faces condemnation by the IMF and, eventually, even the prospect of sanctions.

Hitler's and Napoleon's dreams of global domination are having their sequel in Germany's and France's expansion of their economic power through the IMF and the G-20. You don't have to build an army and invade countries to win world power. You can win it at the conference table.

The IMF and the European Union are picking up the same anti-American game that de Gaulle and Adenauer pioneered. How else could a Frenchwoman, Christine Lagard, Dominique Strauss-Kahn's successor as head of the IMF, and a German, Uwe Corsepius, secretary general of the European Union, be able to stand up to the United States? (France and Germany's combined GDP is $5.9 trillion. Ours is $14.5 trillion.[11])

Unfortunately, our leaders, President Obama and Federal Reserve Chairman Ben Bernanke, are only too happy to meld into this international oligarchy, putting their need for global political, social, and academic acceptance ahead of our economic interests.

How did we cede this power to the IMF and the G-20? The process began under the Bush 43 administration, when the United States agreed to the expansion of the G-8. Not wanting to appear to be shutting out emerging economies, the United States bowed to demands for inclusion of other countries in the exclusive club of global economic leaders. The growing power of China, and, to a lesser extent, India, made it vital to create a larger global economic entity. Okay. We needed to include China and India. Maybe Brazil, too. But Argentina? South Africa? Saudi Arabia? Turkey? Indonesia? Political correctness ran amuck. And how did we end up giving Europe five votes to our one? And empowering the European-dominated IMF to run the group? How did that happen?

Our Congress was never consulted on the decision to form the G-20, on its membership, or on the staffing role of the IMF. Nor did any president ask our elected officials whether we wanted to accept the IMF and the G-20 as our financial overseer, with powers to trump even our own, undemocratic, unrepresentative Federal Reserve Board.

Of course, the IMF currently has no coercive power over the United States, but its real power comes from being able to manipulate the global consensus and bring pressure on policy makers throughout the world to conform to their policies.

However, outright coercion to enforce the IMF dictates may not be far away. Europe is pushing for a trigger mechanism. If a country's current account surplus or deficit goes over a certain limit, for instance, it would require negotiations to get the country back into line.[12] And behind the negotiations would be the prospect of global punishment—sanctions—for those who misbehave.

However, the real IMF and European power grab came as a result of the US feelings of guilt over the fiscal crisis of 2008. Suddenly, the big kahuna—the United States—went through its own massive fiscal crisis when its subprime lending policies triggered a global financial meltdown. Europe looked across the ocean and blamed the United States for the global economic crisis. American diplomats hung their heads in shame. Our central bankers and Federal Reserve Board economists pleaded for help. And then, the apologizer-in-chief, Barack Obama, went abroad and ratified the massive transfer of power and moral authority from our own Federal Reserve to the G-20 and the IMF.

The fact that we led the world into a financial disaster has become a kind of original sin, obliging the United States to take a backseat and go along with new constraints on our economy imposed by Europe to stop us from spreading mayhem around the planet once again.

The Europeans exploited to justify broad intervention into our economy, pressing our own Federal Reserve to tighten up lending standards and limit corporate salaries, and demanding that our Congress cut the budget deficit. Some of these goals are, of course, worthy, but they should stem from a democratic consensus within our own borders, not from the decisions of extranational experts imposing their beliefs on us.

CNN reported, "Europeans [are] emboldened by their belief that the credit crisis didn't originate on their soil. . . . They say that means the more tightly regulated European banking model has triumphed over the more lax laws favored in America." As French President Nicolas Sarkozy said, "self-regulation to solve all problems, it's finished. Laissez-faire, it's finished. The all-powerful market that is always right, it's finished."[13] Fini. Fini. Fini.

CNN sums up the IMF agenda: "greater oversight of hedge funds and investment banks; increasing how much money banks need to keep in reserve;

more transparent and universal accounting standards; and limits on executive pay." The network notes, "all that would be accompanied by a new global network of regulators—regulators that would presumably have power over US banks."[14]

Now, the IMF and the G-20 are functioning "as a kind of global board of directors for the global economy."[15]

The G-20 and the IMF have spread their range wide, firing orders for each nation in the global economy. The United States has "to define ways to boost savings" and must "commit to a sharp deficit reduction by government." Meanwhile, "China, Germany, and Japan [must] reduce [their] reliance on exports." Europe is supposed to "pass investment-friendly tax measures and reopen the debate about making it easier to fire workers—viewed as one way to encourage employees to hire more freely." China needs to "face perhaps the biggest challenge: remaking its economy so it relies far less on exports to the US."[16]

Who are these people, giving orders so freely to the governments of the world, overriding the decisions the people have made in democracies and urging all governments to fall into step?

The IMF and the EU are technocratic and bureaucratic oligarchies, but those who staff and manage them are not necessarily the global elite. Nobel Prize–winning economist Joseph Stiglitz famously described the IMF economists as "third rank students from first rate universities."[17]

The fact that the IMF is replacing democracy is fine with countries like China and Russia, who never believed in democracy in the first place. However, it also finds broad acceptance among Western European and Japanese elites. And, of course, everybody likes cutting Washington down to size.

Europe Never Liked Democracy; It Still Doesn't

This delegation of power to experts essentially grows out of the old monarchical and aristocratic systems. Instead of a hereditary system of nobles and kings, the IMF and EU governing elites style themselves as a meritocracy of educated experts who want to appropriate to themselves the power to decide our futures.

These meritocracies are nothing but a continuation of government by self-perpetuating elites, the new aristocracy.

These new mandarins come from the European and Japanese heritage of civil-service domination of governments where elected officials have little voice and less control.

We comfort ourselves with the idea that North America and Europe are lands of democracy where the people rule. Hardly. No nation even begins to approach the level of freedom and popular sovereignty that we cherish in the United States, even with the growth of our regulatory bureaucracy.

The United Kingdom comes closest. But, even there, the prime minister and his cabinet colleagues control very few appointed positions. Almost all their staffs come from the civil service. But, at least in the United Kingdom, there is a tradition among civil servants of deferring to the elected government and seeking to tailor their actions to the policies that the elected cabinet advocates. In Britain, they are literally civil *servants*.

On the Continent, it is different. The power of the civil-service bureaucracy over the elected representatives of the people dates back to Otto von Bismarck, who ruled first Prussia, then a united Germany. In order to keep workers from demanding real democracy, which he loathed, Bismarck conceived of the welfare state, meting out unemployment insurance, health care, elderly pensions, and the like to the masses to keep them from demanding real political power. Bismarck invented the very concept of retirement, the time for the elderly to live on pensions and savings without having to work for a living.

Fundamental to Bismarck's worldview was a detestation of democracy. He ran his government in the name of the kaiser, through a cadre of civil servants over whom he exercised total control.

When the kaiser was overthrown, ending World War I, he was replaced by the Weimar Republic, whose democratic legacy was Hitler's peaceful acquisition of power at the ballot box. The German elites distrust their democracy and where it might lead them if given its head.

The French also empowered their civil service, selecting students who graduated from a handful of elite schools to run the country. Particularly since the political parties made a mess of governing France, with governments seemingly rising and falling every few months, the French came to rely on experts to run their government. They trusted that their steady policies would be largely unaffected by the ebbs and flows of electoral passion. The French came to regard their voters as crazy. Twenty percent regularly voted communist and even the monarchists continued to attract votes.

Italy was even worse, with the communists winning more than a third of the vote. The last thing the elites in Germany, France, or Italy wanted to do was to trust their own voters.

The German and French models, with their distrust of democracy, have come to characterize not only the government of the European Union but also the governing style of many international organizations.

In Europe, democracy is discredited. Its failure to block the rise of Hitler in Germany and Mussolini in Italy left permanent scars on both countries.

The French blame the democratic governments of the Third and Fourth Republics for their national decline, and credit the limitations of democratic power in the Fifth Republic's constitution for their recent recovery of power.

Dick once asked a member of the Christian Democratic government in Germany why they did not force a referendum on the question of Turkey's admission to the European Union. Letting Turkey in is very unpopular in Germany and would be a great hot-button issue to use to beat the Social Democrats who favor it. "Referenda have not worked out well for us," was his reply, a dark allusion to Germany in the '30s.

When an elected official speaks out in the United States, we give him credit for a legitimacy that stems from his selection by the people. An appointed civil servant has no such credibility. But in Europe, it is quite the opposite. The elected official is usually written off as a demagogue pandering to the voters, while the civil servant is a disinterested expert whose opinion can be trusted. The very word *populist* is a compliment in America and a putdown in Europe.

Indeed, the very nature of a parliamentary system, such as those in Britain, Germany, and most of Europe, implies sharp limits on democracy, and lends itself to government by expert civil servants. While Americans vote for hundreds of thousands of elected officials in our federal, state, county, city, school board, and town governments, Europeans don't. In most Continental parliamentary democracies, there is no effective local government. And, even on the national level, a voter casts only one vote every four or five years. And that vote is for a party. There are no separate votes for prime minister and members of parliament. The elected officials who actually govern are named, not by the voters, but by the parliamentary delegation of the party they elect. There are no primaries. The party, not the voters, decides who will be the prime minister and who will get which cabinet post.

Once the election is held, a parliamentary system is essentially an elected dictatorship. Since, by definition, the prime minister's party controls parliament, he can usually pass whatever he and his cabinet want. If they fail to pass an important measure—a routine occurrence in the American system of checks and balances—a major crisis ensues, often leading to the resignation of the government and the calling of a new election. Since members of the party's parliamentary majority are voting themselves, essentially, out of office if they defeat a government proposal, very few fail to pass.

Most European countries, except the United Kingdom, use proportional representation in selecting their parliaments. If a party, for example, gets 20 percent of the vote, the top 20 percent of its list of possible parliamentary representatives are elected. Voters cannot even choose who should represent them in parliament; the party selects it all. All they can do is vote for one party or the other.

Nor is there any powerful local government to offset national authority. While every city or town has its own mayor and council, their powers are typically sharply limited, their posts more symbolic and ceremonial than real. For example, France was able to proceed to dot its land with nuclear power plants, which now supply 80 percent of its electricity. In the United States, local governments blocked the expansion of nuclear power, fearful of its environmental impact. In France, however, they had no such power.

Japan, too, has long embraced the German/French model. A Japanese prime minister once told Dick that he could only select a secretary and one or two others for his personal staff and that each member of the cabinet gets to fill only one or two positions in his department. The rest of the administrative apparatus were civil servants.

Japanese bureaucracy runs the country as surely as the clerical establishment runs Iran. Elections mean little in either country. It's like high school: The kids vote for the student government, but the principal runs the school.

And Japanese civil servants do not make the least effort to toe the line laid down by the elected officials. Rather, in concert with their allies in the private sector, they fight tooth and nail against the initiatives sponsored by elected officials. Hand in hand with the special interests, the civil servants protect the status quo and look forward to retiring from their low-paid public sector jobs to lucrative positions in the private companies they spent their careers protecting.

To grasp the weakness of elected officials in Japan, it is important to realize that it was not really the government of Japan that chose to attack Pearl Harbor and start a war with the United States. It was the navy that made the decision, just as it was the Japanese army that decided to invade China. Using the façade of the emperor's imperial power, the military bureaucracy, acting on its own and running amok, dragged Japan into that self-destructive conflict. And the heritage of civil-service control hasn't changed much since.

Democracy in Europe is proving ever more elusive in the wake of its sovereign debt and currency crises.

As the price for getting funds from Germany and France to back up—read *bail out*—the debts of Portugal, Italy, Greece, and Spain (called the PIGS in Europe), all euro countries are going to have to subject themselves to budget discipline. *Budget discipline* is a fancy term for overriding the wishes of the voters and abiding by the desires of bureaucrats, bean counters, accountants, and economists, the experts that are overruling democracy. In the name of saving the euro, the entire continent is abandoning democracy. Now, not only developing countries will be under the sway of the IMF and its bean-counting buddies in the European Union, but developed European countries will fall under their sway as well.

Remember, the sovereign debt crisis that is now plaguing southern Europe could easily spread to its larger northern economies. France and Britain are not immune from these problems. Only Germany and Scandinavia seem relatively safe. And, when fear of a debt crisis looms, the bureaucrats of the IMF are only too happy to move in and take control away from the irresponsible electorate and their political leaders.

Even before the IMF moves to expand its powers, the European Union is scarcely a democratic institution. Its executive brands is entirely composed of officials who are appointed by its secretary-general, who, in turn, is named by the Council of Ministers, the governing body composed of the prime ministers of all member countries.

So, voters in each country elect a party to power. The party then selects the members of parliament. The members name the prime minister who, with the other twenty-six prime ministers, appoints the secretary-general who appoints the bureaucracy. By then, any nexus between the will of the voters and the actions of their European Union leaders is far, far removed.

There is no direct election by voters of Europe for secretary-general.

European voters can and do elect a European Parliament, but it is totally powerless. It can act only on bills submitted to it by the EU bureaucracy and may not initiate legislation. It has never rejected an important proposed piece of legislation. A sinecure, it exists to buy the consent of the European political establishment for the EU by paying its members a healthy salary.

Members of the European Parliament (MEPs) get a monthly salary of EUR 8,000 (about $12,000). They also get EUR 4,299 (about $6,000)—per month for staff and offices, and EUR 304 (about $450) for each day they attend at EU sessions.[18]

Typically, MEPs are punctilious in coming to meetings to be sure to pick up their daily checks. Put together, the average MEP can count on an income of almost $200,000 per year, giving them and their parties a big stake in maintaining the EU.

The presidency of the Council of Ministers rotates among its members, changing every six months, giving no one of them much time to accumulate power. The real leverage belongs to the appointed secretary-general, who is the uberbureaucrat.

The current secretary-general, chosen in 2009, is Uwe Corsepius, a longtime German civil servant. Fifty-one years old, he entered the civil service at thirty and never left. He began as a civil servant in the German Ministry of Economy and Labor. After two years, he moved to the International Monetary Fund and two years later, in 1994, became a functionary in the Federal Chancellery in Berlin, first under Helmut Kohl, then under Chancellor Gerhard Schroder, and recently under Angela Merkel.

Elected chancellors of Germany come and go and the party in power changes, but bureaucrats like Corsepius remains in charge.

At the EU, his powers are vast. About two-thirds of the legislation for European members are passed not by their own parliaments, but promulgated by the EU bureaucracy with only perfunctory oversight by the Council of Ministers. The bureaucracy decides everything from antitrust enforcement to fishing policies to trade barriers to environmental regulations to food safety standards to labor policies to consumer practices to farm policy to energy exploration. The bureaucracy is omnipotent.

The EU budget is EUR 146 billion, about $200 billion, a sum that is spent as the bureaucracy dictates.

And now, the bureaucrats at the EU and the IMF are getting the power to override the decisions of the elected officials in southern Europe as a result of the sovereign debt crisis. Soon, all of Europe will be under their sway. The entire subtext of this change: You can't trust the voters.

The United States has moved in the same direction as has Europe, toward increasing civil-service power and less democratic control ever since the New Deal era, when FDR set up agencies to oversee so many aspects of American life. Now, the Department of Agriculture (USDA) tells farmers what they can plant. The Food and Drug Administration (FDA) determines what medicines we can take. The Federal Aviation

Administration (FAA) controls aviation. The National Labor Relations Board (NLRB) goes a long way toward deciding where unions should be established. The Federal Communications Commission (FCC) tells television and radio stations what their content can be. The surgeon general limits tobacco production and advertising. The Securities and Exchange Commission (SEC) runs Wall Street, and the Federal Commodities Futures Trading Commission controls the commodities market. Fannie Mae and Freddie Mac, to our detriment, dominate the mortgage market. The Environmental Protection Agency (EPA) regulates all manner of emissions. The Employee Retirement Income Security Act (ERISA) controls our pensions. The Federal Reserve controls our banking system. The Occupational Safety and Health Administration (OSHA) controls our workplace environment. The Internal Revenue Service (IRS), with its often selective enforcement of a voluminous tax code, dominates our personal financial decisions. This is just part of the regulatory umbrella at the federal level. There is the state and local regulatory superstructure as well as the criminal justice system to control our lives.

Our elected officials, including the president himself, have only indirect control over these powerful bureaucrats.

When Dick worked for President Clinton, he saw firsthand how much power the bureaucrats had, even over the man who nominally appointed them. At every turn, bureaucrats tried to frustrate presidential initiatives. The bureaucracy at Health and Human Services worked overtime to propagandize against the welfare reform program the president wanted. The Department of Education did not want the federal college tax-credit program Clinton wanted. The State Department and the National Security Council opposed the restrictions on foreign lobbyists Clinton favored. The Justice Department opposed the gun controls the president wanted to pass. The Treasury Department didn't want the capital gains tax cut for homeowners he proposed. And on and on and on. Clinton could not get the support he needed even from those whom he had appointed. To get the cooperation of the civil service was just a wistful dream.

But, let's all remember: The United States is a bastion of democracy compared to any other country on earth.

Some will say that experts are right and more qualified than average voters to make complex public policy. As we contemplate a future dominated by bureaucracy, not by democracy, we need to remember the prophetic words of James Harrington, an Enlightenment philosopher, who wrote, in 1656, "The wisdom of the few may be the light of mankind, but the interests of the few are not the interests of mankind."[19]

THE IMF'S ASSAULT ON THE DOLLAR

Even as the European-led IMF tries to minimize America's power by reducing us to one vote on the G-20, it is also orchestrating an assault on the citadel of American economic power: the status of the dollar as the global currency.

During the US economic swoon, the Federal Reserve Board essentially printed money and then borrowed it back to fund our budget deficit. (It is a comforting myth that China lent us the money to pay for our budget deficit. It stopped doing so a while ago. Now the Fed funds our deficit by printing the money we borrow.) The Federal Reserve Board could do so because the dollar is the world's reserve currency. It has replaced gold as the standard of exchange. Nobody challenges it. If we had to change dollars into euros and borrow euros to fund our deficit, for example, the Fed could not have been so free to print dollars. Other nations would not have sold us their euros for our dollars very cheaply, worrying that our currency had lost its value. However, since the Fed controls the global currency, it could just gear up the printing press.

Even though using the dollar as the reserve currency seems unjust to some, the question is: What should replace it? The euro? When Europe is on the verge of financial ruin because of its sovereign debt crisis? The yen? With Japan mired in a twenty-plus-year recession? The yuan? Which China manipulates to keep it deliberately weak?

The IMF has its own plan to replace the dollar with its own currency, called Special Drawing Rights (SDRs), which it would issue. The *Financial Times* explains that the SDR is "a basket of currencies, which today consists of the euro, Japanese yen, pound sterling, and US dollar. An SDR is neither a currency, nor a claim on the IMF. Rather it is a potential claim on the freely usable currencies to IMF members. Apparently, it's something of a virtual currency."[20]

The problem is that the IMF has no power to tax, so there is nothing to stand behind its SDRs, except the taxing power of its member nations. When the *Financial Times* speaks of SDRs as being backed by "a potential claim on the freely usable currencies to IMF members,"[21] it means that the taxpayers of the several nations will back up the SDRs with their tax base—and that means, overwhelmingly the American taxpayer.

So get this straight: The IMF wants to use *our* power to tax *our* citizens to replace *our* currency with *theirs*! Their ultimate hope is to become the global economic government: a bureaucracy, ruled by experts.

The lack of taxing power won't deter the IMF imperialism. The organization is still calling for the replacement of the dollar. CNN reported that Dominique Strauss-Kahn, managing director of the IMF until he was arrested for sexual assault in New York City (charges were later dropped), acknowledged that there are some "technical hurdles" involved with SDRs.[22] But he assured us that having an IMF currency would "help correct global imbalances and shore up the global financial system."[23]

The IMF director said that "over time, there may also be a role for the SDR to contribute to a more stable international monetary system."[24]

CNN explained that the IMF "goal is to have a reserve asset for central banks that better reflects the global economy since the dollar is vulnerable to swings in the domestic economy and changes in US policy."[25]

In addition to SDRs serving as a reserve currency, CNN reports, "the IMF also proposed creating SDR-denominated bonds, which could reduce central banks' dependence on US Treasuries. The Fund also suggested

that certain assets, such as oil and gold, which are traded in US dollars, could be priced using SDRs."[26] Strauss-Kahn requires translation.

• When he says there are "technical hurdles" to replacing the dollar with SDRs, he is referring to the fact that the IMF would need our tax base so that it can replace our currency.

- When he says that SDRs would "correct global imbalances," he means that it would reduce the power of the United States and give European central bankers the power to control the global economy.

- When he says "the dollar is vulnerable to swings in the domestic economy and changes in US policy," he means that our democracy is messy and that sometimes our voters assert themselves in ways in which Europeans and the Chinese cannot, and that we are better off without US voters having any power.

- When he says that he wants the IMF to issue SDR-denominated bonds to "reduce central banks' dependence on US Treasuries," he means that he wants it to be harder for the United States to borrow money, in order to weaken our power.

- And when he says that "certain assets, such as oil and gold, which are traded in US dollars, could be priced using SDRs," he wants to increase the price of oil to American consumers to further weaken us.

These misguided policies would be not only wrong for the United States, but a fiasco for the rest of the world. Imagine a currency not backed by any government or taxing power, supported by an international organization that can do no more than request that its member nations make good on the currency should anyone question it! SDRs would be worth less than wallpaper were they not backed by the taxing power of the United States government!

However, it remains the goal of the IMF to cut the United States down to the level of the other nations and impose its bureaucratic control over us.

The desire of these European bureaucratic elites to rule us and control our economy would not be so bad if they were any good at it, but these same elites set up the international banking system that came crashing down in 2008 and threatens to unravel over the European sovereign debt crisis. It was their structure, created in 1944 at the Bretton Woods Conference, which is falling apart before our very eyes.

The basic precepts that have dominated their economic and financial thinking have proven to be fundamentally flawed. In words that might well be said today, FDR told the nation in his inaugural address in 1933 that "the rulers of the exchange of mankind's goods have failed, through their own stubbornness and their own incompetence." He noted that "faced by failure of credit, they have proposed only the lending of more money."[27] His words precisely define the attitudes of our global economic leaders.

Remember, the experts at the IMF and in European banks led the world into crisis after crisis with their shortsightedness and lack of vision:

- It was their policies that made developing nations cower before global currency speculators, slashing their living standards and consigning billions to poverty.

- They were the ones who bought subprime securitized mortgages and then got phony insurance from AIG to back it up. Their plunge into speculation made a domestic American crisis into a global calamity. We created the subprime mortgage, but they are the ones who bought them.

- It was the vision of the European bankers that led to the establishment of the euro in the first place, which is a currency that could only be as strong as its weakest link, the most irresponsible country in the EU. That turned out to be Greece. When Greece threatened default, all Europe had to jump to the rescue or watch their economies flounder.

- The European banks bought euro-denominated bonds issued by Greece, Italy, Portugal, and Spain, even though it was obvious that these countries couldn't repay their debts.

The time has come to label the global consensus of economic experts for what it is: a self-serving perpetuation of economic myths that undermine real prosperity and growth. Instead, we must embrace the lessons that history has to teach: that less government intervention, regulation, taxation, spending, and dictation will free entrepreneurial forces, whose collective wisdom exceeds the plans and programs of our elites. We must learn to embrace the decisions of the marketplace— judgments based not on public policy but on trial and error and experimentation and experience. In the pursuit of private profit, entrepreneurs often point the way to the public good.

However, less government means less power for bureaucratic elites. So it's not likely to happen in Europe anytime soon.

ACTION AGENDA

At home, we must adopt measures to make the Federal Reserve Board more transparent and accountable. Abroad, the next president must sharply limit American participation in the G-20 process and explicitly reject the role of the International Monetary Fund in setting goals for our national economy.

We must also reject any attempt to use our power to tax to sustain an international currency such as Special Drawing Rights, which is designed to replace the dollar as the international currency. The next president must declare the maintenance of the dollar as the international unit of exchange as a central policy goal of the United States, and this policy must guide our actions in dealing with international organizations and foreign countries.

We must not delegate control of our economy to the IMF and the G-20, and we must take back a large measure of control from the Federal Reserve Board.

PART TWO

Trick or Treaties: How the European Union Is Preempting Congress and Binding Us Through International Treaties

One of the greatest threats to our liberty is the almost unknown treaties the internationalists are pushing, which would bind the United States hand and foot to global policies that we would never pass on our own. Eager to strike while Obama is president, Secretary of State Hillary Clinton and the Democrats who now control the US Senate (which ratifies treaties; the House has no role in treaty making) are rushing to get Uncle Sam's signature on a wide variety of treaties that would change our nation, our governing systems, and our civil liberties.

And these treaties are advancing in stealth. The mainstream media hardly covers them and even conservative bloggers and media outlets are too focused on other issues to offer them the exposure they need.

Here's what the globalists are trying to do:

- Take away the right of Congress or the president to go to war unless the United Nations approves (that is unless we get Russia and China not to veto the resolutions).

- Hold American presidents and cabinet members criminally responsible for going to war without UN approval.

- Limit the right of the US Navy to keep the seas open.

- Require half of the royalties from offshore oil and gas drilling and mineral mining to go to a UN body to distribute as it wishes with no real control by the United States.

- Require us to share our offshore drilling technology with all other nations.

- Require us to assure, through registration and other intrusive methods, that none of the gun owners in America export their weapons to other countries.

- Establish international jurisdiction over firearms in the United States.

- Prohibit the United States from deploying anti-missile defense weapons systems in outer space to counter the threat from Iran, North Korea, and China.

- Require the United States to give foreign aid to poor nations to assure that their children have adequate health care, education, clothing, nutrition, and housing.

- Ban corporal punishment in school and at home in the United States.

- Create a legal basis for suing state and local governments to demand that they increase spending for welfare, education, and health care for children.

- Enact zoning regulations that reduce the need for automobiles and encourage people to migrate from rural areas to denser urban environments.

Who *are* these people to try to require us to adopt their policies? They are the personification of the "moral busybodies" that C. S. Lewis spoke of in his quotation earlier in this book. They are European social workers and socialist policy wonks trying to impose their policies on the United States, bypassing Congress and using international treaties to do so.

The Europeans want to lock us into treaties on each of these subjects, tying our hands and committing us to their policies. They want to override US opinion and bind the United States to numerous international commitments from which future Republican administrations could not extract us.

FOX News explains that "[b]ecause of the Supremacy Clause in Article VI of the Constitution, all treaties are rendered 'the supreme law of the land,' superseding preexisting state and federal statutes. Any rights or laws established by the U.N. convention could then be argued to hold sway in the United States."[1]

Third World countries or authoritarian regimes can ignore these treaties at will. None of the treaties has an enforcement mechanism that would work in China or Russia. But the United States' court system would be obliged to enforce these treaties on our citizens. Because of our courts, we, uniquely among the nations of the world, would have to abide by each dot and comma. Under the Supremacy Clause, the provisions in any of these busybody treaties could be enforced by US court rulings. The treaties would have the effect of a law that our legislators could not change without the consent of all the other nations of the world and which our judges would be bound to enforce.

It isn't Halloween, but the Europeans are playing Trick or Treaty all the same!

It's the same strategy they used to force the European Union down the throats of an unwilling public. On October 29, 2004, the Union's twenty-five member nations agreed to a new constitution turning the EU into a real government with sovereignty, foreign policy, and vast new powers. France and the Netherlands submitted the document to their voters for approval. Both said no in May 2005 and June 2005. Britain, which had scheduled a vote, saw that it would fail there as well and cancelled the referendum. End of constitution?

No! The EU bureaucrats were not so easily deterred. Instead, they met in Lisbon in 2007 and signed a *treaty* among the members incorporating many of the same changes that were in the rejected constitution. Why a treaty? Because it did not need voter approval as a constitution did. Instead, the insiders in each national parliament greased its chances for passage and the Lisbon Treaty glided through. Never mind that it directly contradicted what the voters of the Netherlands and France had said (and what the polls in the United Kingdom indicated). The EU didn't care. They had found a way around public opinion: Don't even ask the people!

Now the European Union wants to use the same modus operandi to find a way around American voters, pass the European social agenda, and impose it on the United States.

OUR CONSTITUTION AND SOVEREIGNTY REPEALED: THE INTERNATIONAL CRIMINAL COURT

Our sovereignty and ability to govern ourselves is under attack by the growing pressure to join the International Criminal Court (ICC). This judicial body, established in 2002, is appropriating the power to itself to overrule all our courts, even when Americans are on trial for crimes against other Americans on US soil, and to put our former presidents, defense secretaries, military leaders, and Congressional leaders in jail for going to war without United Nations approval.

The powers the ICC is claiming for itself would amount to creating a supertribunal above the Supreme Court, the American president, and our elected Congress. It would lead, inevitably, to relegating the United States to a neocolonial status. This time, our ruler would not be a king but a court and the bonds that would bind us would have been of our own making.

Not only is the ICC a breathtaking power grab, but it also represents an end run around our basic constitutional guarantees against an imperious and overreaching judiciary.

Presidents Clinton and Bush refused to sign onto the court. Both men understood that the operations of the court contradict our most fundamental constitutional rights. But President Obama is moving closer and closer to subjecting the United States to its rulings.

The International Criminal Court has no trial by jury. It has no right to a speedy trial. No right to confront your accusers. No presumption of innocence. Is this America's future? It will be if President Obama has his way and the United States joins the International Criminal Court.

The arbitrary and administrative system of justice at the ICC worried Clinton and Bush enough to keep the United States out. But Obama has shown no such concern. Marion Smith, a fellow at the Heritage Foundation, writes, "In November 2009, the United States signaled a fundamental shift in its position toward the International Criminal Court (ICC). The Obama Administration sent Stephen Rapp, US Ambassador-at-Large for War Crimes Issues, to a meeting of the Assembly of States Parties of the ICC as an official observer." Smith wrote that Rapp's attendance at the court "risks conferring legitimacy upon an international institution that may endanger the constitutional rights of US citizens."[2]

Obama sympathizes with the international efforts to dilute American sovereignty. He deeply believes in multilateralism and explicitly rejects the idea of US exceptionalism.

Many of his moves to integrate the United States into a global framework can be undone by a subsequent administration. But if we submit ourselves to the jurisdiction of the International Criminal Court, it can't be undone. This bell cannot be unrung.

The Court Criminalizes War Without UN Approval

The International Criminal Court's name itself is misleading. This court does not exist to try criminals. It exists to try presidents and other top government officials. Its focus is on four basic crimes: genocide, crimes against humanity, war crimes, and aggression. The definitions of each are expansive. Who will decide what a war crime is and what it is not? What aggression is and what it is not? Where crimes against humanity begin and end? The ICC itself will. The Rome Statute, which created it, says grandiloquently that the court "shall satisfy itself that it has jurisdiction in any case brought before it."[3] That's pretty neat. It's a more expansive definition of jurisdiction than any court anywhere in the world can assert or has asserted.

Fundamentally, the ICC is a political court developed to try the leaders of nations on behalf of the global community. Particularly problematic is the individual nature of the charges brought before the ICC. It does not prosecute or judge countries. It judges presidents, prime ministers, and other leaders personally. It uses the totally inappropriate sanction of imprisonment to express disagreement with policy choices. It criminalizes differences of opinion and has the potential to hold former leaders responsible long after they have left office.

When this sanction is applied against a dictator, it has some considerable merit. Milosevic in Serbia, Idi Amin in Uganda, or Saddam Hussein in Iraq deserved such treatment. But when the accused is the fairly and freely elected leader of a democracy who went to war pursuant to the decisions of the elected Congress, to hold the leader personally responsible for the crime of aggression, simply because the UN did not see it his way, is absurd. And let's not forget that the UN makes its decisions in its Security Council, whereby a Chinese or Russian veto can block action.

Essentially, the crime of aggression makes it illegal for any president to send in troops if Russia or China disagree, and raises the specter that the president, after he leaves office, could be arrested and imprisoned for doing so!

Empowered by international anger against the Bush administration for its invasion of Iraq without UN approval, the left wants to use the ICC to bring the world's foremost military power to heel.

So, why would American citizens, particularly liberals who are normally so conscious of protecting the rights of the accused and so suspicious of government investigatory powers, be willing to see us submit to the International Criminal Court without such protections?

The ICC has acquired the reputation of being a human-rights court to hold accountable those government leaders who act unilaterally and aggressively with military intervention on the global stage. It is essentially a political court, part of an overall objective of global government.

Particularly alarming is the inclusion of the crime of aggression in the jurisdiction of the ICC. Aggression is defined as "the use of armed force by one State against another State without the justification of self-defense or authorization by the Security Council."[4]

So, if the United States Congress and our president, both elected democratically by our people, choose to go to war without a UN resolution of the "justification of self-defense," their leaders are committing the crime of aggression and can be prosecuted by the ICC.

Charges of aggression may be brought before the ICC through a referral from the UN Security Council (which would be subject to a US veto). They can also stem from a complaint by a member nation against another country that participates in the ICC. Even lacking such a referral, the permanent prosecutor built into the ICC structure can decide to bring a complaint against the current or former political leaders of a nation if he feels they have used military force inappropriately. The only requirement is that the prosecutor wait six months before bringing the action.

States that are party to the ICC can opt out of its jurisdiction over crimes of aggression, but we all know that this slippery slope could change once the United States becomes a party to the court.

Of course, under this expansive definition of aggression, the war in Iraq, which was authorized by the US Congress but not by the United Nations, would be considered illegal and Bush, Cheney, Rumsfeld, et al. could be prosecuted.

Smith writes that "this scenario . . . highlights the political nature of the ICC's mandate and reach."[5]

Former UN ambassador John Bolton has it right when he says that "Fundamentally, the Rome Statute takes an enormously important executive power and

puts it into an international institution that is outside the control of any democratic process."[6]

Marion Smith and other conservatives raise several key objections to American participation in the ICC:

- The ICC determines its own jurisdiction. It can inject itself into any dispute it so chooses. If the United States participated, it could try Americans for crimes against other Americans on US soil, even if they had been acquitted in the US courts.

- Americans could be brought before the ICC if they are charged with crimes on the soil of a participating nation. Smith recounts how, "[i]n 2009, ICC Chief Prosecutor Luis Moreno-Ocampo commenced an investigation of alleged US and NATO atrocities committed in Afghanistan. Afghanistan is one of the 110 countries that are party to the Rome Statute, which gives the ICC jurisdiction over Afghan territory."[7]

- The ICC lends itself to becoming a kind of kangaroo court for political issues. Opponents of the war in Iraq have tried to use the court to air their grievances against the American military and former president George W. Bush actually cancelled a trip to Switzerland where he was to be the keynote speaker at a Jewish charity gala "due to the risk of legal action against him for alleged torture." Reuters reports that "pressure [had] been building on the Swiss government to arrest him . . . if he enters the country."[8] On December 2, 2011, Amnesty International called for "several African nations to arrest and detain former President Bush for authorizing the use of waterboarding and other forms of torture." Bush, whose record on humanitarian and anti-AIDS relief for Africa is extensive, was visiting Ethiopia, Tanzania, and Zambia "to raise awareness about cervical and breast cancer and HIV/AIDS."[9] The ICC prosecutor is also investigating Israel for alleged crimes in Gaza, even though neither Israel nor the Palestinian Authority is a participant in the court. There is, of course, no comparable investigation of Hamas for firing rockets at Israeli civilians.

No Constitutional Rights at the International Criminal Court

Beyond the political goals of the court and the ambitions of its founders to make it a form of international governance lies the fact that the court will follow the Continental European model rather than the Anglo-American one in administering justice and trying defendants.

The European model of criminal justice differs from ours in that it places much more power in the hands of the state than our founding fathers were comfortable with. The Napoleonic Code forms the basis of the European criminal justice model, while the common law that began in Britain forms the basis for ours.

The European model is based on statutes passed by their elected bodies, which are designed to cover all possible eventualities. The incredibly detailed Continental justice system applies these statutes meticulously.

However, the Anglo-American model puts broad discretion in the hands of judges to interpret the law and to apply it to the case at hand. Most of European law is statutory. Most of Anglo-American law is common law, made by judges as they apply general principles to specific factual patterns.

When it comes to criminal justice, the United States and Britain place a very high priority on juries of ordinary citizens to sift through the facts and decide on guilt or innocence. It is the job of these twelve ordinary people to figure out who is lying and who is telling the truth. In some cases, such as those dealing with the possibility of capital punishment, the jury even decides the penalty. This fundamental form of democracy is a key distinguishing feature of our entire governing system.

The Anglo-American system rigidly separates the judicial function from the prosecutorial power. Justice is achieved by a three-way process involving the prosecutor, the defense attorney, and the judge and jury. The prosecution and defense battle it out and an impartial judge and jury collaborate to make the decision and mete out the sentence.

The prosecutor cannot even bring a felony case in most jurisdictions unless a grand jury approves the bill of indictment. And, of course, he will not prevail at trial unless a jury votes his way, usually unanimously.

The European system, which is used in the International Criminal Court, is totally different. There are no grand juries or trial juries. The investigator, the prosecutor, and the judge are usually the same person. Justice is not based on the results of an adversary system with an impartial referee. It stems from an investigation by the judicial and prosecutorial authority and an application of the law to his findings. The defense has very limited rights and is often not much more than an observer as the judge processes the case and renders his decision.

In addition, the ICC has none of our constitutional safeguards against unjust imprisonment or prosecutorial overreach. It would not have the Fourth Amendment's guarantees against unreasonable searches and seizures or the Fifth Amendment's protection against self-incrimination, its requirement of due process, or its prohibition of double jeopardy. Indeed, the ICC would have the explicit power to try defendants who are acquitted in American criminal courts. Theirs would be a super jurisdiction not delimited by what national courts decide. There is no guarantee of a speedy and public trial in the international court as there is in our Sixth Amendment. Nor is there any right to a jury trial.

When the British asked the United States to submit to the jurisdiction of the tribunal that it had established to stop the slave trade, President John Quincy Adams warned against our participation. His warning echoes the current criticism of subjecting the United States to ICC jurisdiction. Despite Adams's well known hatred of slavery and support of abolition, he wrote that making Americans subject to the jurisdiction of the International Slave Trade Tribunal would subject them to being "carried away by the . . . officers of a foreign power, subjected to the decision of a tribunal in a foreign land, without benefit of the intervention of a jury of accusation, or of a jury of trial, by a court of judges and umpires, half of whom would be foreigners, and all irresponsible to the supreme authorities of the United States."[10]

Obama: Putting the United States Under the Thumb of the International Criminal Court

The ICC began with the so-called Rome Statute, which was adopted by 110 nations. Written in 1998, it lays out the structure for the court and governs its procedures and jurisdiction. The United States signed the Rome Statute in 2000, as Clinton's term was coming to a close. President Clinton refused to send it to the Senate for ratification because of his concern over certain key provisions.

So, when the ICC was established in 2002, the Bush administration, likewise, refused to participate and notified the United Nations' secretary-general that the United States did not intend to ratify the Rome Statute or join the ICC and that "the United States has no legal obligations arising from its signature"[11] on the Rome Statute.

Bush was particularly worried that when US soldiers or other personnel served in nations that were part of the ICC they could be turned over to the court for trial. His administration negotiated a series of so-called Article 98 agreements with over one hundred countries that hosted US personnel ensuring that they would not turn them over to the ICC without US consent.

Obama is moving ever closer to ICC participation. Globalpolicy.org reported in 2010 that "the American government has signaled a willingness to engage in closer cooperation with the International Criminal Court, ICC."[12] They noted that "since assuming the US presidency at the start of 2009, Barack Obama has fostered a policy of cautious engagement with the court. Last November, the United States participated for the first time in the annual meeting of ICC member states, the Assembly of States Parties (ASP). It also announced that it would send a delegation to the ICC review conference in Kampala, which seemed to signal a departure from the policy of previous administrations."[13]

The Kampala Conference, held in 2010, brought the United States closer to ICC membership. The Conference noted that "during the Review Conference, 112 pledges with the purpose of strengthening the Rome Statute system were made by 37 states parties including the United States and the European Union. In addition, the Conference adopted the Kampala Declaration, reaffirming states' commitment to the Rome Statute and its full implementation, as well as its universality and integrity."[14]

Secretary of State Hillary Clinton defended US participation in the Kampala Conference, saying that it gave us a chance to influence their deliberations even if we did not join the court. She said, "the US must become more involved with the ICC in order to positively affect the court and address 'some of the challenges that are raised concerning (US) membership.' "[15]

Her justification for involvement in the ICC decision-making process is completely without merit. If the United States doesn't participate in the ICC, the court will wither on the vine like a latter-day League of Nations. The entire purpose of the court is to cut

America down to size. If we don't play ball, we don't have to worry about what the court decides to do. We will not be subject to its jurisdiction. It is only if we plan to participate, as Obama evidently does, that we have to worry about the rules of the game.

The most terrifying part of the ICC is the peek it gives us into the plans for global governance being hatched on the European left and in the United Nations.

UN envoys to the Climate Change Conference in Durban, South Africa, have just recently proposed a global climate court. FOX News describes how the court would be responsible for enforcing a sprawling set of rules requiring developed countries to cut emissions while compensating poorer countries in order to pay off a historical climate debt.[16]

The proposals were presented to the 194 nations at the Durban conference on December 10, 2011. FOX News relates how the "the draft document [proposing the court] . . . gives a glimpse into the long-term vision some nations hold for the creation of an international legal framework on climate change."[17]

The International Court of Climate Justice would seek to guarantee the compliance[18] of developed countries like the United States, Britain, Canada, Australia, and much of Europe with requirements for the reduction of greenhouse gas emissions.

FOX News reports that the court would be charged with making developed countries pay their climate debt to poor countries by helping them with " 'finance, technology and capacity building' so they can 'adapt to and mitigate climate change' while helping eliminate poverty."[19]

Oy vey!

The international bureaucrats want to use the idea of global courts to take away our sovereignty and override our democracy.

The powers they are granting to the ICC amount to a complete ability to overrule the actions of the US Congress, the president, and the Supreme Court. Americans can be prosecuted even if the Supreme Court in the United States says they are innocent. Presidents and Congressional leaders can be hauled before the court for making war if the court feels the conflict was illegal and not sanctioned by the United Nations. And the rules of the court totally circumvent the guarantees embedded by our founders in the United States Constitution and its Bill of Rights.

Yet the very same leftists who cheered when the Warren Supreme Court expanded the rights of criminal defendants in American courts are now loudly calling for American participation in the ICC ubercourt.

That's because the International Criminal Court has nothing to do with criminals. Were its arbitrary system of justice to be loosed on drug dealers or murderers, the left would have a fit. But since its power is aimed at the elected leaders of the United States, they applaud the move toward global governance!

The global governance crowd also wants to cash in on the minerals, particularly oil, which lie embedded under the sea off our shores. Under the guise of protecting freedom of the seas, which is something that our navy does quite well, they want to assert international jurisdiction through the Law of the Sea Treaty (usefully named LOST), so that they can rake in billions in royalties.

THE THREAT OFFSHORE:
THE LAW OF THE SEA TREATY

Not content with regulating nations, the Law of the Sea Treaty attempts to constrain what we do offshore.

Negotiated in the 1970s, the treaty was part of the New International Economic Order heralded at the United Nations, an order designed, according to *Forbes*, to take "money from productive First World democracies and [give] it to collectivist Third World autocracies."[20] When the diplomats had finished hammering out the treaty, President Reagan refused to sign it, to the horror of international diplomats, bureaucrats, and activists.[21]

But, as *Forbes* notes, the dreams of the international diplomats and bureaucrats die hard. "Unfortunately, treaties attract US diplomats like flames attract moths. It's hard for the State Department to imagine an international agreement to which America is not part."[22] So, Bush 41 and Clinton renegotiated the treaty including language meant to fix its defects. But, because it was still a bad deal for America, the agreement was never ratified by the Senate.

Now the treaty is coming up again for ratification as Obama and Senate Foreign Relations Committee Chairman John Kerry try to ram it through while the Democrats still control the Senate. The Republican ranking member on the committee, Senator Richard Lugar of Indiana, a certified RINO (Republican In Name Only), is backing the treaty and can be counted on to help get it passed.

Replacing the US Navy with a Treaty

The basic intent of the treaty is fine but unnecessary. It seeks to establish freedom of the seas by international agreement. While this sounds great, it might have the perverse effect of limiting our ability to navigate the world's oceans. Former UN ambassador John Bolton explains that "if the Senate ratifies the [Law of the Sea] treaty, we would become subject to its dispute-resolution mechanisms and ambiguities. Right now, since we are the world's major naval power, our conduct dominates state practice and hence customary international law—to our decided advantage."[23]

After all, Bolton notes, all we want to do is to use our navy "to enhance international peace and security, deter conflict, reassure allies, and collect intelligence."[24] He worries that if we buy into the LOST framework, we would have to take our chances on "endless legal maneuvering and the submission of conflicting claims to the treaty's international tribunal, where our prospects are uncertain at best."[25]

Bolton also warns of Chinese efforts to game the LOST system. LOST awards each signatory a two-hundred-mile offshore exclusive economic zone for deep-sea mining operations that is well beyond the twelve-mile territorial waters that define its sovereignty. While these economic zones would be international waters under the treaty, former UN ambassador Bolton writes that "China is exploiting the treaty's ambiguities to declare 'no go' zones in regions where centuries of state practice clearly permit unrestricted maritime activity."[26]

China takes the position that it can keep American intelligence-gathering operations out of its economic zone, even though LOST makes no mention of such a restriction.

Bolton explains Beijing's game: "China simply does not want the US military to gather intelligence near its shores. [It] wants to deny American access . . . so it can have its way with its neighbors." Bolton notes that "Beijing is building a network of 'anti-access' and 'area denial' weapons, such as integrated air defenses, submarines, land-based ballistic and cruise missiles, and cyber and antisatellite systems designed to make it exceedingly hazardous for American ships and aircraft to traverse China's exclusive zone or peripheral seas."[27]

Nevertheless, advocates of LOST say that it would give us a seat at the table when matters of international naval law are discussed and a guarantee of freedom of navigation. But is the guarantee more secured by a treaty or by the power and practice of the US Navy?

Steven Groves of the Heritage Foundation writes that "the navigational rights and freedoms enjoyed by the United States and the Navy are guaranteed not by membership in a treaty, but rather through a combination of long-standing legal principles and persistent naval operations."[28]

Groves points out that the US Navy is constantly asserting its right to sail anywhere on the world's oceans simply by doing it without challenge. He points out that "the evidence indicates that the navigational provisions [of LOST] are already locked in to the extent that any aspect of international law can be."[29] He says that signers and nonsigners of LOST "have generally adhered to the convention's navigational provisions in good faith and that those provisions have endured, not eroded."[30]

The Third World Cashes In on American Offshore Oil Royalties

But the real intent of LOST is economic. The less developed nations of the world, and their bureaucratic allies in the UN and in Europe, want to cash in on American offshore oil drilling. According to Article 82 of the treaty, the United States would have to forfeit royalties generated from oil and gas exploration on the continental shelf beyond 200 miles. The US calls this area the *extended continental shelf*. This money, considered international royalties under LOST, would go to the International Seabed Authority, created by the treaty and based in Kingston, Jamaica.

The US Extended Continental Shelf Task Force estimates that the treaty would lead to forfeiting "many billions, if not trillions of dollars."[31]

Royalty payments to the International Seabed Authority would have to begin in the sixth year of production at each offshore site. Starting in the twelfth year, the Heritage Foundation reports, "about half of the revenue that would otherwise go to the US Treasury would instead be sent to the [International Seabed] Authority."[32]

Who would get our money? Whomever the assembly created by LOST designated. The assembly would have more than one hundred and sixty members and

the United States, which would provide an estimated quarter of the Seabed Authority's revenue, would only have one vote in deciding on its distribution. Would the money go to dictatorial regimes like China or to terror-sponsoring countries like Cuba and Sudan (all treaty signatories)? Heritage notes that "thirteen of the twenty most corrupt nations according to Transparency International are signatories to LOST."[33]

Why should we sacrifice these royalties? And, if we are moved to give them away, why should we give up the power to say to whom they should go?

We would not only be required to give up the money we would earn from offshore drilling; we might also have to transfer our mining technology to the Seabed Authority, which would be free to give it to competitor nations.

The Seabed Authority would supervise a mining subsidiary called, right out of *Star Trek*, the Enterprise. LOST provides that the Seabed Authority should "promote and encourage the transfer to developing states of such technology and scientific knowledge." It also provides that the Authority "shall initiate and promote . . . the transfer of technology to the Enterprise and to developing states" and that it shall "facilitate the access of the Enterprise and of developing States to the relevant technology."[34]

It gets worse. The treaty also provides that "if the Enterprise or developing States are unable to obtain deep seabed mining technology, the Authority may request all or any of the contractors and their respective sponsoring State or States to cooperate with it in facilitating the acquisition of deep seabed mining technology."[35]

So, what is to stop the authority from demanding technology transfers as the price of its okay to let companies proceed with offshore mining?

Not only must we share the revenues from our deep-sea mining operations with whomever the Seabed Authority directs, but we might also have to give them our proprietary technology as well.

A Backdoor Treaty on Global Warming?

Enter the environmentalists! In the years since LOST was first drafted, climate change and global warming has become the new international cause *du jour*. William C. G. Burns of the Monterey Institute of International Studies argues that LOST "may prove to be one of the primary battlegrounds for climate change issues in the future."[36] More reason to stay away!

He explains that while nobody thought of climate change when the treaty was written, it contains a very expansive definition of marine pollution, which could be read as including "the potential impacts of rising sea surface temperatures, rising sea levels, and changes in ocean pH as a consequence of rising levels of carbon dioxide in sea water," which could "give rise to actions under the Convention's marine pollution provisions."[37]

And, if the United States ratifies LOST, Burns raises the specter that its provisions on pollution and climate change could be enforceable in American courts. LOST specifically provides that its decisions "shall be enforceable in the territory of each State Party."

Could its provisions be enforced in US courts? In *Medillin v. Texas* 552 US 491 (2008), Supreme Court Chief Justice John Roberts, writing for the majority, held that international agreements are not enforceable in American courts unless Congress has made them so by specific legislation. But he also wrote that if a treaty is "self-executing," as the language in LOST suggests that it is, then it could be enforced in our courts.[38]

Thus, if we ratify LOST, we will be bound hand and foot. On land, our local planning and zoning boards will have to enforce land-use policies designed by the international environmentalist community, and at sea, we will be bound by an International Seabed Authority over which we would have no power.

The decisions of our elected officials won't count for much at all. Another nail in the coffin of government of the people, by the people, and for the people!

GUN CONTROL IN DISGUISE: THE PROPOSED UN SMALL ARMS TREATY

The United Nations is trying to conduct an end run around Congress and jam through gun controls, which it would impose on the United States. Capitalizing on an antigun president and secretary of state and a Democratic majority in the Senate, the UN is actively hammering out an international small arms treaty cracking down on the exportation of guns throughout the world.

There is, of course, no question that small arms—AK-47s, grenades, handguns, automatics—are proliferating in all countries. But mostly governments are selling the weapons. China, the United States, Russia, Israel, and a host of other countries conduct a lively commerce in weapons and arms. But the proposed UN treaty would take advantage of public concern about the spread of arms to crack down on private arms sellers and owners whose contribution to the worldwide arms epidemic is minimal.

And the Obama administration is getting serious about the Small Arms Treaty. In January 2010, the United States joined 152 other countries in endorsing a UN Arms Treaty Resolution that will establish a 2012 conference to draft a blueprint for enactment. Secretary of State Hillary Clinton has pledged to push for Senate ratification.

Former US ambassador to the United Nations John Bolton sees the treaty as a way to impose gun controls on the United States. "The administration is trying to act as though this [the UN Treaty on Small Arms] is really just a treaty about international arms trade between nation states, but there's no doubt—as was the case back over a decade ago—that the real agenda here is domestic firearms control. After the treaty is approved and it comes into force, you will find out that it . . . requires the Congress to adopt some measure that restricts ownership of firearms. The administration knows it cannot obtain this kind of legislation purely in a domestic context. . . . They will use an international agreement as an excuse to get domestically what they couldn't otherwise."[39] And, if Congress won't pass such laws, the courts will force it to do so. The treaty's provisions must be enforced!

The terms of the treaty are still under discussion, but FOX News reports that it would create a new bureaucracy to "regulate international weapon sales, and require countries that host firearms manufacturers to set up a compensation fund for victims of gun violence worldwide."[40] FOX News notes that the new treaty would require "every country to submit a report to the [new agency] outlining 'all activities undertaken in order to accomplish the implementation of this Treaty, including . . . domestic laws, regulations and administrative measures.' "[41]

FOX News reports that the treaty would also require "countries to set up their own government agencies to track any guns that could be exported."[42] The treaty draft reads: "Parties shall take all necessary measures to control brokering activities taking place within its territories . . . to prevent the diversion of exported arms into the illicit market or to unintended end users."[43]

A major US gun manufacturer believes that the draft treaty "leaves room for the [UN] to declare the registration of all American-made guns to prevent illegal exportation."[44]

Defenders of the Small Arms Treaty note that the UN resolution, which opened the door for negotiations on the compact, specifically denied any intention to force gun control on domestic firearms owners. It reads, in part, "Acknowledging also the right of States to regulate internal transfers of arms and national ownership, including through national constitutional protections on private ownership, exclusively within their territory . . ."[45]

On October 14, 2009, Secretary of State Hillary Clinton reversed the policy of the Bush administration, which had opposed a Small Arms Treaty. Reuters reported that she announced that "the United States would support the talks as long as the negotiating forum, the so-called Conference on the Arms Trade Treaty, 'operates under the rules of consensus decision-making.' [She said] 'Consensus is needed to ensure the widest possible support for the Treaty and to avoid loopholes in the Treaty that can be exploited by those wishing to export arms irresponsibly,' "[46]

Clinton's emphasis on "consensus" is intended to give the United States the right to veto any provision in the treaty. But it ignores the fact that the treaty is subject to "mission creep" once it is signed and ratified and that it is completely unnecessary.

If the agency administering the new treaty decides that it requires registration and other restrictions on gun ownership, it can do so. And international treaties under UN jurisdiction often expand their scope as the international bureaucrats widen their reach. The treaty's emphasis on exportation of guns could easily be expanded to require that all Americans register their firearms so that the international busybodies make sure none are exported.

But this discussion misses the essential point: Joe down the block isn't exporting arms. It is the governments of the United States, Russia, China, Israel, and a number of others. Their arms flood the world. For the nations in the United Nations—themselves the sellers and buyers of small arms—to sign a treaty stopping *us* from selling arms to Africa and other purchasers is hypocritical and inane.

THE EUROPEAN UNION WANTS TO STOP LITTERING IN SPACE!

DISCLAIMER: Nothing in this chapter is a joke!

The moral busybodies in the European Union are worried that there is too much litter or debris in space and they are determined to clean it up. NASA estimates that there are 22,000 pieces of space junk as big as a softball and more than half a million bigger than a marble.[47]

But the EU efforts to tidy up outer space may have the effect of making it illegal for the United States to deploy antimissile systems in space, weapons that may be the only effective counter to nuclear ballistic missile threats from Iran and North Korea. Indeed, some suggest that the code is a form of "lawfare"—warfare through changes in the law that would unilaterally disarm the United States in the face of a growing space capability by China and a looming menace of nuclear-tipped ballistic missiles by rogue states such as Iran and North Korea.

Professing worry about all the junk orbiting the earth, the European Union wants to restrict space activities to minimize space debris so it is proposing a "code of conduct for Outer Space Activities." According to Taylor Dinerman of the Stonegate Institute (formerly Hudson Institute), the code would "have the effect of banning all 'space weapons' or at least ones that create debris or space weapons whose use will result in an out of control spacecraft that is the functional equivalent of a piece of debris."

And where did space debris come from? Dinerman reports that "a large portion . . . is the result of the Chinese Anti-Satellite weapons test of February 2007, when a Chinese space weapon hit an old Chinese weather satellite and blew it to pieces. The debris from this test has been falling out of orbit since then, but, as with all forms of space debris, it is a slow process, and if a piece were to hit a satellite or another piece of debris, more 'space junk' would be created." That China could obliterate a satellite was ominous news indeed for the US military.

We depend heavily on satellites to operate our military machine and civilian economy. The Pentagon uses the Global Positioning System (GPS) to move and locate its troops and equipment and gathers intelligence from spy satellites. Dinerman describes how our "civilian economy depends on communications satellites, on GPS and on remote sensors for almost everything: electronic funds transfers, weather forecasting, pollution monitoring and most importantly to keep hundreds of millions of Americans connected with each other wherever they are."

Dinerman and other critics see the European initiative as an effort to use treaties and codes of conduct to hamstring the US military. He writes, "what this Code would in fact ban is what the Europeans, the Russians and the Chinese see as American 'space weapons.' The Code is designed to prevent the United States and other liberal democracies from deploying systems actively to defend their own satellites, while it would allow Russia, China and just about anyone else to continue their space weapons programs, probably with only minimal cosmetic changes."

As sanctions prove ineffective in stopping Iran from developing nuclear weapons or North Korea—which already has the bomb—from building delivery vehicles, space-based defenses become more important. Interceptor missiles launched from the ground and sea—current US capabilities—can only intercept enemy missiles as they travel through space or as they descend on their target. But space-based interceptors can kill enemy missiles in the launch phase before they enter space. These missiles travel much more slowly, are easier to hit, have not MIRVed into multiple warheads, and the debris falls on the country launching the attack.

For all these reasons, then-President George W. Bush opted out of the Anti-Ballistic Missile Treaty, an action that gave the United States the legal ability to construct and deploy space-based weapons. President Obama, of course, has not acted on this, but a new Republican president is likely to move in that direction, especially considering the Iranian and North Korean threats.

Leftists and socialists in Europe—the same crowd that opposed deploying intermediate range missiles in Europe during the Cold War—are anxious to prevent the United States from deploying weapons in space. So they have resorted to the subterfuge of a "code of conduct" aimed at stopping deployment in the name of preventing debris.

The scary thing is that President Obama and Secretary of State Hillary Clinton may sign away our rights to deploy space-based interceptors without asking Congress for permission.

Michael Krepon, writing in the September 12, 2011, issue of *Space News*, warns that the Obama administration might use the Code of Conduct as a way to bypass the Senate. "Space diplomacy offers the Obama

administration a welcome reprieve from trench warfare, since executive agreements like the space Code of
Conduct are not treaties, do not require the approval
of two-thirds of the Senate and are a clear presidential
prerogative."

Clinton said in January 2012 as she announced that
the United States would begin discussions with the
Europeans on the Code of Conduct: "the long-term
sustainability of our space environment is at serious risk
from space debris and irresponsible actors. Ensuring
the stability, safety, and security of our space systems
is of vital interest to the United States and the global
community."[48]

Curiously, Clinton's statement came a week after
Ellen Tauscher, undersecretary of state for arms control
and international security, appeared to reject the code.
"It's been clear from the very beginning that we're not
going along with the code of conduct," she said at the
time; "it's too restrictive."[49]

We can only speculate on what went on during the
week between these two contradictory statements.
Most likely Europeans and leftists pushed back against
Tauscher's statement and Obama and Clinton caved in
the face of their pressure.

Clinton was careful to say that she would not
agree to any treaty that limited American military

deployments in space, but such limitation—dear to the hearts of liberals—is the fundamental motivation for the debris ban.

The draft code would pledge signatories to maintain the use of space "for peaceful purposes without interference, fully respecting the security, safety and integrity of space objects in orbit."[50] The nations would pledge to "prevent harmful interference in outer space activities" and to "seek to prevent outer space from being an area of conflict even if they were engaged in military activities in space."[51]

The plain language of the code indicates how easily it could be used to preclude military uses of space, anti-satellite capability, and the positioning of antimissile missiles on orbiting platforms.

We must not let European lawfare disarm us unilaterally in the face of growing Chinese, Iranian, and North Korean threats!

THE UNITED NATIONS TELLS US HOW TO RAISE OUR KIDS

Not content with regulating our offshore coastline, telling our president and Congress when to go to war, regulating firearms in our country, and preventing us from defending ourselves in outer space, the United

Nations' moral busybodies want to tell us how to bring up our children.

Twenty years ago, the Clinton administration signed the UN Convention on the Rights of the Child. Fortunately, Congress did not ratify it, but now leftist Democrats like Senators Barbara Boxer (D-CA) and socialist Bernie Sanders (D-Vt) are seeking to ratify the Convention before the Republicans take over the Senate and kill it.

The Convention does several constructive things, like ban child pornography, child prostitution, and child soldiers. But the United States has already accepted these provisions, and signed them, and the Senate has ratified our participation. The broader Convention, however, is another story. It establishes an eighteen-member panel in Geneva composed of "persons of high moral character" who are charged with reviewing the rights of children in participating nations.

The treaty, which covers all children under eighteen, declares that "the best interests of children must be the primary concern in making decisions that may affect them. All adults should do what is best for children. . . . This particularly applies to budget, policy, and law makers."[52]

The document goes on to state that "when countries ratify the Convention, they agree to review their laws relating to children. This involves assessing their social services, legal, health and educational systems, as well as levels of funding for these services. Governments are then obliged to take all necessary steps to ensure that the minimum standards set by the Convention in these areas are being met."[53]

In the United Kingdom, the governing Conservative/ Liberal Democrat coalition got a good indication of what the treaty could lead to. When Prime Minister David Cameron tried to cut welfare benefits to £26,000 a year for a family (about $43,000) and £18,200 for a single person (about $33,000), the United Kingdom's Childrens Commissioner Maggie Atkinson said that the reductions may violate the UN Convention on the Rights of the Child.

The *Guardian* reported that "Atkinson pointed out that children's rights to social security are guaranteed under the United Nations convention on the rights of the child. The UK is party to the convention, and in December 2010 the children's minister, Sarah Teather, committed the government to giving 'due regard' to the convention when making new policy and legislation."[54]

Britain now faces the prospect that it may not be able to legislate its own level of welfare payments because the social workers in the European Union feel that $43,000 is not enough for a family to live on. (Median household income in the US is $50,000 and the comparable statistic for Britain is much lower.)

Article 12 of the treaty—respect for the views of the child—requires that "when adults are making decisions that affect children, children have the right to say what they think should happen and have their opinions taken into account. . . . This Convention encourages adults to listen to the opinions of children and involve them in decision-making." In a bow to reality, the convention notes that "children's ability to form and express their opinions develops with age and most adults will naturally give the views of teenagers greater weight than those of a preschooler, whether in family, legal or administrative decisions."[55]

This provision could create a due-process requirement that adults hear what their children have to say about their decisions that "affect" them. If parents did not give children an opportunity to comment on their parents' divorce or social relationships, they could find themselves in violation of the UN Treaty, a treaty that a US court would be obliged to enforce!

Michael Farris, president of ParentalRights.org, says that the treaty's effect would be far-reaching. "Whether you ground your kids for smoking marijuana, whether you take them to church, whether you let them go to junior prom, all of those things . . . will be the government's decision. It will affect every parent who's told their children to do the dishes."[56]

But Farris understates the danger. The "government" would not be meddling in our lives and our families. It would be an international treaty. Our elected representatives would be powerless to modify its provisions and our president could only do so if the other signatories released us.

Worried that your children are hanging out with a bad bunch? Article 15 guarantees children "freedom of association." It states, "Children have the right to meet together and to join groups and organizations, as long as it does not stop other people from enjoying their rights."[57] So you may not be able to ground your children since it would deny their "freedom of association."

Spanking and slapping are out! They would become violations of international law! Article 19 says that "any form of discipline involving violence is unacceptable."[58]

Countries that skimp foreign aid to poorer nations may run afoul of Article 24, which specifies that "rich countries should help poorer countries achieve . . . the best health care possible, safe drinking water, nutritious food, and a clean and safe environment" for children.

Congress and the president may not want to vote for extra foreign aid, but the treaty provides that the courts can make them do so to meet America's treaty obligations!

The treaty creates numerous legal rights for children. While admirable, these "rights" could lead to lawsuits forcing governments to increase budgets for welfare or education even if the taxpayers reject them just as constitutional rights of prisoners have led the courts to demand early release of certain felons to mitigate overcrowding. The treaty grants children the right to "help from the government if they are poor or in need" (Article 26).[59]

Article 27 requires governments to "help families and guardians who cannot afford to provide an adequate standard of living for children with help, particularly with regard to food, clothing, and housing."[60]

Article 28 confers a right to a free primary education and requires that "wealthy countries should help poorer countries achieve this right." The busybodies who drafted the treaty demand that "governments must ensure that school administrators review their discipline policies and eliminate any discipline practices involving physical or mental violence, abuse or neglect."[61] Can we imagine Miss Jones, a third grade teacher, being brought up on charges for speaking harshly to Johnny or Jennie?

The lax policies in juvenile facilities, the chance for escape, and the tendency toward early release led most states to elect to try youthful offenders above a certain age—typically fifteen or sixteen—as adults and to sentence them to adult prison if they are convicted. Article 37 would overrule these laws. It provides, "Children should not be put in prison with adults."[62]

Supporters of the treaty note that children are subjected to horrific abuse in Third World countries. Particularly in Muslim countries, reports of acid being thrown in their faces are common.

In revving up support for the treaty to get it ratified in the Senate, Barbara Boxer said, "children deserve basic human rights . . . and the convention protects children's rights by setting some standards here so that the most vulnerable people of society will be protected." She added, "Now, all you have to do is look around the world and see these girls that are having acid thrown in their face," implying that the US refusal to ratify the treaty led to abuses elsewhere.[63]

But Boxer's illustration—despicable acid throwing— begs the question: How does the United States' refusal to ratify the treaty cause other nations to violate its provisions? Globalists argue that if the leading nations of the world set an example then others will follow.

But the United States already sets quite an example. We protect the rights of children far better than most nations on earth. All the treaty will do is provide a basis for litigation in the United States to overrule local governments, force increased spending and taxes, mandate additional foreign aid, and meddle in discipline and family decision making.

Remember that the treaty, should we ratify it, would become supreme over any state or federal law.

President Obama bemoans the fact that the United States is alone in the world in not ratifying the treaty (except for Somalia). Liberals urge us to get with the program,

But FOX News points out that even "when acceding to the convention, countries are able to sign so-called RUDs—reservations, understandings, and declarations—that can hinder or negate responsibilities they would otherwise be bound to follow. Most majority Muslim nations express reservations on all provisions of the convention that are incompatible with Islamic Sharia law, which takes much of the teeth out of the treaty. Acid attacks on girls continue in Afghanistan, which is already party to the convention."[64]

FOX News reports that the United Nations itself admits that the treaty could not be enforced in many countries. " 'When it comes to signatories who violate the convention and/or its optional protocols—there is no means to oblige states to fulfill their legal obligations,' said Giorgia Passarelli, a spokeswoman for the

UN High Commission on Human Rights, which over-
sees the child-rights body. Passarelli said that the committee has kept a constant spotlight on rights violators
and fed into decisions made by the Security Council,
especially involving child soldiers. But even then, she
added, such pressure does not always prevail."[65]

But in the United States, the treaty could be fully
enforced through our national court system. The
possibilities for litigation are endless and it would be
inevitable that the treaty would lead to a new level of
intrusive government intervention in the most intimate
of family practices.

As one reads the treaty, one wonders how we raised
children for so long without one!

BUREAUCRATIC REGULATION TRIUMPHANT: THE UNITED NATIONS' WAR ON THE AUTOMOBILE

Threats to freedom usually advance masked, their real
purpose concealed behind a façade of good intentions.
The world's environmentalists, loudly proclaiming
their stewardship of God's planet, seek to impose global
bureaucratic regulation on every state, city, town, or
hamlet in the United States through the global Agenda
21 project.

Their goal is to crowd us all into small spaces so we drive our cars less and reduce our carbon emissions. They dislike sprawl and want to impose their vision on the rest of us.

Agenda 21, adopted at the 1992 United Nations Conference on Environment and Development (UNCED), held in Rio de Janeiro, Brazil, is "a comprehensive plan of action to be taken globally, nationally and locally by organizations of the United Nations System, governments, and major groups in every area in which human impacts on the environment."[66]

Mike Brownfield, writing for Heritage.org, notes that Agenda 21, three hundred pages long, sets forth "hundreds of specific goals and strategies that national and local governments are encouraged to adopt."[67] Each of these steps has a common goal: to discourage us from driving.

Brownfield describes it as a "voluntary plan . . . [that] calls on governments to intervene and regulate nearly every potential impact that human activity could have on the environment."[68] Agenda 21 wants to get governments to "rethink economic development and find ways to halt the destruction of irreplaceable natural resources and pollution of the planet."[69]

Behind this motherhood-and-apple-pie concept, Agenda 21 is a very serious threat to our liberties and, above all, to our self-government. While voluntary, its standards give liberal regulators a guideline for enacting laws and rules that circumscribe our freedom in important ways. As Brownfield warns: "Ready to trade in your car for a bike, or maybe a subway instead? Interested in fewer choices for your home, paying more for housing, and being crammed into a denser neighborhood? You can have all this and more if radical environmentalists and 'smart growth' advocates have their way and local, state, and the federal government impose the policies set forth in the United Nations' Agenda 21."[70]

CNN describes how "[e]ven though the US government is not legally bound by the initiative, local governments across the country have implemented some of its strategies for sustainable development. Smart growth, transportation planning, and limited rural development are all Agenda 21 goals."[71]

Agenda 21 is an end run around our democratic processes. It was inspired by environmentalists, written by technocrats, adopted by diplomats, and is being used by bureaucrats to justify their preemption of private property rights and democratic control over our local governmental institutions.

In the name of Agenda 21, local governments are increasing regulation of all development and property, masking their social planning behind the noble language of Agenda 21 about protecting the earth's resources.

One of the agenda's key themes is the fight against urban sprawl, where low-density growth extends over a large geographic area (e.g., Los Angeles). Environmentalists worry that sprawl encourages extensive driving with the consequent massive release of carbon into the atmosphere, perpetuating global climate change.

Brownfield warns that this "translates into restrictive zoning policies that are aimed at deterring suburban growth. Ultimately, they suppress housing supply and drive up home prices, in turn imposing unnecessary costs, especially on middle- and lower-income households. These policies contributed to and aggravate the real-estate bubble by putting inflationary pressures on housing prices."[72]

Wendell Cox, a visiting fellow at the Heritage Foundation; Dr. Ronald D. Utt, a senior fellow at the Roe Institute for Economic Policy Studies at the Heritage Foundation; Brett D. Schaefer, a fellow at the Margaret Thatcher Center for Freedom at the Heritage Foundation; and Shelby Cullom Davis of the Heritage Foundation have collaborated on an extensive analysis of the Agenda 21 policies, published in rightsidenews.com.

They say that the program tries to "impose land use regulations that would force Americans into denser living arrangements, curtail freedom of choice in housing, discriminate against lower-income Americans, and compel people to pay more for their houses and give up their cars in favor of subways, trolleys, buses, and bicycles."[73]

Agenda 21 doesn't like farms or rural areas. It worries that they waste energy. They would much rather have us all live in high-density cities and be less dependent on cars. When Agenda 21–inspired smart-growth plans are adopted, online magazine americanthinker. com warns, they can lead to "a massive reshuffling of property rights. . . .

- Farmers may lose subdivision rights;

- conservation land adjacent to population centers may be rezoned into commercial employment centers;

- and low-density land in small towns is re-designated as growth area and rezoned to accommodate diverse housing including high-density apartments and condominiums."[74]

Americanthinker.com relates how the Planning Department of Carroll County, Maryland, is following a plan right out of Agenda 21, calling its recommendations *smart-growth* policies.

Richard Rothschild, Carroll County commissioner, is highly critical of the plan. "Smart growth," he says, "is not science; it is political dogma combined with an insidious dose of social engineering. Smart growth is a wedding wherein zoning code is married with government-sponsored housing initiatives to accomplish government's goal of social re-engineering. It urbanizes rural towns with high-density development, and gerrymanders population centers using housing initiatives that enable people with weak patterns of personal financial responsibility to acquire homes in higher-income areas. This has the effect of shifting the voting patterns of rural municipalities from right to left."[75]

Americanthinker.com spells out what the Carroll County plan, called Pathways, includes:

- "Rezoning of thousands of acres of beautiful, low-density agricultural farmland and protected residential conservation land into office parks

- Down-zoning of agriculture land to prevent future subdivision by farmers

- Up-zoning of low-density residential land around small towns into higher density zoning to permit construction of hundreds or possibly thousands of inclusive housing units, including apartments and condominiums

- Inclusive housing with placement of multi-family construction on in-fill lots within existing residential single family communities

- Endorsement of government-sponsored housing initiatives (subsidies)"[76]

Americanthinker.com reports that "Carroll County, Maryland is one of 1,168 cities, towns, and counties worldwide that are members of the International Council for Local Environmental Initiatives (ICLEI), which is an international association of local governments as well as national and regional local government organizations that have made a commitment to sustainable development. The ICLEI mission statement closely resembles that of Agenda 21. In fact, the ICLEI has Special Consultative Status with the UN Economic and Social Council and coordinates local government representation in the UN processes related to Agenda 21."[77]

The United Kingdom has been down the smart-growth road. Under the socialist Labour government following World War II, it adopted the Town and

Country Planning Act, "which forced nearly all sub-sequent development into existing urban footprints." Rightsidenews.com reports that the programs "have been an economic disaster. The citizens of the United Kingdom now have the smallest and most expensive housing of any advanced country in the world."[78]

In the United States, the antisprawl smart-growth program has worked to "deter suburban growth for all but the well-to-do," in the words of rightsidenews.com. "Growth control efforts underway in these communities were driven not only by a distorted view of the environment, but also by the desire of those already in place to prevent newcomers from arriving and spoiling the rural ambience of their suburban communities."[79]

Agenda 21: Taxing Rain; Limiting Toilet Flushes

The American Policy Center cites other examples of Agenda 21–inspired policy run amuck.

- Maryland governor Martin O'Malley wants to ban all septic tanks, which move the American Policy Center warns "will destroy the ability to live in rural areas." Continuing his war on toi-lets, O'Malley would "triple sewer 'flush' taxes on property bills—a tax on toilet flushes. Any county that doesn't comply will face a loss of state funding."[80]

- Houston, Texas, taxes rain and Knoxville, Tennessee, is thinking of following suit. Because rainwater runoff from private property pollutes streams, Houston charges a fee that private property owners have to pay when it rains. The city gets $400,000 a year by taxing rain. The American Policy Center reports that "some churches in South Carolina pay an annual rain runoff fee of as much as $2,600."[81]

- Six states—Hawaii, Virginia, Maryland, Vermont, New Jersey, and New York—have enacted Benefit Corporation laws, which give companies that follow Agenda 21 and sustainable development principles the right to go to the head of the line for permits, licenses, and other opportunities, according to the American Policy Center. And California, Colorado, Michigan, North Carolina, and Pennsylvania are considering such bills.

The federal EPA may put its clout behind Agenda 21. Some have speculated that it might deny grant funds to states and cities that do not adopt smart-growth policies.

When smart growth plans are adopted by statute, americanthinker.com notes, it "enable[s] municipalities to change zoning laws and engage in other regulatory actions that devalue property, restrict off-conveyances, and otherwise erode property values without payment of any compensation to the property owner."[82]

And President Obama has jumped on the Agenda 21 bandwagon, issuing an executive order (not reviewable by Congress) on June 9, 2011, establishing the White House Rural Council (WHRC). Theblaze.com links the executive order to Agenda 21, saying that it is designed "to begin taking control over almost all aspects of the lives of 16 percent of the American people."[83]

TheBlaze.com notes that section one of the order reads: "Sixteen percent of the American population lives in rural counties. Strong, sustainable rural communities are essential to winning the future and ensuring American competitiveness in the years ahead."[84]

The language about "sustainable rural communities" is right out of Agenda 21, whose watchword is "sustainability." The Obama order carries with it the threat of financial coercion to induce rural areas to toe the Agenda 21 line. It orders the White House Council to work "on streamlining and leveraging Federal investments in rural areas, where appropriate, to increase the impact of Federal dollars and create economic opportunities to improve the quality of life in rural America."[85]

TheBlaze.com wonders if the order contains "a hint . . . that a 'rural stimulus plan' might be in the making? Will the Federal government start pumping money into farmlands under the guise of creating 'economic opportunities to improve the quality of life in rural America?' "[86]

Apart from the wisdom of imposing antisprawl "smart-growth" policies on rural America lies the basic question of democratic self-government. The Obama executive order implies a big role for the federal government in incentivizing local communities to adopt the Agenda 21 proposals to move away from low-density development toward crowded urban areas.

Newt Gingrich has helped to raise our awareness of the dangers of the Agenda 21 project. In a 2011 Republican presidential debate, then-candidate Gingrich said, "I would adopt a very strong policy towards the United Nations of dramatically taking on its absurdities. I would explicitly repudiate what Obama has done on Agenda 21 as the kind of interference from the United Nations."[87]

Gingrich noted, "Everywhere I go today, people . . . are very worried about Agenda 21. . . . It's part of a general problem of the United Nations and other international bureaucracies that are seeking to create an extra constitutional control over us. And I reject that model totally."[88]

Gingrich called Agenda 21 "a United Nations proposal to create a series of centralized planning provisions where your local city government can't do something because of some agreement they signed with some private group who are all committed to taking control of your private property and turning it into a publicly controlled property."[89]

As Gingrich points out, the real danger of Agenda 21 is that it takes land use and planning decisions out of the hands of the voters and gulls them into ceding them to zoning boards in the name of "smart growth" and "global sustainability." At the local level, it reflects the same contempt for democracy and voter decisions that the growth of IMF power represents on the international level.

We Don't Need Agenda 21 to Cut Carbon Emissions

However, environmental efforts like Agenda 21 are just not needed.

Underscoring the Agenda 21 and sustainability initiatives are concerns about global climate change. The reason they want to reduce low-density rural living is that they want to discourage driving. And their effort to turn America away from cars is linked to their concerns about the impact of the carbon emissions of motor vehicles on global climate.

We can debate whether climate change is happening. (We think it is.) Or whether it is largely or partially man-made? (We are agnostic on that one.) But even if you vote *yes* on both, the fact is that drastic changes in our zoning, energy, land use, and environmental laws just aren't necessary to reverse it. The United States, which has rejected the cap-and-trade system and refused to impose special taxes on carbon emissions, has had a spectacularly successful record in cutting its output of carbon despite its failure to adopt these liberal proposals.

Knowledgeable people realize that planning and coercive legislation are not necessary to salvage the planet even if it is endangered by climate change. Market forces and public education will do the job quite nicely, as they are. Nonetheless, environmentalists still press for programs like Agenda 21 because they are socialists who like central planning and government control, not because of any need to keep the planet green. Green is just their latest excuse to promote an agenda of government control and regulation.

No less an environmental authority than Lester R. Brown, president of the Earth Policy Institute and recipient of the United Nations Environment Prize in 1987, says that "between 2007 and 2011, carbon emissions from coal use in the United States dropped 10 percent. During the same period, emissions from oil use dropped 11 percent. The net effect of these trends was that US carbon emissions dropped 7 percent in four years."[90]

"And," Brown proclaims, "this is only the beginning. The initial fall in coal and oil use was triggered by the economic downturn, but now powerful new forces are reducing the use of both."[91]

Brown paints a green vision of the future. "We are now looking at a situation where the 7 percent decline in carbon emissions since the 2007 peak could expand to 20 percent by 2020, and possibly even to 30 percent. If so, the United States could become a world leader in cutting carbon emissions and stabilizing climate."[92]

Brown credits several factors with the sharp turnaround:

- The hugely successful efforts of green groups to block the building of new coal-fired plants, creating a de facto moratorium on such plants.

US Energy-Related Carbon Dioxide Emissions[93] 1950–2010 with Projection for 2011

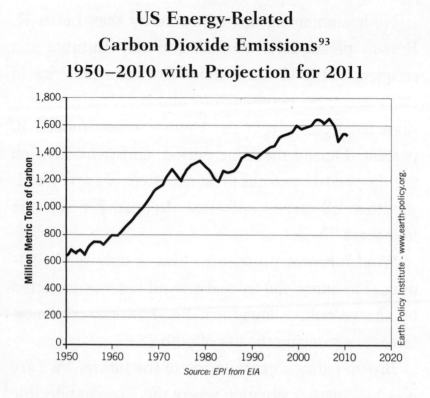

Source: EPI from EIA

- Environmental efforts have led to a decision to close 68 of our 492 coal-fired power plants.

- Wind energy has increased dramatically. Over the past four years, 27,000 megawatts have come on line and another 300,000 are awaiting construction. If this extra wind power comes on line, it will be enough to supply 80 million homes with electricity.

- 22,000 megawatts of solar panel energy are under development.

Cumulative Installed Wind Power Capacity in the United States 1980–2011[94]

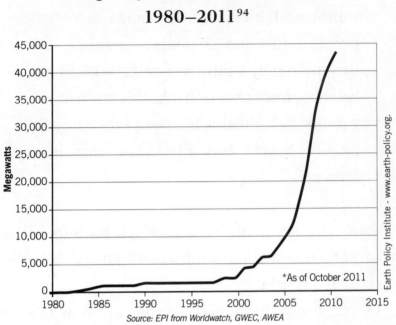

*As of October 2011

Earth Policy Institute - www.earth-policy.org.

Source: EPI from Worldwatch, GWEC, AWEA

- The size of America's car fleet is shrinking and "the fuel efficiency of new cars, already rising, will soon increase sharply. The most recent efficiency standards mandate that new cars sold in 2025 use only half as much fuel as those sold in 2010. Thus with each passing year, the US car fleet becomes more fuel-efficient, using less gasoline."[95]

- Brown writes that even as the size of the automobile fleet drops, "miles driven per car are declining because of higher gasoline prices, the continuing recession, and the shift to public transit and bicycles." He notes that "when people retire and no longer commute, miles driven drop by a third to a half." With so many baby boomers now retiring, this too will lower gasoline use. Finally, he sees a rapid growth in plug-in hybrid and all-electric cars in the future.[96]

And, as noted, natural gas, which releases half as much carbon as coal and a third less than oil,[97] is replacing coal at a rapid pace.

Okay. So why do we need Agenda 21? Why take the power to control our lives away from voters and give it to regulators? The free market system with its high gasoline prices (likely to go higher as political instability spreads to Saudi Arabia and, possibly, Kuwait) is deterring driving, so why put regulations in place that are not needed?

And public education is working. The way a free society adjusts to change is that it educates people to focus on the problem and make voluntary, responsible adjustments in their individual lives. That's what the ultimate green slogan, "think globally and act locally," is all about.

We need to beware of efforts to strip us of our democratic rights and our ability to make our own decisions, as individuals and as a community, in the name of protecting the environment. Natural market forces and public education leading to voluntary individual actions are doing just fine in protecting our precious planet.

ACTION AGENDA

Keeping our republican system of government has been the goal of our national political process ever since it began. Sometimes our adversaries were foreign: the British in 1812, the Germans in World Wars I and II, the Japanese in the Second World War, the Islamists in the War on Terror. Often, they have been domestic: the slave power in the antebellum South, unbridled crony capitalism in the industrial revolution, ongoing racism in the post-Reconstruction South, domestic communism in the '30s and '40s, and the expanded reach of big government under Obama.

Now, a new threat again comes from abroad: the overreach of international bureaucratic organizations, invading our democracy, regulating our economy, and trying to structure our most intimate land use decisions.

But the danger, as is usually the case with foreign threats, is increased by the sycophantic echo these international bureaucrats find among America's own political leaders. Within our own nation, elites have always distrusted democracy and wanted to control the often unruly masses. The financial elites distrust their economic populism. The intellectual elites distrust their social populism.

And the Obama administration, which has always rejected the very idea of American exceptionalism, is happy to subordinate American governance to international regulation. In a recent speech in Kansas, President Obama attacked the concept of "rugged individualism," saying "it's a simple theory—one that speaks to our . . . healthy skepticism of too much government. It fits well on a bumper sticker. Here's the problem: It doesn't work."[98]

To Obama, what works is international coordination, income redistribution, wealth transfer to poorer nations, and a consensus of economic experts. He regards democracy with frequently expressed alarm. During the 2008 campaign, he famously worried about the political power of alienated, white, blue-collar voters, saying, "it's not surprising . . . that they get bitter, they cling to guns or religion or antipathy to people who aren't like them or anti-immigrant sentiment or antitrade sentiment as a way to explain their frustrations."⁹⁹

Who can trust such people? Who can base the decisions of the world's dominant nation upon their prejudices and bitter scapegoating? In international eyes, and in the views of America's own intellectual elites, the United States is the untamed gorilla, throwing its enormous weight around with abandon and a total lack of discipline, upsetting the delicately balanced global applecart.

However, the criticisms of international bureaucrats are not directed only against the United States. They distrust democracy in general. Their barbarians-at-the-gates worldview seeks to limit the power of the people and sublimate it to the control of their betters.

We must recognize that the threat to our freedoms comes from abroad and from antidemocratic elites here at home. They arrive not in warships or bombers, but in the form of treaties, regulations, courts, resolutions, and communiqués that entice our leaders to sign away our freedoms and enlist in a global regime of bureaucratic domination.

Specifically, we must:

- Stop Obama from signing and the US Senate from ratifying the International Criminal Court Treaty.

- Stop the Senate from ratifying the Law of the Sea Treaty

- Stop Obama and Clinton from signing and the Senate from ratifying the United Nations Small Arms Treaty

- Stop Obama and Clinton from agreeing to the European Code of Conduct in Outer Space

- Stop Obama and Clinton from signing and the Senate from ratifying the United Nations Convention on the Child.

- Stop our local zoning and planning boards from following the precepts and advice of Agenda 21.

But we must fight these encroachments on our freedom, democracy, and sovereignty. Our very independence is at stake.

But the United States is also being screwed by individual foreign countries, China first among them. Indeed, a huge portion of the blame for our inability to shake the effects of the global financial meltdown lies with the Chinese government. China makes its living by ripping us off.

PART THREE
China

THE PIRATES OF BEIJING

There is simply no other way to put it: The United States is locked in a stealth Cold War with China that is just as brutal, just as anti-American, and just as important to win as the Cold War was with the former Soviet Union.

The strategic objective of China's undeclared economic war on the United States?

To supplant the United States as the largest and most successful economy in the world, to match and then ultimately surpass our military prowess, to undermine our financial markets, and to overtake our military and commercial technology.

That's all.

In short, China wants to force the United States into an inferior global position and project China into a superior one.

It's that elementary.

It's that scary.

It's that audacious.

This cloak-and-dagger war is currently being fought on several battlefronts:

- Chinese currency manipulation that drains our economy and jobs

- Hacking into American corporate computers and stealing industrial and technological secrets

- Sending industrial spies to the United States to steal trade secrets and technology

- Hacking into American defense systems to steal military information and technical data

- Hacking into the US electrical grid to give China the capacity to disable it

- Refusing to enforce intellectual property rights and allowing blatant pirating of our videos, recordings, and software

Despite its intensity, this is by no means a traditional war between two hostile countries. Instead, it's an aggressive unilateral offensive by China, which passively and purposely is ignored by the United States.

We don't seriously fight back.

We don't stop them.

We just look the other way.

THE OBAMA ADMINISTRATION'S POLICY OF APPEASING CHINA IS HURTING THE UNITED STATES

Instead of forceful retribution for China's brazen tactics, the Obama administration simply changes the subject and prattles on about the importance of establishing free trade and free markets. Obviously, free trade with China is an important and long overdue objective. No one argues with that. But the only reason that we don't have free trade with China is that they refuse to trade fairly. In order to achieve anything near free trade, the United States has to confront the fundamental issues that give China the upper hand, that is, currency manipulation, pirating of our intellectual property, spying on our military, and, most important, our own fear of biting the hand that feeds us—or at least the one that lends us money.

To suggest that there is an acceptable pathway to legitimate free trade without challenging the grossly unfair and illegal strategy of the Chinese government is laughable. It's mixing apples and oranges. While we're yelling about losing an orange, China is plowing over our apple orchards.

QUIET DIPLOMACY ISN'T WORKING

All the while that China is working to overtake us, the Obama administration objects to any real sanctions against it, insisting instead that "quiet diplomacy is a better way to influence Chinese policy and warning that overt sanctions could lead to a destructive trade war."[1]

Obama's quiet diplomacy has led to a loss of over two million American jobs and drastically escalated the trade deficit with China.

That quiet diplomacy has not deterred China from its recent imposition of antidumping and antisubsidy tariffs of up to 21 percent on American SUVs that are exported to China.

That quiet diplomacy has not stopped China from stealing our intellectual property and using it to improve its own economy, which has grown to be the second largest in the world.

That quiet diplomacy has not stopped China from developing a world-class espionage service that successfully infiltrated our military systems and walked off with the top-secret design of the American W-88 nuclear warhead that sits atop the missiles carried by our Trident submarines.[2]

So much for quiet diplomacy. It might better be called *glaring appeasement.*

And as for concerns about a destructive trade war, here's a message for President Obama and his chief diplomat, Secretary of State Hillary Clinton. Earth to Washington: We are already in a trade war and guess what? It's driven by China.

And we're losing it.

So eager is Washington to keep the Chinese happy, that we sugarcoat every statement about them. And the Obama administration panders to them at every opportunity.

Take the Chinese currency manipulation issue. Because the Chinese government artificially depresses the value of its currency, the *renminbi,* it gains a huge trade advantage because, as the *New York Times* explains, "a cheaper renminbi makes Chinese goods less expensive when they are shipped to the United States. It also makes American goods more expensive in China. Both would increase America's trade deficit with China, which is on pace to reach a record high this year."[3]

Yet, on December 27, 2011, the Treasury Department declined to cite China for engaging in currency manipulation. The department based its decision on the fact that the renminbi had increased its value against the dollar by 12 percent in the last eighteen months and that China had promised in two meetings that it would make the renminbi's exchange rate more flexible.[4]

American manufacturers decried the administration's decision. Scott N. Paul, executive director of the Alliance for American Manufacturing, said, "I'm disappointed that President Obama has now formally refused six times to cite China for its currency manipulation, a practice that has contributed to the loss of hundreds of thousands of American manufacturing jobs."[5]

It appears that only the Obama administration cannot see the big red blinking light of Chinese currency violations.

And would anyone in their right mind rely on the promises of the Chinese government to the United States? Someone ought to remind the folks at Treasury of the promises of free trade made by the Chinese when they entered the WTO. If they believe the Chinese promises, we have a bridge to sell them.

There is one reason and only one reason why the Obama administration is not labeling the Chinese as currency manipulators: It's afraid of offending them. Afraid that they will retaliate.

Speaking of retaliation, it's time for the United States to retaliate against the Chinese for all their anti-American policies and activities.

We've done it before. The United States cited China as a currency manipulator in the past. From 1991 to1994, the Treasury Department identified China and several other countries as violators. However, once we entered the WTO in 1994, we stopped citing anyone.

Now is the time to start doing it again, because we still need a further 40 percent revaluation of the renminbi (also known as the *yuan*) in order to even the stakes. Looking the other way is not going to make that happen.

Because the Chinese have no intention of allowing a free-market currency any minimal progress that has been made in improving the Chinese currency was in reaction to the threat of Congressional action in 2010.

In March 2010, after talks with the Treasury, Chinese officials showed their true colors. Resisting pressure from the United States, Zhong Shan, the deputy commerce minister, stated the official Chinese position: "The Chinese government will not succumb to foreign pressures to adjust our exchange rate."[6]

For once, the Chinese were telling the truth.

All the while, as we continue our misguided policy of engaging in pointless and unsuccessful quiet diplomacy, China is keeping its eye on the ball. And, make no mistake about it, to China, the sole purpose of the ball is crystal clear: to topple the global preeminence of the United States.

The unfortunate truth is that in pursuing its reprehensible goals, China is robbing us blind, using the most blatant combination of old-fashioned protectionism and cutting-edge cyberspying.

And what's even more unfortunate is that we're letting them get away with it.

Think about it.

CHINA'S UNFAIR TRADE PRACTICES ARE PROLONGING OUR RECESSION

Why isn't the United States recovering from its recession?

Why did our over-the-top stimulus spending fail to stimulate our economy?

And why hasn't an almost tripling of our money supply done much to increase either consumer demand or corporate borrowing?

Answer: Because China is siphoning it all off through a variety of assaults.

The trade deficit created by China is sucking us dry.

Imagine the US economy as a big metal bucket. Normally, it is filled with consumer demand, sometimes lapping over its brim. However, the long and deep recession has drained away the once buoyant and insistent demand for goods and services.

Since 2008, we haven't been buying as much as we did before the recession. The stark and pervasive consequences of the recession—severe unemployment and massive losses in retirement accounts, stock market portfolios, home equity, and overall wealth— have drastically altered consumer spending habits. Instead of using our disposable income on restaurants, travel, and consumer goods, we're paying down debt and increasing our savings and retirement accounts at a much greater pace than before the financial melt-down.[7] While that strategy is likely to increase our individual security somewhat, it ultimately hurts the economy when the practices are so widespread. When we can't sell the goods and services that are produced here, we lose jobs. Since the height of the recession in 2008, there have been modest increases in consumer spending and a slight easing in consumer savings, but there's still a long way to go to reach pre-2007 levels.

So, the government steps in. Understandably anxious to restore the consumer demand that is so fundamental to economic health, the federal government and the Federal Reserve Board have turned their spigots up to full power to refill the depleted bucket with money to rekindle consumer demand.

From one spigot flows almost a trillion dollars of stimulus spending. That cash flows directly to American households and to contractors working on government-funded projects. It cascades into the bucket like a waterfall of relief.

From the second spigot, the Federal Reserve Board prints money, pumping more than a trillion and a half dollars into the bucket to revive economic growth.

You'd think that the bucket would be filled fairly quickly as the water pours in, but it doesn't ever fill up. In fact, the level of consumer demand never rises much at all.

What's wrong here? Well, if you take a moment to look under the bucket, you'll find that there are several holes in the bottom that are emptying the water out as fast as the Treasury and the Fed can pour it in.

The holes in the bucket represent our trade deficit with China. As fast as we can stimulate consumer demand, China siphons off the money by underpricing its products and underselling our American manufacturers. That costs us jobs and increases our trade deficit with China. We are importing $300 billion more Chinese goods into the United States than we are exporting our products to China.

Some blame this trade deficit for our overall economic problems.

Even as our monetary policy makers pour more print money into our economy, China intercepts it by selling cheap (and often unsafe) products to fuel its own economic growth, at our expense.

University of Maryland economist Peter Morici explains that America holds its own in competition with the other countries of the world. Our two Achilles heels are our dependence on imported oil and our acquiescence to Chinese trade practices. He notes that together, "oil and Chinese imports account for virtually the entire [US] trade gap. The failure of the Bush and Obama Administrations to . . . address subsidized Chinese imports are major barriers to reducing unemployment."[8]

Morici says that "the trade deficit is the most significant barrier to jobs creation and growth in the US economy . . . the US economy suffers from too little demand for what US workers make." It's not the shell shock of the Great Recession that is holding us back any longer. He argues "Americans are spending again—the process of winding down consumer debt that followed the Great Recession ended in April [2011]; however, every dollar that goes abroad to purchase oil or Chinese consumer goods, and does not return to purchase US exports, is lost domestic demand that could be creating American jobs."[9]

The story doesn't end there.

China then recycles the money it siphons off from our economy by lending it back to us, and charging a hefty interest of $34 billion this year or about 1 percent of our total budget.

In a continuous circular flow, China saps us of the economic stimulus that our government spending should generate, then lends it back to us to make more money and gain more leverage over us. In turn, it uses this advantage to be sure that we never plug the holes in the bottom of our bucket for fear of angering China.

Why don't we stop this? What exactly is it that we are we worried about?

Our leaders in Washington sit up at night apprehensive that Beijing won't lend us back our own money and leave us unable to pay our own debts. China already holds about $1.1 trillion of United States debt,[10] almost 10 percent of our total indebtedness. Yet, every year, we have to hope and pray that China, once again, will lend the United States $40 billion more.[11] So, whatever they do, the folks in Washington won't dare antagonize the Chinese. As a result, the watery cycle continues to flow like some great, baleful fountain.

And we continue to speak softly, but we definitely don't even carry a stick, let alone a big one.

But the truth is that China *needs* to borrow from us even more than we need it to lend us money. When China buys dollars, it forces up the exchange rate against the renminbi. That lets China keep its currency undervalued so that they can rip us off in foreign trade. The more dollars they buy, the more there is demand for the dollar, the more the price of the dollar rises against the renminbi, got it?

Once China has all these dollars, what is it going to do with them? It can't change them back into renminbi because that would cheapen the dollar and defeat the whole purpose of their manipulation. So, China needs someplace to invest its dollars. The stock market in the United States? Maybe, but it's too volatile, so China chooses to buy Treasury bills, in effect, lending us money.

China has to keep lending us money or it can't manipulate its currency and undercut our products anymore! Why doesn't Obama get this fundamental fact? Guess they didn't teach that to community organizers.

LETTING CHINA INTO THE WORLD TRADE ORGANIZATION WAS A HUGE MISTAKE

It wasn't always this way. China's edge in trade with the United States is relatively recent. Twenty years ago, it ran a measly $10 billion trade surplus with the United States. Ten years ago, it was only $83 billion. Now, it is over $300 billion.[12]

All this has happened since we agreed to let China into the World Trade Organization (WTO) a decade ago, relying on its promise to remove trade barriers. At the time, the consensus was that this would have a positive effect on the US economy. Reuters recalls how "prior to China's accession to the World Trade Organization . . . free trade proponents argued that the move would create American jobs and eliminate the country's trade deficit. Neither prediction has proven accurate."[13] Instead, the aftermath has been downright devastating.

In December 2011, reporting to Congress on the state of affairs of our trade with China after ten years of membership in the WTO, Assistant Trade Representative Clare Smith noted that China is now the world's biggest exporter and continues to erect trade barriers that hurt the United States.

"The level playing field promised as part of China's WTO accession has not arrived," Smith said at the hearing. "WTO membership has resulted in a massive shift of jobs and wealth from the United States to China, which has come at a huge cost to us."[14]

Consider this: Since China joined the WTO, 40 percent of the factories in the United States with 250 or more employees have closed.[15]

They're screwing us.

Reuters notes that "while [all our economic troubles] can't be laid at China's door, it is not a coincidence

that after decades of more gradual decline, US manufacturing took a nose dive after China's entry into the
WTO."[16]

It certainly wasn't what we expected. A good entry
for what has proven to be the stupidest comment ever
made on the subject comes from Roger Kapp, then
president of the US-China Business Council and who
supported China's entry into the WTO. He predicted
that "opening China's markets to US products and services . . . is the biggest single step we can take to reduce
America's growing trade deficit with China. We're not
talking about a 'gift' for China . . . we're talking about
bringing home the bacon."[17]

Some bacon! If it's bacon, we're the pig!

While the US government and American businesses
are not happy about China's continued trade barriers,
China's inclusion in the WTO has unquestionably been
a very positive step for the Chinese. "Membership
in the WTO, which sets global rules for trade and
investment, has proved to be an unmitigated success
for China, priming the economy for its fastest-ever 10
years of growth."[18]

But China's "unmitigated success" was based largely
on its unmitigated chutzpah.

China started playing unfairly right from the start.
Soon after it joined the WTO, China began to rip us

off, piling up ever-higher trade surpluses, in part due to the horrendously low wages it paid its workforce (a ratio of twenty to one versus American workers). A lot of its edge came from what Reuters describes as "a raft of subsidies . . . [from] an undervalued yuan currency, to artificially cheap or even free land in some cases, low-interest loans, and even subsidized energy bills." And all the while, "the US government and major companies say or do little in response."[19] Don't want to alienate China!

And, of course, the absence of worker and consumer safety or environmental regulations in China comparable to those we have in the United States keeps the Chinese production costs even lower.

Milton Magnus, president of Leeds, an Alabama manufacturer, tells it like it is: "We're in the middle of an economic war with China. The Chinese want what we have and we're just sitting back and giving it to them."[20]

Ain't that the truth!

This story wouldn't be so bad if China competed and won fairly, as Japan does: making better products at lower cost than do our domestic companies or developing its own technology. Japan's sin is not letting our products into their country, not artificially underpricing our products.

CHINA WINS BY CHEATING, STEALING, LYING, AND RIPPING US OFF

Here's how:

- Cheating by artificially subsidizing its currency so that they can undercut our prices.

- Stealing through a massive program of industrial espionage, hacking, and corporate shakedowns.

- Lying by covering up these activities, disclaiming all knowledge of their corrupt practices, and posing as a legitimate country on the global stage, while accusing us of discrimination and neanderthal trade policies when we catch them in the act.

- Ripping us off by refusing to protect our intellectual property rights and pirating our videos.

CHINA'S RULERS NEED ECONOMIC GROWTH TO STAY IN POWER

The mandarins of Beijing are obsessed with economic success. To them, it is not just a question of national well-being or even prestige. It's about political survival.

Increasingly, China no longer has an overarching ideological reason for existing. So, what's holding it together? Strict communism is long buried and, while there is a move back to the left these days, nobody takes seriously the faded rhetoric of a global workers' revolution. China, of course, is by no means a democracy. Its power most definitely does not come from the consent of the governed. They're not even consulted.

However, even under the Chinese system, the discipline imposed by the secret police and autocratic censorship can only go so far in holding together a country of 1.3 billion people. No, China is now basically held together by its economic success. If pervasive unemployment or rampant inflation were to grip the nation, the current regime would likely lose power. It stays in control because it fills the nation's pockets and stomachs.

China's political stability is only purchased by the coin of economic prosperity. As long as China makes money, its government can rest secure. Once it stops, would the dictators in Beijing find themselves being led to the exits by an outraged populace? Yes? No? The leaders of China are in no mood to find out.

Thus they are determined to keep China growing economically. Their very survival depends on it. Political and economic control operate in tandem. If they have to cheat, lie, and steal to do so, they believe, in perhaps the only remaining vestige of their dated communist ethic, that the ends do, indeed, justify the means.

CHINA MOVES BACK TO THE LEFT

Some in the West have gotten complacent about China as they see it adopting capitalism and allegedly moving away from absolute state control, but they haven't looked at China lately. The reforms of Deng Xiaoping are fading further and further into the past. And there is compelling evidence that China is indeed reversing a thirty-year move away from doctrinaire communism and back toward state control again, in part to challenge the United States for global leadership.

Professor Han Deqiang of the University of Beijing writes poetically that China is reversing its former drift to free markets: "The river runs to the east for thirty years, the river runs to the west for thirty years, and now it will run east for another thirty years," Han, founder of a leftist utopia website says; "the transition is already occurring but people are failing to notice."[21]

The river that Han says once ran east for thirty years was the move toward communism and collectivism

CHINA · 155

that dominated the country after Mao's takeover in the late 1940s. Then Deng came to power in the 1980s and reversed direction, moving China closer to capitalism. Now, thirty years later, Gordon G. Chang, writing in *Forbes*, warns that Chinese President "Hu Jintao . . . is presiding over an era marked, on balance, by the reversal of reform."[22]

Chang warns that "[t]he Communist Party of China has already abandoned Deng Xiaoping's transformational policies, which were encapsulated by the phrase 'reform and opening up.' China . . . has entered another era."[23]

He notes that Hu has blocked high-profile foreign acquisitions in China, renationalized key segments of the economy, and shut out foreign competitors from the Chinese market as he has embraced a new economic paradigm of closing the country down.[24]

China's economic system is generally described as state capitalism, which Ian Bremmer defines as "a system in which the state functions as the leading economic actor and uses markets primarily for political gain."[25] Bremmer emphasizes the importance of a close working relationship between the people who govern and the people who head the biggest industries.

That's what's going on in China. It's been evolving for quite a while.

As China sought to emerge from the global economic collapse of 2008, it had its own massive government spending/stimulus plan, but the money went into increasing the state sector, leaving the private sector to fend for itself. Chang says: "The state's stimulus plan is favoring large state enterprises over small and medium-sized private firms and state financial institutions are diverting credit to state-sponsored infrastructure. As they say, 'The Communist Party is now the economy.' "[26]

Chang notes, "Now that the political system [in China] is on the verge of an historic political transition with a whole new set of leaders taking over—the transfer of power to Xi Jinping is slated to begin in about a year—we are seeing more and more officials take the safe course and pay tribute to Maoism and endorse regressive economic policies, especially because the current leader has set a hardline tone during his tenure."[27]

WHAT CHINA WANTS, IT STEALS

China's economic success story may once have been simply the result of cheap labor, hard work, and industrial initiative. But no longer. Now it stems from the vilest sort of chicanery, swindling us by appealing to our idealistic commitment to free trade, while pilfering our technology, pirating our products, and plundering the fruits of our own inventiveness. China doesn't create much new technology. It just steals ours.

Donald Trump, a longtime and vocal critic of China, minced no words in discussing their tactics: "China is raping this country."[28]

What's particularly galling is that China's theft of our industrial secrets and technologies is not the random product of rogue companies or ingenious individual hackers with time on their hands. No, it's much worse. It stems from a deliberate Chinese government policy of looting. Stealing from the United States is China's gateway to economic and military supremacy.

As a result of this exploitive maneuvering, China is benefitting royally from the American entrepreneurial spirit, our capital investments at home and in China, our creativity, and our commercial successes. While the United States spent $402 billion on research and development in 2010 and China spent only $103 billion,[29] China had no need to spend the extra $300 billion. It evened things up by swiping our technology, legally and illegally.

And it's no secret. A US government report recently concluded that China's "technological advances and increased exports are disproportionately due to foreign investment capital and technology rather than to indigenous technological advances."[30]

In other words, the Chinese technological gains are not the product of its own commitment to develop new technology or to any brilliance in research and development. It's much easier than that; their increasing technological prowess is stolen from us.

Let's put it in perspective. First, the Chinese put us at a disadvantage by selling us cheap consumer goods made by poorly paid workers that depress the consumer market for our own products. But that's still not enough for them. Now China is aggressively challenging the United States' lead in technology, described by Reuters as "the remaining power base of the US manufacturing sector."[31]

And there's nothing fair about this fight. They're stealing our technology and products to compete against us with the same products!

We've seen it before. In a sense, China is following in Russia's footsteps. Right after World War II ended with the big bang of two American atomic bombs, most people assumed the American monopoly of nuclear power would last for many years or even decades. Soviet science was nowhere near the level of sophistication required to produce an atomic bomb. So, Stalin decided to steal one. Russia conducted a sophisticated espionage network right inside the Los Alamos Laboratory, where our scientists developed the bomb.

Because of their invasive and successful spy network, Russia was able to explode its first atomic bomb just four years after we did, and then set off a hydrogen weapon just one year after ours was exploded.

The Soviet espionage coup changed the world and led to a forty-year standoff between freedom and communism that very nearly engulfed the planet in a self-destructive nuclear war

Now the Chinese have emulated the Russians by basing their efforts at economic and military advancement on a foundation of espionage and currency manipulation. They make their money the old-fashioned way. They steal it.

CHINA STEALS OUR TECHNOLOGY

If China sees something that looks profitable, it doesn't hesitate to appropriate it, even if it is owned by and developed by its own citizens. Everything is up for grabs by the state. In a recent series, the *New York Times* reported a case of a private Chinese company, Cathay Industrial Biotech, that produced an ingredient valuable in a variety of industrial products, including diabetes drugs and lubricants.

The company's success caught the eye of American vendors and investors. "The patents Cathay won prompted DuPont, a leading global producer of nylon, to become one of Cathay's biggest customers. And the $120 million that Goldman Sachs and other backers have pumped into Cathay in recent years primed investors in China and abroad to eagerly await a public stock offering that had been planned for earlier this year."[32]

They're still waiting.

"According to Cathay, a factory manager stole its secrets and started a rival company that has begun selling a suspiciously similar ingredient, undermining Cathay's profits. Instead of planning to go public, Cathay is now struggling to stay in business.

"In this counterfeit-friendly nation, employees run off with manufacturing designs almost daily. But, according to Cathay, this was copying with a special twist: The new competitor, Hilead Biotech, is backed by the Chinese government."[33]

According to the *Times*, Hilead was formed "with the help of the state-run Chinese Academy of Sciences . . . received a $300 million loan from the national government's China Development Bank."[34]

Not surprising, the Chinese government has sided with Hilead in patent infringement litigation and actually revoked some of Cathay's patents.[35]

That's how things work in China. What the government wants, the government gets. No questions asked. So the American companies, Dupont and Goldman Sachs, who attempted free market economic tactics are just out of luck. Their good-faith support of Cathay means nothing to the Chinese. They are not looking to help American companies. No way. To the contrary, they are looking to sustain their economy through state capitalism, their system that advances the state as the dominant economic force through ownership of large and successful companies and control of capital.[36]

It has done this by exploiting the global financial crisis to buy foreign companies at cheap prices and by regulatory practices that give domestic Chinese companies a tremendous advantage.

And it's worked.

Profits in state-owned companies have risen by 22 percent per year from 2003 to 2009, when they accounted for 2.1 percent of national GDP, up from 0.3 percent in 1998.[37]

And we'll undoubtedly see this catapult even higher as the Chinese expand their newest model of state capitalism.

But we still have yet to reconfigure our understanding of China to bring it up to date. We haven't fully integrated the systemic corruption that underlies their recent economic successes into our analysis of what's going on in China.

We're not used to their deceitful and often illegal tactics, especially the idea of a government-sponsored commercial espionage program. When companies hack into American computers and steal industrial secrets or partner with US firms to spy on and steal their technology, we reflexively assume that it is just one private company trying to get an edge over another. We don't condone that.

But, more often than not, these companies are unmistakably fronts for the Chinese government, every bit as much as they were for the Soviet government during the Cold War.

The Chinese government has a deliberate and well-organized policy of spying on successful American companies.

But it doesn't end with spying on our companies and appropriating their technology. It goes much further.

CHINA STEALS OUR MILITARY TECHNOLOGY

As part of its drift to the left, China also is mounting a considerable military challenge to America's global leadership, seeking, in particular, to establish a conspicuous Chinese sphere of influence over the South China Sea, in direct competition with Vietnam, the Philippines, Indonesia, Malaysia, Singapore, and, of course, Taiwan. To do this, China has diligently updated its military technology in the past few years.

"Bolstered by the development of a new stealth fighter, an aircraft carrier and a record number of space launches over the past year, China is on pace to achieve its goal of building a modern, regionally focused military by 2020, according to the Pentagon."[38] The Defense Department reports that China has invested in improving its military capabilities: "Beijing has closed critical technological gaps and is rapidly modernizing its military equipment."[39]

Why are they doing this? A lot of it has to do with China's ongoing belligerence toward Taiwan. The Pentagon says it is "all with an eye toward preventing possible US and allied intervention in a conflict with Taiwan. It also warns that the military expansion could increasingly stretch to the western Pacific in a move to deny US and allies' access or movement there."[40] "The pace and scope of China's sustained military investments have allowed China to pursue capabilities that we believe are potentially destabilizing to regional military balances and that increase the risk of misunderstanding and miscalculation and may contribute to regional tensions and anxieties,"[41] said Michael Schiffer, the deputy assistant secretary of defense for East Asia.

Emblematic of China's new military assertiveness was its launch of its first aircraft carrier on August 10, 2011. Three more are planned. As Congresswoman Michele Bachmann noted in the Republican presidential debate on November 9, 2011, US taxpayers paid for the carrier as part of their $34 billion in annual interest payments to China.[42] In fact, our interest payments come to about a quarter of the Chinese military budget and about one-half of 1 percent of China's GDP.[43]

That can pay for a lot of modern military presence.

And where is China getting the technology for its military advancement and its economic surge? It steals it from us.

Here's how:

a. By systematically training and deploying computer and Internet hackers, China steals secrets from American companies. Hacking in China is not some lawless activity by a bunch of bored computer geeks. It is a state industry on whose success rides China's economic future. Hacking has been nationalized. The government invests vast amounts of money in the hacking industry, using it to swipe our technology, often without our knowing about it.

b. More conventionally, through a system of industrial spies that would rival any ever fielded by the KGB or CIA or MI-5, China pilfers technology from the United States, stealing our most closely held intellectual and scientific secrets. This espionage is not a sidelight of China's efforts to modernize, it is the main way in which China advances technologically—by espionage and theft! Its program for economic growth reads increasingly more like a Robert Ludlum or John le Carré novel than an Adam Smith or Milton Friedman economic text.

c. China demands that foreign firms doing business there cough up their trade and technology secrets as the price of admission to their market. No other country does this. The companies are so eager to access China's market of 1.3 billion customers that they willingly comply, even though it means that their most intimate trade secrets are soon likely to be stolen.

d. China uses cyberspying and hacking to gain access to American military secrets and our electrical grid. In the event of an armed conflict, China may have achieved the ability to close down the United States economy by interfering with our electrical grid.

e. China is believed to be responsible for the hacking of Google, known as Operation Aurora, in order to access the email accounts of Chinese dissidents.

CHINA HAS THE BIGGEST SPYING OPERATION IN THE WORLD

Espionage is a huge priority of the Chinese government. According to the *Diplomat*, "the communist-controlled People's Republic of China operates the single largest intelligence-gathering apparatus in the world—and its growing appetite for secrets has apparently become insatiable.

"From economic and military espionage to keeping tabs on exiled dissidents, China's global spying operations are rapidly expanding."[44]

The United States knows exactly what they are doing, but only timidly confronts China for fear of angering it. But some US officials step out of line and tell it like it is: "In early November, the US chief of counterintelligence issued a report that was unusually blunt in accusing China of being the world's 'most active and persistent' perpetrator of economic spying."[45]

Fortunately, when we catch Chinese spies in the United States, we're not timid. We try them in federal court and put them in jail. Since 2008, fifty-eight people have been indicted and charged with espionage related to China, according to an Associated Press study of Justice Department.[46]

However, there are still plenty of Chinese spies out there stalking us. US intelligence agencies have identified twenty groups who are responsible for cyberattacks against the US government and defense contractors. A dozen of these spy groups are affiliated with the People's Liberation Army (PLA), six are affiliated with universities, and the source of the remaining two is not yet clear.

HACKING OUR TECHNOLOGY

They're watching us.

They're profiting from us.

They're after us.

From economic and military espionage to keeping tabs on exiled dissidents, China's global spying operations are rapidly expanding.

In China, hacking is an instrument of government policy, vital to China's economy and central to its challenge to America's global domination. And the Chinese government has always recognized the crucial role of the Internet in its theft.

A US government report recently explained why spies capitalize on the efficiency of the Internet. "There is a lower risk of detection than attempting to collect

the data in person. Spying becomes faster and much cheaper, as a result, because broadband networks allow for the instantaneous transfer of massive amounts of data in just seconds, instead of delivering the files in physical form."[47]

And there's no shortage of hackers in China. The Associated Press reported, "Thousands of Chinese computer enthusiasts belong to hacker clubs and experts say some are supported by the military to develop a pool of possible recruits. Experts say military-trained civilians also might work as contractors for companies that want to steal technology or business secrets from rivals."[48]

And the hackers are very, very effective:

- Between June and September of 2011, AP reports, "Cyber attacks traced to China targeted at least 48 chemical and military-related companies in an effort to steal technical secrets."[49]

Symantec, a computer security firm based in California, found that the Chinese targets included chemical and other companies that "make advanced materials used by the military."[50] According to Symantec, "the purpose of the attacks appears to be industrial espionage, collecting intellectual property for competitive advantage."[51]

The hackers sent emails to companies that were implanted with software called Poison Ivy in their computers. Symantec said it traced the attacks to a computer system owned by a Chinese man in his twenties in the central province of Hebei. The man told a contact that he would perform hacking for hire.[52] But no one believes, for even a minute, that he was acting alone. AP reports that "security consultants say the high skill level of earlier attacks traced to China suggests its military or other government agencies might be stealing technology and trade secrets to help state companies."[53]

And, of course, we now know that to be the case.

Symantec says the same hackers were also involved in attacks earlier this year on human-rights groups and auto companies.

- McAfee Inc., another security firm, announced in August 2011 that it had discovered a five-year long hacking campaign that it called Operation Shady Rat. The AP reports that it was run "against more than 70 governments, international institutions, corporations and think tanks."[54] McAfee found hackers operating from China stole information from oil companies in the United States, Taiwan, Greece, and Kazakhstan about operations, financing and bidding for oil fields.[55] The same malware has been "implicated in numerous attacks."[56] McAfee called it the handiwork of a nation-state intent on acquiring, among other things, American military designs. Military contractors in the United States made up a disproportionately large share of the companies selected—twelve in all.[57]

The hackers were nothing if not subtle and tricky. They invented a dodge in which small numbers of emails were delivered to only a few people in each company, touting meeting requests from reputable business partners or, in some cases, "updates to antivirus software or for Adobe Flash Player. When users fell for the trick and opened the message attachment, they unknowingly installed Poison Ivy on their machines." The website techcentral.ie reports that "after that, the attackers were able to issue instructions to the compromised computers, troll for higher-level passwords to gain access to servers hosting confidential information, and eventually offload the stolen content to hacker-controlled systems."[58]

- Google has charged that "a server in China" compromised the "gmail accounts of senior US

officials." Richard N. Clarke, former top antiterrorism official, made it clear that "the targeting of specific US officials is not something that
a mere hacker gang could do." He reports that
"the German government claims that the personal computer of Chancellor Angela Merkel
was hacked by the Chinese government. Australia has also claimed that its prime minister was
targeted by Chinese hackers."[59] Symantec says
that these attacks were not at the level of sophistication of the Stuxnet computer worm planted,
probably by Israel, to destroy Iran's nuclear program, but it notes that "there are similarities
with other advanced threats such as a narrow
attack focus, fake software updates, and meeting
requests."[60]

- In March 2011, a still unknown hacker, but pre-
sumed to be a foreign government, judging by its
skill, "breached the systems of the RSA, whose
electronic security tokens are used across many
industries," the New York Times reported.
"RSA's parent company, EMC, has said that
replacing tokens and cleaning up the mess had
cost it roughly $90 million so far . . . Hackers
used information obtained in the RSA attack to

break into Lockheed Martin, the largest military contractor in the country."[61]

In all, the director of the Office of National Counterintelligence estimates the total loss to American business from foreign espionage, primarily Chinese, at $50 billion per year (on top of a $300 billion trade deficit). A report issued in November 2011 by federal authorities details what is described as an "onslaught of computer network intrusions" that "originated in China and Russia."[62]

What were they after? "business information; military technologies, especially marine systems; and drones and civilian and dual-use technologies, including clean energy and health."[63] The report noted that "the governments of China and Russia will remain aggressive and capable collectors of sensitive US economic information and technologies, particularly in cyberspace."[64]

The government report predicted an "escalating online arms war" between hackers and those trying not to get hacked. "The proliferation of portable devices that connect to the Internet and other networks will continue to create new opportunities for malicious actors to conduct espionage," the report said.[65]

According to Bloomberg, "Representative Mike Rogers, the chairman of the US House Intelligence

Committee, said last month that hacker attacks by China had reached an 'intolerable level' and called on the US and its allies to 'confront Beijing.'"[66]

The *Washington Post* reported that "Michael Hayden, a former director of the CIA and the National Security Agency, said that the scope of China's efforts to spy on the United States is stunning. 'I say that as a professional intelligence officer, I step back in awe at the breadth, depth, sophistication and persistence of the Chinese espionage effort against the United States of America.'"[67]

It goes on and on.

Eweek.com reports that Homeland Security Secretary Janet Napolitano determined that her department's networks already "have been probed by adversaries attempting to breach systems."[68] She noted, "Cyber-attacks have already come close several times to shutting down parts of the country's critical infrastructure."[69] When asked at a *Washington Post* forum how many attacks may have occurred, Napolitano told the audience, "thousands."[70] She said that some cyber-assaults had come close to crashing key infrastructure.

In addition, there have been attempts on "Wall Street, transportation systems, and things of those sorts."[71] Napolitano said. Eweek.com reports that "in fiscal year 2011, the United States Computer Emergency

Readiness Team responded to more than 100,000 incident reports and released more than 5,000 actionable cyber-security alerts and information products."[72]

They're persistent.

HACKING OUR NATIONAL SECURITY

Apparently, even the Pentagon has been penetrated by China. In their book, *Bowing to Beijing*, Brett M. Decker and William C. Triplett II write that "in 2007, angry US defense officers leaked an internal review reporting that the Chinese military had attacked Pentagon computer networks, including the one serving Defense Secretary Robert Gates."[73] Decker and Triplett add, "We now know that the attack on the Pentagon network was more serious than initially reported, to the point that one expert, James Lewis, director of the technology and public policy program at the Washington think-tank Center for Strategic and International Studies, called it an 'espionage Pearl Harbor.'[74]

"In 2010, Mr. Lewis told *60 Minutes* that 'terabytes of information' had been downloaded from all the high-tech agencies, all the military agencies—the State Department, the Department of Energy (which runs our nuclear weapons labs), and the Department of Defense. Asked how big a 'terabyte' is, Mr. Lewis replied, 'The Library of Congress, which has millions of volumes, is about twelve terabytes. So, we probably lost the equivalent of a Library of Congress worth of government information in 2007.' If the American intelligence community conducted a damage assessment afterward, it has not publicized the details."[75]

Decker and Triplett also report a cyberattack that penetrated the entire computer system of the US Naval War College. "Air Force Gen. Richard Goetze, a professor at the military school who previously was the commander in charge of developing America's strategic nuclear war plan, told his students the Chinese 'took down' the war college's network. Even the school's website and email systems went down. For weeks afterward, military officers—both students and professors—at the school were forced to use private email accounts such as yahoo and gmail instead of their official addresses, exposing government business to untold security risks. This embarrassing attack exposed a serious Pentagon vulnerability, as the Naval War College was where the Defense Department created a cyberwarfare center specifically to counter the threat from hackers. Two days after the incident, US Strategic Command raised the security alert level of America's entire military computer network. Alan Paller, a security expert at the

SAND Institute, observed, 'The depth of the penetration is more than anybody is admitting.' "[76]

But, unfortunately, China's military interest in hacking US computer systems goes beyond the theft of information. It often focuses on the sabotaging of our defenses. Selling millions of bogus weapon parts and electronics to the Pentagon is one way to do that. And they're doing it.

A Senate committee recently found that phony Chinese parts were discovered in our most advanced weapons systems, potentially crippling us on the battlefield when we try to deploy them. This is frightening.

The Senate Armed Services Committee says that its researchers uncovered 1,800 cases "in which the Pentagon had been sold electronics that may be counterfeit."[77]

In total, the UK's *Telegraph* reported that the committee said that "it had found more than a million fake parts [that] had made their way into warplanes such as the Boeing C-17 transport jet and the Lockheed Martin C-130J Super Hercules. It also found fake components in Boeing's CH-46 Sea Knight helicopter and the Theatre High-Altitude Area Defence (THAAD) missile defense system."[78]

Senator Carl Levin (D-Michigan), the committee chairman, called the 1,800 counterfeit parts "the tip of

the iceberg." He said, "we have only looked at a portion of the defense supply chain."[79]

And we know that most of them are coming from
China. The committee reported that 70 percent of the
phony parts originated in China while another 20 percent came from the UK and Canada, which, it said,
were "known resale points for Chinese counterfeits."[80]

These phony parts have created a potentially cata-
strophic possibility that they could cause weapons to
fail at a time when they are urgently needed. According
to the *Telegraph*, "in Chinese bazaars, 'military grade'
microchips are openly advertised, although these chips
are often commercial chips that have been modified and relabeled. Military grade chips are designed
to withstand far greater extremes of temperature and
humidity, and there are fears that the fake Chinese
parts could suddenly fail."[81]

The ranking Republican on the committee, Senator
John McCain (R-Arizona), highlighted the problem.
"We cannot tolerate the risk of a ballistic missile interceptor failing to hit its target, a helicopter pilot unable
to fire his missiles, or any other mission failure because
of a counterfeit part."[82]

The *Telegraph* reported that apparently one reason
for this problem is a 1990s decision by the "Clinton
administration to cut costs by asking the Pentagon to

buy 'off-the-shelf' electronics, rather than designing its own systems."[83]

How much is the episode of the phony chips and parts due to deliberate Chinese sabotage of our military capacity and how much is due to military bargain hunting? We don't know. But, where Beijing is concerned, it is usually unwise to embrace an innocent explanation of its conduct.

Sometimes, like a wolf in sheep's clothing, Chinese companies that are really arms of the government or of its defense and intelligence operations masquerade as private companies and seek access to the American market, pretending to be just a regular corporate player.

One high-profile case involved the three thwarted attempts of a Chinese corporation, Huawei Technologies Co. Ltd., to buy the US telecommunications company 3Com for $2.2 billion. Concerns about the company's links to the Chinese government and terrorists killed the deal.

Of course, the Chinese claim that our refusal to permit them to enter into the telecom business in the United States is an example of our commercial discrimination against them.

But, according to Gertz, Huawei Tech is "a major international bad actor linked up with terrorists and rogue states."[84] Gertz reports that Huawei is closely aligned with the state and was formed by a former Chinese general to provide high-tech communications to the People's Liberation Army.

"A report by the CIA-based Open Source Center states that Huawei's chairwoman, Sun Yafang, worked for the Ministry of State Security (MSS) Communications Department before joining the company" and got a $228.2 million grant from the Chinese government to Huawei for research and development.[85]

Yet, despite Huawei's obvious links to the Chinese government and to its intelligence community, Beijing is actively pressing the Obama administration to allow the company, government subsidy and all, to compete in the US telecommunications market. Lawmakers have cited national security concerns to oppose the bid.

But the co-presidents of Huawei USA are still pretending it is a private company. In a letter to the *Washington Times,* they said that "despite US government allegations, Huawei is an 'employee-owned' company, and China's government and military do not hold any shares or control the company."[86]

Bunk, says the Pentagon, which is not buying the Chinese story. Michelle Van Cleave, the former national counterintelligence executive, warns that "big companies like Huawei are business giants, but they're also stalking horses for Chinese intelligence. They can provide both cover and entree for intelligence operations. China's agents are targeting sensitive US technologies through lawful purchase, theft and guile, including acquisitions and investments."[87]

Van Cleave recalls that "two years ago, [Britain's domestic intelligence service] MI-5 warned that equipment installed by Huawei in British Telecom's networks could be used to disrupt critical services like power and transportation. The same could be true here if we don't watch our backs."[88]

The *Washington Times* reports that "a September 2009 cable quoted Chinese Vice Minister of Finance Zhu Guangyao as saying that the blocking of the Huawei-3Com merger 'roiled' Chinese leaders."[89] Good. They need more roiling.

Huawei was already well known by American intelligence agencies for its anti-American, pro-Taliban work and for its theft of American technology.

According to Gertz, as one of his first actions, former Secretary of Defense Donald Rumsfeld ordered an American aircraft to join British warplanes in a "raid on an Iraqi air defense network that had been targeting US aircraft patrolling the skies over Iraq. Some fifty jets bombed an air defense control center for fiber optic cables that Huawei technicians had installed in violation of UN sanctions." Huawei also assisted the Taliban by installing a phone system in Kabul, Afghanistan.[90]

These folks are not our friends.

Even more alarming was Huawei's brazen theft of proprietary material from US high-tech company Cisco Systems, including network switching technology.

In 2003, Cisco Systems sued Huawei, and it later settled the suit in 2004 after an agreement that Huawei would stop using pirated software and infringing on Cisco's patents.[91]

But, according to Gertz, in 2008, the Department of Homeland Security "found a ring of Chinese counterfeiters with knockoffs of Cisco hardware (including fake Cisco labels) that was traced to the Chinese. At the time, the FBI apparently expressed concern that the Chinese might be using the Cisco counterfeit technology to 'penetrate the US government and private sector.' "[92]

The federal government seized more than $76 million worth of Cisco knockoffs that had been sold to the General Services Administration, the US Naval Academy, the US Naval War Center, the Naval Undersea Warfare Center, and defense contractor Raytheon.

The deal was ultimately blocked by the Department of Justice, despite the strong support of Secretary of the

Treasury Hank Paulson, who had helped structure the proposed deal while he was still at Goldman Sachs.

Any doubt that it was not a good idea for Huawei to control a major high-tech company in the United States?

Unfortunately, there's more to worry about.

DISABLING AMERICA

Even more chilling is the possibility that China might use hacking as a weapon of war, bringing our electrical grid to a standstill, paralyzing the entire country. Writing in the *Wall Street Journal*, Richard Clarke, the former top antiterrorism official in the Bush administration, revealed that "in 2009, the control systems for the US electric power grid [were] hacked and secret openings created so that the attacker could get back in with ease. Far from denying the story, President Obama publicly stated that 'cyber intruders have probed our electrical grid.'"[93] According to the *Diplomat*, the hackers "left behind software that could be used to cause disruptions or even shut down the system."[94]

Why would the Chinese be so interested in our electrical grid? Clarke notes ominously that "there is no money to steal on the electrical grid, nor is there any intelligence value that would justify cyber espionage:

The only point to penetrating the grid's controls is to counter American military superiority by threatening to damage the underpinning of the US economy. Chinese military strategists have written about how in this way a nation like China could gain an equal footing with the militarily superior United States."[95]

While defense experts worry about the risk that a foreign adversary could explode a nuclear weapon in the atmosphere over the United States—a so-called electromagnetic pulse—jamming our electrical grid, the Chinese may have acquired the ability to do so without a bomb blast, simply by hitting the proper keys on their computer keyboards!

CLOAK-AND-DAGGER SPYING

It's not all high tech. Sometimes, China uses time-honored, old-fashioned spying techniques, planting an undercover agent in a corporate setting to steal our corporate and military secrets and export them to China. This happened in the case of Kexue Huang, a Chinese scientist who infiltrated two major US corporations and sent confidential information about organic pesticides and food to China.

Apparently, Kexue "John" Huang, forty-eight, a Chinese national who had been granted legal permanent resident status in the United States, was one such operative. According to federal prosecutors, from "January 2003 until February 2008, Huang was employed as a research scientist at Dow, where in 2005 he became a research leader in strain development related to unique, proprietary organic insecticides marketed worldwide."[96] Huang published Dow's trade secrets in China and directed other scientists to conduct research on Dow's other secrets. Huang, who pled guilty to violating the Economic Espionage Act, then moved his operation to Cargill, where he admitted to stealing a key component used in the manufacture of a new food product.[97]

A Chicago grand jury indicted Hanjuan Jin, a software engineer at Motorola, on charges of stealing trade secrets.[98] ABC reported that Jin was "accused of stealing hundreds of millions of dollars in trade secrets from Motorola. [She] was arrested at O'Hare about to leave for Beijing, according to federal law enforcement agents, with Motorola defense-related information they say was to end up in Chinese government hands."[99]

In March 2011, a Newark, New Jersey, grand jury indicted Sixing "Steve" Liu, forty-eight, on eight counts of exporting defense-related technical data to China without a license, one count of transporting stolen goods across state lines, and two counts of making false statements to law enforcement agents. Liu, a Chinese national who has lived in the United States for eighteen years, worked at L-3 Communications' Space & Navigation division in New Jersey.[100]

According to the US Attorney's Office in Newark, Lui downloaded classified material onto his laptop and transferred it to China. As part of a research and development team, Liu, who holds a doctoral degree in electrical engineering, "worked on navigation and positioning devices used in artillery and missile systems by the US Department of Defense (DoD). Liu was never issued a company laptop or approved to access or possess the company's work product outside of its New Jersey facility."[101]

On November 12, 2010, Liu boarded a flight from Newark Airport to the PRC. Upon his return from the PRC on November 29, 2010, US Customs and Border Protection (CBP) officers found Liu to be in possession of a non-work-issued computer that was later found to contain numerous L-3 Communications documents relating to those systems.

While in the PRC, Liu gave presentations at several universities, a PRC government research entity, and a PRC-government-organized conference. Liu's presentations related to technology that he and his co-workers at Space & Navigation were developing for DoD.

Although listed as a representative of the company on the conference's website, Liu never sought the company's approval to deliver the presentation, which was contrary to the company's security rules. In fact, Liu told one senior employee of the company before leaving for the trip that he was going to Chicago on vacation.

Liu also made false statements upon his return to the United States to Homeland Security Investigations agents about the purpose of his travel to China and the extent of his work on projects for DoD.

In March 2011, law enforcement agents searched Liu's residence in Deerfield, Illinois. During the search, agents discovered a binder containing numerous proprietary documents relating to a munitions project that Liu had worked on while at the company, including schematics, formulas, simulation software coding, and set-up instructions, which he had taken from the company's New Jersey facility.

The US Department of State's Directorate of Defense Trade Controls verified that the information on Liu's computer is export-controlled technical data that relates to defense items listed on the United States Munitions List (USML). Under federal regulations, items and data covered by the USML may not be exported without a license, which Liu did not obtain. The regulations also provide that it is the policy of the United States to deny licenses to export items and data covered by the USML to countries with which the United States maintains an arms embargo, including the PRC.[102]

"As early as April 2009, the company provided training to Liu regarding export control laws. Numerous documents that Liu possessed on the non-work-issued computer were prominently marked as containing sensitive proprietary company information and/or export controlled technical data."[103]

The indictment claims that Liu was transferring the classified information for years before he was caught.

Then there was the case of Shu Quan-Sheng, a Chinese-born naturalized US citizen who sold controlled space-launch technology to China. Shu Quan-Sheng operated a company that was funded by grants from the Department of Energy and NASA. According to Reuters, he "has been involved in China's effort to upgrade its space exploration and satellite technology capabilities. Beginning in January 2003, Shu Quan-Sheng provided technical assistance and expertise in acquiring foreign technology to several Chinese government entities involved in the design, development, engineering and manufacture of a space launch facility in China, according to the charges."[104]

Shu Quan-Sheng worked closely with his Chinese counterparts in the space sector. "Specifically, Shu provided the PRC with assistance in the design and development of a cryogenic fueling system for space launch vehicles to be used at the heavy payload launch facility located in the southern island province of Hainan, PRC. The space launch facility at Hainan will house liquid-propelled heavy payload launch vehicles designed to send space stations and satellites into orbit, as well as provide support for manned space flight and future lunar missions, according to a criminal complaint filed in the case. Among those PRC government entities involved in the Hainan facility are the People's Liberation Army's General Armaments Department and the 101st Research Institute (101 Institute), which is one of many research institutes that make up the China Academy of Launch Vehicle Technology, as overseen by the Commission of Science Technology and Industry for the National Defense."[105]

Shu Quan-Sheng was sentenced to fifty-one months in prison.

Most of these spies were nominally working for private Chinese companies, but, with the degree of state control of the private sector growing, their actions carry the taint of government spying.

They're not doing this on their own. This is state business. Big business.

Sometimes, they even recruit Americans to do the job for them. Several years ago, Gregg Bergersen, a weapons analyst with the US Defense Security Commission, gave the Chinese information about all the specific weapons that we had supplied to Taiwan. Bergerson sold out cheap; he was paid $7,000.

And they're not just hacking into US companies at home. They don't stop there. If you do business in China, watch your back. Companies that locate there are particularly at risk of seeing their intellectual property walk out the door, especially if they are in a joint venture with the Chinese, voluntarily or otherwise. The comrades help themselves and take whatever they want of American know-how.

The director of the US-China Clean Energy Forum noted that "the number one risk [of IP theft in China] is your partner because you invariably go into business in China with a Chinese partner and often more than one." He says, "these are the people who are most likely to steal your intellectual property, which is actually a huge plus because if you know who it is that is going to steal your stuff, you can protect yourself more readily."[106]

A huge plus is that you know that it is most likely your business partner (who is probably your closest associate in China) who will steal from you? Somehow, it's not very comforting.

And, while you're at it, you'd better watch out for your customers too. US clean energy company AMSC, also known as American Superconductor Corporation, learned the lesson the hard way when one of its biggest clients defrauded it by hijacking its proprietary technology, then reneging on its contractual obligations to purchase the product and actually cancelling orders. Once they appropriated AMSC's property, they didn't need the company anymore. According to the *Financial Times*, AMSC accused its best customer of "gaining access to some of its wind turbine software codes and using those codes without authorization."[107]

It was a devastating financial blow to AMSC. The Chinese company, Sinovel, "was once AMSC's biggest client, accounting for more than 70 percent of the company's revenues last year. But earlier this year Sinovel stopped accepting contracted shipments of wind turbine components. The companies had several long-term supply contracts in place, and each side accuses the other of contractual violations."[108]

So that's how Chinese customers behave towards our companies: What's yours is theirs.

AMSC is now suing Sinovel in a Chinese court for $400 million for theft of its intellectual property. Good luck with that one!

SCREWED!

HOW CHINA FORCES US COMPANIES TO SHARE TECHNOLOGY AS THE PRICE OF ADMISSION

The Chinese government, eager to acquire Western and, particularly, American technology, routinely blackmails US companies. It's an accepted part of doing business, and it's not illegal.

Here's how they do it: If the US company is interested in selling its products to the vast Chinese domestic consumer market, there's a price to pay. This is most certainly *not* a free trade country. And the price of admission is fairly standard. In return for coveted access to Chinese consumers, American companies must agree to give the Chinese valuable technology. There's no compensation for this transfer. And, they're very serious about it. Make no mistake about it: You won't get to do business in China unless you comply. If Western companies refuse to hand over their most advanced and intimate technical secrets, they better just pack up and go home.

National Public Radio reported that "technology transfer[s] . . . are a key part of doing business in China. Whether you're GE and you want to build electronic systems for China's first large passenger jet or you're GM and you want a piece of China's electric vehicle market, China demands that you share technology."[109]

And *share* is NPR-speak for getting ripped off!

It's interesting that China and Japan have adopted quite different approaches to competing with the United States. Japan never encouraged direct investment in their homeland by American companies. Reuters reports that, in the '80s and '90s, "some key US multinationals made a great deal of noise in public, and in the US Congress, about unfair Japanese trading practices. Their interests were aligned with the smaller domestic manufacturers."[110]

But China plays the game differently, encouraging direct investment by American and multinational companies in large part to get their hands on the technology that makes them tick. It's a win-win situation for the Chinese.

Because Japan wouldn't let American companies in, "no one made any money off Japan Inc," said Diane Swonk, chief economist at Mesirow Financial. But, because the Chinese do, a lot of "people are making a lot of money off China Inc."[111] And they want it to continue.

That's why their Chinese-generated profits make "big American companies with investments in China afraid to criticize Beijing because of the controls it has over just about any access to the Chinese market. They fear too strident a stance could mean they will lose contracts or even be ostracized as Google Inc was after a dispute with China over censorship and hacking."[112]

Everyone's afraid of China, with good reason. If you don't play their ball game, you don't even get onto the field. So most people keep quiet regardless of how outrageous the Chinese government acts. It's too dangerous.

"The Chinese government controls all the levers of the economy, from import and export licenses on up," said Victor Shih, an assistant professor of politics at Northwestern University. "There are so many ways for the Chinese government to retaliate it is no surprise businesses are so reluctant to criticize it."[113]

A good example of this kind of coerced technology transfer involved the construction of high-speed trains in China. *Wall Street Journal* reporter Norihiko Shirouzu reports that four foreign companies helped China build high-speed trains. Good-bye technology. China didn't steal it. It "re-innovated" it, putting a new façade on the technology the four dumb firms gave it and are now calling it their own, "creating tensions with the companies who fear they're now having to compete with China."[114]

The saga began in 2004, when the four companies—Siemens (Germany), Alstom (France), Bombardier (Canada), and Kawasaki (Japan)—agreed to transfer technology so that China could build a high-speed train that could reach 155 mph. China paid Kawasaki $760 million and paid the other companies too.

Then, in 2009, China changed the rules. Reuters recounts how "the [Chinese] government began requiring that prospective bidders for Chinese high-speed rail projects form minority joint ventures with state-run manufacturers and hand over their latest designs and that 70 percent of the equipment had to be produced locally."[115]

The foreign companies knew what that meant but they were in too deep to move out. "While aware of the flow of technology to the Chinese side, Kawasaki saw its joint venture as an opportunity to gain access to China, which was rapidly expanding its high-speed rail network. China has been by a long way the world's largest market for new rail lines in recent years."[116]

"Now, Chinese companies build faster, cheaper trains than their former mentors make and compete against them in global markets. Kawasaki has complained that trains built by Sifang are based on its own technology. Similarly, Siemens was elbowed aside by its erstwhile partner, the China National Railway Signal and

Communication Corp, when it came to constructing the high-profile Beijing-Shanghai high-speed link."[117]

Now China is not only using that technology to build its own high speed trains, it is even trying to sell trains to the United States, Brazil, and Russia, competing with the original companies by using their own technology. The Chinese claim they improved it. The companies say that's nonsense, but even the Chinese admit that their technology for trains is based on the foreign innovations. They have an artful way of saying it. "We attained our achievements . . . by standing on the shoulders of past pioneers."[118] It's more like they picked the pioneers' pockets!

The companies are stuck between a rock and a hard place. If they take a hard line and sue the Chinese company for blackmailing them and stealing their valuable property, it would take decades to resolve the issue. And, in the meantime, the Chinese would undoubtedly block their ability to sell any of their products in China. It's highly unlikely that the Chinese courts will rule against their own citizens, so it makes no sense to fight back. It won't work. Now, the innovative technology developed by American creativity has a "made in China" label.

As P. T. Barnum put it, "There's a sucker born every minute."

Chinese chicanery is not limited to the railroad industry. It's pervasive throughout the Chinese economy. A US government report confirmed that "the transfer of advanced US technology is the price of market access in China for US high-tech companies."[119]

It's no secret. Everyone knows it, and, regrettably, everyone apparently accepts it. It's the elemental prerequisite for admission to the Chinese markets—like a license or application fee. Except that it is not at all innocuous. It's not at all fair. But it's the way business is done in China.

Our own government concedes it. After an extensive study of firms doing business in China, the report concluded that "the majority of industry representatives interviewed for this study clearly stated that technology transfers are required to do business in China . . ."[120]

It's their way or the highway. The Chinese government understands that they have the upper hand and blatantly extort those companies who want to enter their markets. They're ruthless.

The government study further noted that "China's is a buyer's market. As such, the leverage of such an enormous potential market allows Chinese officials to frequently play foreign competitors against one another in their bids for joint venture contracts and large-scale, government-funded infrastructure projects in China. The typical result is usually more technology being transferred as competitors bid up the level or type of technology that they are willing to offer."[121] Put simply, US industries feel that "one cannot not be in China lest a competitor establish a foothold. US high-tech firms seem willing to pay the price in technology transfers—in exchange for limited market access."[122]

They're giving away the store. And still the Chinese want more.

"Under the rubric of promoting 'indigenous innovation,' China has introduced a string of policies—ranging from patent laws and technology standards to procurement policies and product approval rules—that many foreign technology companies believe are a huge threat to their intellectual property.

" 'With these indigenous innovation industrial policies, it is clear that China has switched from defense to offense,' says Jim McGregor, a Beijing-based consultant and former director of the American Chamber of Commerce in China.

" 'Many single-industry and single-product companies could be destroyed in the process. Global markets are likely to become increasingly distorted, and the end result could be a chilling effect on innovation globally.' "[123]

Apparently, "most US and other foreign investors in China thus far seem willing to pay the price of technology transfers—even state-of-the-art technologies—in order to . . . 'establish a beachhead' in China with the expectation that the country's enormous market potential eventually will be realized."[124] They see it as a quid pro quo that will result in a huge new market for their products, even if there is a downside. So, the higher China raises the stakes, the higher they jump.

Their goals are clear. As a December 2010 article for the *Harvard Business Review* noted, China's rules "limit investment by foreign companies as well as their access to China's markets, stipulate a high degree of local content in equipment produced in the country, and force the transfer of proprietary technologies from foreign companies to their joint ventures with China's state-owned enterprises."[125]

Sometimes the technology transfer involves forcing the foreign corporation to give up its industrial secrets outright. More often, it involves "the establishment of a training or R&D center, institute, or lab, typically with one of China's premier universities or research institutes."[126]

The report concluded that "unless significant changes are made to China's current investment regulations and import/export policies, US commercial technology transfers to China are likely to continue, potentially enhancing Chinese competitiveness in high-technology industry sectors such as aerospace and electronics."[127]

If firms want to give away their technology, that would seem to be their business. While Japan tries to stop its companies from giving away the store and Europe seems not to care in the least, the United States has adopted a midway course.

Some American companies have wised up and are refusing to let China have their technology. For example, there's Bob Chesebro, whose Wisconsin factory makes socks. His big technological edge is that he has a machine that sews the toes closed, a task that "in China . . . is still often done by hand—a labor-intensive task."[128] GE may be willing to give away its technology, but Bob's not. In fact, he guards against any possibility of access to his equipment by the Chinese.

Reuters reports that, "his equipment ends its days as scrap metal in a dumpster behind his plant. 'We have taken the view that if we sell these machines we're just going to put them in the hands of people who will compete against us,' he said."[129]

Good for Bob Chesebro!

However, while the United States polices technology transfers that have military application, frequently denying firms the right to export these technologies, what happens when the technology that is transferred to China can be adapted for military use? Our "export control review process is not designed to evaluate continuing US commercial technology transfers to China that are demanded or offered in exchange for market access,"[130] the government report noted.

The government report warns that "although it is not possible to make a clear determination of the US national security implications of commercial US technology transfers to China, the continuation of the trends identified in this study could pose long-term challenges to US national security interests."[131]

This study also warned that "continued pressures on foreign high-tech firms to transfer advanced commercial technologies, if successful, could indirectly benefit China's efforts to modernize its military."[132]

Particularly in the area of aviation, China is using its commercial relationships with American companies to leapfrog its airplane technology into international competition. However, many US business leaders claim that the dangers of sharing technology are minimal, given the state of Chinese technological development.

The *New York Times* reports that "for the most part, Western aviation executives say the Chinese are simply too far behind in both civilian and military airplane technology" [133] to compete with the United States, commercially or militarily.

General Electric Gives Away Our Technology

But there's no doubt that China is determined to catch up and become a serious commercial competitor to US-based Boeing and Europe's Airbus, as well as a serious military competitor to the United States. And, just as P. T. Barnum stated, China has, once again, found a new sucker: General Electric, America's largest corporation.

GE desperately wants to be a leader in the ripe Chinese market, and they have kowtowed to the Chinese over and over again, especially when it comes to their aviation products. What China wants, GE hands over.

According to the *New York Times*, "no Western company has been more aggressive in helping China pursue that dream [of becoming a technological giant in aviation] than one of the aviation industry's biggest suppliers of jet engines and airplane technology, General Electric."[134]

Please note that you won't see this story on NBC or MSNBC. They're partly owned by General Electric!

GE has entered into a joint venture with the Chinese that has serious military implications. To help China develop its commercial aircraft, GE has partnered with a state-owned Chinese company, the Commercial Aircraft Corporation of China, an enterprise that, according to the *Times*, "supplies China's military aircraft and weapons systems."[135]

As part of the deal, GE will be sharing some of its most sophisticated technology, particularly in the realm of avionics, "the electronics for communications, navigation, cockpit displays and controls. G.E. will be contributing its leading-edge avionics technology—a high-performance core computer system that operates as the avionics brain of Boeing's new 787 Dreamliner."[136]

The *Times* notes that there is a "risk that Western technologies could help China play catch-up in military aviation—a concern underscored last week when the Chinese military demonstrated a prototype of its version of the Pentagon's stealth fighter, even though the plane could be a decade away from production."[137]

Some lawmakers have expressed concerns about the military impact of the technology transfer. Congressman Randy Forbes (R-VA) has asked Defense Secretary Leon Panetta to investigate whether the GE deal will help China acquire integrated modular avionics systems that, military.com reports, "were originally developed for the United States' F-22 Raptor and the G-35 Joint Strike Fighter stealth jets."[138]

Congressman Forbes noted that "given [the technology's] military origin, I am deeply concerned that once in [China] it will wind up aiding the military aviation programs of the People's Liberation Army Air Force, which is even now developing its J-20 fifth-generation fighter that appears intended to threaten US air supremacy in East Asia."[139]

While GE officials maintain that there will be no technology transfer to the Chinese military, its efforts to prevent the venture from aiding the military in China are pathetically weak. The joint company in Shanghai will have separate offices and will "be equipped with computer systems that cannot pass data to computers in Avic's military division"[140] according to GE.

Hello!

Has anyone told GE about the claims of Chinese cyberattacks on the US military? On American companies?

Does GE really think that the Chinese can't or won't hack into their computers? In their own country?

Open your eyes, GE.

Oh, and there are other protections, says GE. Get this: Anyone working in the joint venture must wait two years before they can work on military projects at COMAC/AVIC. Now that will really protect our secrets. And, presumably, this agreement will be very enforceable in Chinese courts.[141]

GE's attempt to build a, well, Chinese Wall between its civilian cooperation with AVIC and the company's military activities are ridiculously weak and virtually invite technology transfer.

The Secrets GE Is Giving Away Could Have Great Military Value

Not everyone thinks that this relationship is a good one for the US or that there is little danger. Military.com warns that "partnerships between Western aviation firms and Chinese aviation companies aimed at developing civil aviation technology could unwittingly be helping China develop next-generation military technology. 'Joint ventures with jet engine market leaders like General Electric (GE) have the potential to give the Chinese aerospace industry a 100 piece puzzle with 90 of the pieces already assembled.' "[142]

That viewpoint is echoed elsewhere. Online journal *DoD Buzz* quoted US Naval War College professor Andrew Erickson on China's quest to build high-quality jet engines: "enough is left out [of what GE gives China] so that the exporting companies can comply with the letter of the export control laws, but in reality, a rising military power is potentially being given relatively low-cost recipes for building the jet engines needed to power key military power projection platforms including tankers, AWACS, maritime patrol aircraft, transport aircraft, and potentially, subsonic bombers armed with standoff weapons systems."[143]

The RAND Corporation also weighed in on this issue, and came out squarely against GE's Pollyannaish defense of its agreement. RAND recently concluded that "foreign involvement in China's aviation manufacturing industry is contributing to the development of China's military aerospace capabilities." This contribution is "increasing China's ability and possibly its propensity to use force in ways that negatively affect US interests and would increase the costs of resisting attempts to use such force."[144]

There's another issue, too. GE's sharing of commercial aviation technology with China is enabling China to compete with America's Boeing, at a time when US manufacturing base is suffering and American jobs in that sector are declining even further.

A good example is the synthetic vision technology that GE installed in China's new commercial airplanes, which provides a simulation of the view for takeoffs and landings without any bad weather distortions. This system will presumably save money for the airline industry by virtually eliminating weather-related delays.

However, it's going to the rival of an American company, not to any US corporation. And most of the jobs it will create will be in China, not in the US.

How will this affect the future of the American avionics industry?

It's hard to tell. One knowledgeable observer has his doubts. "It's unclear whether anyone in the US government took a look at the GE deal in terms of US competitiveness—the future of the aviation industry 10 or 20 years out," says an executive who advises companies working in China. He worries that a heavily subsidized Chinese jet program, enhanced with US avionics, could eventually clobber Boeing. "China has an incredible ability to distort markets, and we can't be reacting after the distortion has taken place."[145]

Regardless of the effect on US markets, GE has no regrets. Lorraine Bolsinger, chief executive of GE Aviation Systems, told the *Washington Post* that "China's airplane market is booming, and the deal was too important to pass up . . . even at the cost of sharing the avionics technology.

"We are all in and we don't want it back."

She said new airplanes don't come along that often, and that the chance to be part of developing a major new aircraft is not to be missed—even if most of the jobs will be in Shanghai or elsewhere in China.

"We don't sell bananas.

"We can't afford to take a decade off."[146]

Well, now we know where GE stands.

GE added insult to injury when it was revealed that the corporation made profits of $14 billion in 2010, but paid not a penny in corporate income taxes. Using a 57,000-page tax return, its tax lawyers wiggled their way out of paying anything to the country that permitted them to prosper.[147]

GE knows its way around Washington. Except for the Chamber of Commerce, it outspent every other corporation and special interest group in the United States in 2010, spending almost $40 million on lobbyists in Washington. In the first three quarters of 2011, GE spent over $21 million.[148]

Remember that General Electric is headed by Jeffrey Immelt, President Obama's jobs czar, chairman of the President's Council on Jobs and Competitiveness. Several months after his appointment, Immelt showed just how good he was at job creation. GE moved its 115-year-old X-ray/medical imaging division from Wisconsin to Beijing, where it hired sixty-five engineers and support staff.[149]

Apparently, nobody told Jeffrey that he was supposed to generate jobs in the United States, not China.

GE's going further. As part of a commitment to invest $2 million in China, GE envisages the creation of over one thousand jobs for the Chinese.[150]

Exporting jobs abroad is nothing new for either Immelt or GE. Since he took over in 2001, the number of the company's overseas employees has steadily increased. In the last decade, the overseas jobs rose by 8 percent. In 2000, 46 percent of the GE employees worked overseas. Today, it is a robust 54 percent.[151] In fact, GE now has more employees abroad than it does in the United States.

General Electric is not alone in giving away vital American technology with potential military uses to China in return for access to their markets. Other companies are doing the same thing, and sometimes it involves technology underwritten by the US taxpayers.

Fortunately, some members of Congress are sounding a warning against this continued corporate give-away of our military technology to China. Senator James Webb (D-VA) charged that "Westinghouse Electric has transferred more than 75,000 documents to Chinese counterparts as the initial phase of a technology transfer agreement in exchange for a share in China's growing nuclear market. These documents relate to the construction of four third-generation AP1000 reactors that Westinghouse is building in China. US taxpayers supported the development of the AP1000 as well its predecessor, the AP600, through decades of nuclear energy research and development at the Department of Energy (DOE). Moreover, the DOE Nuclear Power 2010 program provided years of government support for the design and licensing of this reactor."[152]

Webb also said that "Ford Motor Company is looking to share certain proprietary technologies for electric vehicles in exchange for selling cars in China. The electric vehicle sector has enjoyed significant federal R&D funding, loan guarantees, and public-private partnerships funded by US taxpayers. In 2009, Ford Motor Co. received a $5.9 billion loan guarantee from the Department of Energy to advance its vehicle technology manufacturing program."[153]

Oddly, one of the offenders in the transfer of important technology with military applications to China is
none other than our own government. Congressman
Frank Wolf (R-VA) notes that "Dr. John Holdren, head
of the White House Office of Science and Technology
Policy [has] spent 21 days in China on three separate
trips in one year—more than any other country." He
also said, "I was troubled to learn from the press last fall
about NASA Administrator Charlie Bolden's imminent
departure for a weeklong visit to China to discuss areas
of cooperation between NASA and the PLA (People's
Liberation Army) space program."[154]

China's space program has developed rapidly. Just
ten years ago, China launched its first manned spacecraft. Now it is launching components for an advanced
space station. As Wolf notes, "the PLA is not our friend
as evidenced by their recent military posture and
aggressive espionage against US agencies and firms."[155]

Wolf said he was alarmed at the administration's
"apparent eagerness to work with China on space
issues."[156] He said that "we should be wary of any
agreements that involve the transfer of technology or
sensitive information to Chinese institutions or companies, many of which are controlled by the government
and the PLA." Wolf continued: "space is the ultimate
'high ground' that has provided the US with countless

security and economic advantages over the last 40 years."[157] Now he is concerned that the administration may be giving it away to Beijing.

As chairman of the Appropriations Subcommittee on Science, Wolf pushed through Congress language in the NASA and Office of Science and Technology Policy budgets prohibiting them from using federal funds to "participate, collaborate, or coordinate bilaterally in any way with China or any Chinese-owned company."[158] Now he feels that the Obama administration is violating the new law he passed and he wants to hold them accountable. But no administration official has even discussed publicly what happened during the trips to China of their top science and space officials.

CHINESE CURRENCY MANIPULATION

By far the biggest part of the effort by China to rip off the United States is through its manipulation of its currency.

Every other major country in the world permits its currency to trade freely on the global currency market. You can walk into any bank or currency exchange and get their national currency in return for your dollars. Euros, yen, pounds, Canadian dollars, all exchange freely for US currency, rising and falling in value as the international market dictates.

But not China. The mandarins in Beijing will not allow you to cash in your yuans for dollars. They control all the trading in their own currency. Why? Because they are scared to death of what their money would sell for if it were properly valued. With their economy growing at almost 10 percent a year, Chinese yuan would be especially valuable on the global market. Experts agree that it would sell for 40 percent more than it does today.

So, right now, the yuan trades at 6.4 to the dollar. But a realistic figure would be more in the neighborhood of 4 to the dollar. But China won't have it!

Why not? Because then Chinese products would cost up to 40 percent more in the United States. That cute outfit selling for forty dollars would suddenly cost fifty-six. Those neat sneakers retailing at eighty dollars would now set you back one-hundred twelve.

Concurrently, American products would be 40 percent cheaper in China. Our cars, laptops, phones, iPads, iPods would undoubtedly undersell theirs in their domestic market. So China works overtime to hold down the value of its currency.

How does China do it? It buys dollars. The more dollars that are bought on the international currency markets, the higher the demand for the dollar, the more valuable it will be. And the more yuans are sold, the less valuable they will become. Never mind that the demand for dollars is artificial, fabricated by the Chinese government; the laws of supply and demand kick in and the dollar becomes more expensive and the yuan becomes cheaper.

Where does China get the money for this massive currency swap? From us. Remember the bucket we talked about earlier? It takes the money that it siphons off through the holes in the bottom and uses it to purchase dollars, driving up the value of our currency relative to theirs. Then it uses that lower-value yuan to sell us more products, enlarging the hole in the bottom of the barrel. And the entire process continues, only faster and faster.

Before the General Agreement on Tariffs and Trade (GATT), negotiated in 1947, countries routinely imposed tariffs on one another's products. French wines had to pay a 30 percent tax to get into the United States, which encouraged Americans to buy California wines. After GATT and the lower tariffs required by the World Trade Organization (WTO), which succeeded GATT in 1995, tariffs become virtually illegal. (Very low duties were still sometimes permitted.) Fundamentally, all the nations of the world committed to free and open trade.

And they all honor that commitment, except the pirates of Beijing.

China, admitted to the WTO in 2011, after years of begging, demanding, and hectoring, doesn't widely impose tariffs, but it does artificially strengthen its currency, which amounts to the same thing.

Largely due to its policy of subsidizing the yuan, the US trade deficit with China reached $273 billion in 2010 and is headed to $300 billion in 2011.[159]

The manipulation of the yuan's value has had a critical effect on our economy. The Alliance for American Manufacturing, a labor-management partnership, says that a "28.5 percent appreciation in the yuan would create 2.25 million American jobs and reduce the annual trade deficit by $190.5 billion."[160]

Under heavy pressure from the United States, China grudgingly says that it is "committed to gradual currency reform and notes that the yuan has risen 30 percent against the dollar since 2005,"[161] 6 percent in the past year.[162]

Even if we accept China's figures, it has still closed less than half of the artificial gap in value between the dollar and the yuan that its own policy of manipulation has created.

China's artificially weakened currency, low-wage labor force, and government subsidies to industry are a combination that American firms find impossible to beat. It's effective, but don't call it free trade. It's the furthest thing from real free trade left on earth.

In the face of this currency manipulation, American presidents have dithered, none more so than Barack Obama, who campaigned against exporting our jobs overseas. Saying that he prefers dialogue with China to punitive measures, Obama has only recently admitted that China was, indeed, gaming the international trade system. In five periodic reports, required by Congress, the Obama administration has, according to Reuters, "stopped short of formally labeling China a manipulator, which would require it to pursue stepped-up negotiations aimed at getting Beijing to revalue the yuan."[163]

Even Democrats are disgusted with the administration's refusal to take the currency manipulation seriously. Defying the administration, a bipartisan majority in the Senate passed legislation in October 2011 cracking down on China's currency manipulation.

The bill would require the "Commerce Department to consider whether undervalued currencies act as an effective export subsidy that justify the United States applying countervailing duties in response."[164] If the department finds that undervaluing of currencies is an export subsidy, the US would be required to seek redress through negotiations or, failing that, to impose tariffs on Chinese goods in retaliation.

FOX News explains the impact of the legislation: "Up to now, the Treasury Department has had to declare that a country was willfully manipulating its currency to trigger a response, something the Bush and Obama administrations have avoided doing. The [Senate] legislation would require Treasury to determine only that another country's currency is misaligned, then give its government 90 days to make corrections before countervailing duties are imposed."[165]

The legislation also makes it easier "for specific industries to petition the Commerce Department for redress under claims that the misaligned currency of China or another country amounts to an export subsidy."[166]

However, the bill may never see the light of day.

House Republican Speaker John Boehner recently called the Senate bill dangerous,[167] casting doubt on its chances in the House. Indeed, Boehner may never bring it up for a vote.

Republicans are really split on this legislation. The China Currency Bill passed the Senate by 63–35 with Republicans voting against it by 16–30. Such divisions, in this era of enforced party unity, are very rare.

Here's the list of Republicans who voted for the bill, putting the need for American jobs first:[168]

Brown (R-MA)	Hoeven (R-ND)
Burr (R-NC)	Isakson (R-GA)
Chambliss (R-GA)	Johanns (R-NE)
Cochran (R-MS)	Portman (R-OH)
Collins (R-ME)	Risch (R-ID)
Crapo (R-ID)	Sessions (R-AL)
Graham (R-SC)	Shelby (R-AL)
Grassley (R-IA)	Snowe (R-ME)

And these Republican senators voted no, trying to stop effective action against Chinese currency manipulation:

Alexander (R-TN)	Hatch (R-UT)
Ayotte (R-NH)	Heller (R-NV)
Barrasso (R-WY)	Hutchison (R-TX)
Blunt (R-MO)	Inhofe (R-OK)
Boozman (R-AR)	Johnson (R-WI)
Coats (R-IN)	Kirk (R-IL)
Corker (R-TN)	Kyl (R-AZ)
Cornyn (R-TX)	Lee (R-UT)
DeMint (R-SC)	Lugar (R-IN)
Enzi (R-WY)	McCain (R-AZ)

McConnell (R-KY)   Rubio (R-FL)

Moran (R-KS)   Thune (R-SD)

Murkowski (R-AK)   Toomey (R-PA)

Paul (R-KY)   Vitter (R-LA)

Roberts (R-KS)   Wicker (R-MS)

This rare split in Republican ranks reflects the gulf between purist free-market conservatives and those who are more pragmatic. In this case, the purists are deceiving themselves. Opposing these sanctions is like supporting unilateral disarmament.

And, even if the House passes the bill, Obama won't say whether he will sign it. In fact, he won't talk about the bill at all, even though it was passed by his own party in the Senate. (Likely he wanted to give Democratic senators a chance to put themselves on record by voting for the trade sanctions without having actually to implement them.)

China replied to the Senate action, calling it protectionism and blasting the United States. BBC reports that "recent comments in the Chinese media have shown fierce opposition to the [Senate] bill, saying the trade imbalance between the two countries is a result of US economic policies and not the exchange rate. 'China calls on the US to discard protectionism, stop politicizing economic issues and take concrete action to create an enabling environment for the development of bilateral economic relations and trade,' said Ma Zhaoxu, a spokesperson for the foreign ministry."[169]

The Chinese embassy hired one of the top DC lobbying firms to fight the bill in Congress. For the past several years, it has paid Patton, Boggs a retainer of $35,000 per month. Top staff members at the embassy have created a Congressional Liaison Team of twelve members that have been calling Congressional offices and holding briefings for members of Congress.[170]

Some voices in the United States have echoed the criticisms that warn of a trade war with China if the House passes the Senate bill and Obama signs it. They liken the trade sanctions to the imposition of the Smoot-Hawley tariff in 1930, which, by all accounts, accelerated the Great Depression by imposing high tariffs on foreign imports, which, in turn, led to retaliation against American products and thus increased our unemployment rate.

FOX News' John Lott argues that "if passed, the . . . [Senate bill] would force China to raise the value of the yuan. And if they refuse to comply, we will increase the tariffs on what we buy from them, equivalent to putting a special tax on the goods we buy."[171]

Lott says that "China's currency manipulation is a mistake. Yet, their mistake doesn't mean we should make one also. If Chinese leaders are stupid enough to subsidize Americans by selling their goods and assets too cheaply, why should we stop them?"[172]

Lott also argues that "increasing the value of the yuan or higher tariffs will make things worse, temporarily increasing our unemployment rate. Some companies and workers will win from the higher yuan, but others will lose. Many sectors are highly integrated and American products rely on components manufactured or assembled in China. Apple is such a company. If tariffs are imposed, the price of Apple iPads and iPhones will rise."[173]

American businesses are divided on the bill. The *New York Times* reports that "lobbyists for General Motors, Caterpillar, steel producers, textile manufacturers, toy makers, poultry farmers and other businesses . . . [are] supporting or opposing the tariffs depending on their own business relations with China. Generally, large manufacturers like Caterpillar that operate in China have opposed it, warning of a backlash. Smaller businesses, like a tube maker in Ohio or a ceramics maker in upstate New York, have supported tariffs because they say China has artificially lowered its prices and gained an unfair edge."[174]

And it's the large firms that have the lobbyists and make the campaign contributions, perhaps explaining the shared reluctance of Republican Speaker Boehner and Democratic President Obama to see the Senate bill become law.

Fears of a trade war with China are ridiculous. True, whenever the United States has imposed tariffs on Chinese products, Beijing has retaliated against American goods. When President Obama imposed tariffs on tires to protest Chinese trade policies, Beijing replied with levies on American poultry. However, with the United States buying almost $300 billion more from China than we sell it, a trade war would be suicidal for the Chinese.

China's GDP stands at $5.9 trillion US dollars. So, if China sells us $370 billion a year, that means that 6 percent of its economy depends on its trade with the United States. Beijing cannot risk so hefty a slice of its economy by an all-out trade war in which both sides raise tariffs.

We, on the other hand, have a much lower stake in any possible trade war. We only sell China about $100 billion a year, less than 1 percent of our total economy (our GDP is about $14.5 trillion).

Any negotiation involves a certain game of chicken, but this is one game only we can win. Who do you think will blink first? The country with 6 percent of its economy on the line or the one with less than 1 percent? If there were ever a real trade war, China's economy would probably collapse.

GOP presidential contender Mitt Romney grasps the need to stand up to China. "They are threatening a trade war?" Romney asked incredulously during an interview with the author. "Their exports to us are up here," he said raising his right arm high in the air. "And ours to them are down here," as he lowered his left hand. "You want a trade war? Bring it on!"[175]

The WTO would undoubtedly get the case of US versus China if the Senate bill passes. How would it rule? Jonathan E. Sanford, writing for the Congressional Research Service, notes that the IMF has strong rules against currency manipulation, but no real powers of enforcement. The WTO is in the opposite situation. It does not have rules against manipulation of currency but does have very formidable enforcement powers. If a country does not go along with its decisions, it can force other nations to impose tariffs on that nation's products.[176]

There is a way to get the WTO to act against China's currency manipulation. When the World Trade Organization was created, in 1996, it signed an agreement with the IMF (amended in 2006) saying that the two bodies "shall cooperate in the discharge of their respective mandates" and "shall consult with each other with a view to achieving greater coherence in global policy making."[177]

While Sanford notes that "it is unreasonable to expect that the WTO should be expected to enforce the rules of the IMF" against currency manipulation, "one might expect that conversations about the ways the activities of one organization might be hindering the other in 'the discharge of' its assigned duties might transpire."[178]

Sanford says that the agreement between the two organizations "might provide that their disparate treatment of currency manipulation is inconsistent with their promise to 'cooperate in the discharge of their respective mandates' and to promote 'greater coherence in global economic policymaking.' "[179]

The agreement between the IMF and the WTO could be changed by a simple majority vote in each institution.[180]

No guarantees, but it might work.

Or it might be likely enough to work that the Chinese can't take a chance and allow a trade war to develop. If the US government passes the Senate bill, it will likely force China to add up the odds and negotiate in (for them) good faith to readjust its currency.

ACTION AGENDA

First, let's pass the Senate bill on Chinese currency manipulation and get Obama to sign it. Some Republican leaders—like House Speaker John Boehner—are reluctant to act because of their commitment to free trade. But how is free trade consistent with currency manipulation?

More likely, Boehner and the Republicans are feeling heat from big American companies that do business in China and echo its party line in order to stay in Beijing's good graces. In part 11, we discuss how the revolving door between our government and lobbying firms that work for foreign governments undermines our ability to act in our own national interest.

However, pressure from the people, especially Republicans, can undermine the power of the most formidable special interests.

Bombard Boehner and your local Republican Congressional representatives with demands to pass legislation against Chinese currency manipulation. Let them have it! Show them that you are fed up with being screwed by China's currency shenanigans and demand that we put an end to them!

Some Republicans oppose the China currency bill out of a genuine, if misguided, commitment to free trade, but most of this bunch are just on the take, getting campaign contributions from companies that are in China's pocket. They are putting the interests of China ahead of those of the United States! Give them a call. They'd love to hear from you!

What if we lose in the WTO and the organization endorses currency manipulation? University of Maryland economist Peter Morici recommends that the United States impose a tax on currency conversions from dollars to yuan "in an amount equal to China's currency market intervention. That would neutralize China's currency subsidies that steal US factories and jobs. The amount of the tax would be in Beijing's hands—if it reduced or eliminated currency market intervention, the tax would go down or disappear. The tax would not be protectionism; rather, in the face of virulent Chinese currency manipulation and mercantilism, it would be self defense."[181]

More difficult will be how to stop hackers from stealing our most basic industrial technologies. Already, corporate America is bolstering its defenses against hacking. The New York Times reported that "a nationwide survey of company technology managers, conducted by Forrester Research, found that computer security had increased as a share of the total information technology budget of companies, to 14 percent this year from 8.2

percent in 2007. Of those surveyed this year, 56 percent said it was a high priority to 'significantly upgrade.' "[182]

Federal spending on cybersecurity is set to rise from $9 billion now to $13.3 billion by 2015.[183] The news media is filled with stories of hurried efforts by corporate and government information databases to protect themselves from hack attacks.

And the FBI is on the case. The *Chicago Sun-Times* reports that "the FBI has placed economic espionage on both a national and local level second on its list of priorities, right behind fighting terrorism."[184]

Stopping hacking is very, very difficult. On August 3, 2011, hackers loosely affiliated with a group called Anonymous hacked into the computers of ManTech International, a $2.6 billion computer security company that had just won an FBI contract to stop hacker intrusions. With sneering sarcasm, they released internal company documents they had pilfered with the comment, "It's really good to know that you guys are taking care of protecting the United States from so-called cyber threats."[185]

From their conduct, we can infer that this hacking was attributable to the work of adolescent computer prodigies. But, if we can't even stop them, how much more difficult would it be to stop the Chinese government?

Amid all the tens of billions being spent, one question is seemingly never asked: Where the heck are the State Department and the White House? Why are we not demanding that China stop hacking us? Why is this issue not front and center in our discussions with Beijing? Why are we not threatening all sorts of retaliation against them if they don't restrain hacking?

It is ridiculous to think that we can completely stop Chinese hacking. We may not even be able to stop the majority of their attempts to access our industrial, scientific, technological, and defense secrets. The emphasis must be on diplomatic and economic pressure on China to cut it out.

The diplomats usually answer that we can't tell if the hacking is coming from the Chinese. After all, they deny it. But everybody knows they're lying. Everyone understands that only a nation-state can have this kind of capability to hack, and that only China and Russia are in this business (and that China is far more oriented toward hacking than Moscow).

House Intelligence Committee Chairman Mike Rogers (R-MI) said that "when you talk to these companies behind closed doors, they describe attacks that originate in China, and have a level of sophistication and are clearly supported by a level of resources that can only be a nation-state entity."[186] So, why are not

President Barack Obama and Secretary of State Hillary Clinton raising hell? Where is the government to defend us?

What pressure could we bring? China is very, very vulnerable to the United States. As noted, its economy is totally dependent on its ability to sell in the US market. Ours is not nearly as dependent on its ability to access Chinese consumers.

And the debt? What about Chinese holdings of US debt? Doesn't that give them enormous leverage? Not really. As noted, China has to buy our dollars to keep their currency weak and their goods underpriced. And, once it has the dollars, it has little choice but to buy our bonds with them.

So, let's use the leverage we have. Let's not be timid and talk ourselves into a position of weakness. Remember the immortal words of former Secretary of State Henry Kissinger: "The weak grow strong through effrontery. The strong grow weak through inhibitions."[187]

But despite our rather strong bargaining position, the Obama administration, like the Bush and Clinton presidencies before it, has done little to demand that China stop ripping us off.

Congressional Republicans are begging Obama to stand up to Beijing. House Intelligence Committee Chairman Rogers put it well when he said, "Beijing is waging a massive trade war on us all, and we should band together to pressure them to stop. Combined, the United States and our allies in Europe and Asia have significant diplomatic and economic leverage over China, and we should use this to our advantage to put an end to this scourge."[188]

ABC News reported that "Rogers said the United States could use trade or diplomatic avenues in response to Chinese cyberespionage. He and others have suggested pursuing the issue at the World Trade Organization or in other international forums."[189]

Former Republican presidential candidate Senator John McCain (R-AZ) makes a similar point. "We have to make it clear to the Chinese that there are costs to engaging in this kind of activity. We ought to make it very clear to the Chinese that their past and present behavior is unacceptable."[190]

ABC News quotes James A. Lewis, a cyberexpert at the Center for Strategic and International Studies, as saying that the United States should not be afraid to pressure China. "You could begin to release details of cases where we have strong pointers towards Chinese cyberespionage. You could expel an attaché. You could say you're reviewing provisions of agreements or treaties. You could impose tighter requirements on Chinese coming to the United States to study."[191]

But we aren't doing any of these things.

Richard Clarke, a former antiterrorism official, has warned that China has hacked our electrical grid, a step that has ominous military implications. He asks: "What would we do if we discovered that Chinese explosives had been laid throughout our national electrical system? The public would demand a government response. If, however, the explosive is a digital bomb that could do even more damage, our response is apparently muted—especially from our government. Congress hasn't passed a single piece of significant cybersecurity legislation."[192]

Clarke warns that "in the realm of cyberspace, the administration is ignoring its primary responsibility to protect its own citizens when they are targeted for harm by a foreign government."[193]

Clarke compares the US response to these Chinese incursions to the British government's. "Three years ago, the head of the British Security Service wrote to hundreds of corporate chief executive officers in the United Kingdom to advise them that their companies had in all probability been hacked by the government of China. Neither the FBI nor the Department of Homeland Security has issued such a notice to US executives, but most corporate leaders already know it."[194]

Former CIA director and current Defense Secretary Leon Panetta joined the chorus of warnings when he told Congress that the United States was vulnerable to "an electronic Pearl Harbor."[195]

The administration's response to these threats is nothing short of pathetic. Deputy Defense Secretary William Lynn says that it is limited to "a pilot program with a handful of defense companies to provide more robust protection for their networks." As Brett M. Decker and William C. Triplett II noted in their book *Bowing to Beijing*, "the commanders of the Chinese Army must be quaking in their desk chairs."[196]

At the end of October 2011, President Obama met with legislative leaders and called for a cybersecurity bill to deal with the hacker/espionage threat. Obama spoke of the need for "prompt legislative action to ensure the US government has the authorities it needs to keep the nation safe."[197]

Democrats want legislation for "new rules to force companies to notify consumers when breaches put personal data at risk and authorize the Department of Homeland Security to ensure minimum standards are met in monitoring for possible attacks."[198]

Republicans are more oriented to giving "companies incentives to boost cyber defenses and not rush to impose new regulations except in sensitive sectors like nuclear power, electricity and water treatment plants."[199]

Senator Jim Webb (D-VA) has introduced legislation barring companies from giving China technologies that were developed with the support of the American taxpayer." While Webb's legislation does not single out China, it does apply to nations that "by law, practice, or policy require proprietary technology transfers as a matter of doing business," in other words, China.[200]

However, nobody is really focused on demanding that China cut it out. No pressure. No threats. Not even any harsh language from the administration. The closest Obama has come to even addressing Beijing's trade practices was a comment that "we have seen a lot of questionable competitive practices coming out of China when it comes to the clean energy space . . . we're going to look very carefully at this stuff and potentially bring actions if we find that the basic rules of the road have been violated."[201]

And, by refusing to take a position on legislation that passed the Senate to declare China a currency manipulator, Obama sends a signal to Beijing that he is not serious about countering their unfair and illegal trade practices.

And, when his Treasury Department ruled, for the sixth time, that China was *not* manipulating its currency, Obama completely undercut our country's position and its interests.

In the long run, legislation and even retaliation won't be able to restrain China from hacking, stealing, and appropriating our technology. Only vigorous presidential action will work.

But Obama is nowhere to be seen on the issue.

Even after our intelligence agencies identified twenty separate sources of hacking entities tied to the People's Liberation Army and Chinese universities, the administration's response is to continue diplomatic attempts to stop this.

Are they kidding?

And why are they still treading softly? Because they are afraid that China will get mad at us and stop lending us money.

According to the *Wall Street Journal*, "diplomatic considerations may limit the US interest in taking a more confrontational approach because some US officials are wary of angering China, the largest holder of US debt."[202]

And, ultimately, big business in the United States tends to soft-pedal its complaints about China. Anxious to access its vast market, Wall Street and the Fortune 500 companies don't want to alienate Beijing. Obama, who often dances to their tune, responds to their concerns by casting a benign eye over China's abuses, reining in retaliatory proposals, and failing to confront the Chinese leadership on the issue.

But small businesses—traditionally outside Obama's orbit—are exercised about the issue. They generally support sanctions against China and resent the unfair competition Beijing offers.

While Congress does need to pass legislation to protect our country against cyberthreats, it is only through presidential leadership that we will be able to discipline China and use our massive economic leverage over Beijing to get it to obey the international rules of trade and commerce.

PART FOUR

Pakistan

WITH FRIENDS LIKE THESE, YOU DON'T NEED ENEMIES

When we think about Pakistan, the overt hostility of China is almost refreshing. We realize that Beijing is intent on bringing us down, but the Pakistanis masquerade as our friends, live off our foreign aid, and talk about how they cooperate with us in fighting terrorism. But all the time, it is increasingly obvious that they are screwing us.

The amazing generosity of the United States is strikingly evident in our dealings with Pakistan. Over and over again, we provide them with enormous financial support to help both their military and their people.

And over and over again, Pakistan screws us.

When Pakistan is in trouble, the United States is like a good neighbor who shows up at the door to lend a hand. A good example was our response to the devastating floods in Pakistan that killed 1,600 people in 2010. The United States Agency for International Development (AID) immediately rushed in with a

$20 million check to provide relief to the six million people, including three million children, who were affected.

And yet, despite the fact that the United States was the largest single donor to the UN relief effort for Pakistan, many Pakistanis openly complained that the United States was not doing enough to help them. And some even suggested that if we didn't do more, they'd reconsider their help to us in the War on Terror.

In addition to the humanitarian aid, we also provide them with billions of dollars in development assistance and with vast amounts of money to improve their military and help us in fight against the terrorists in the region.

They're supposed to be our allies and we try to help them.

And how do they respond?

They hate us.

Consider the following two facts:

- The United States gave Pakistan $4.4 billion in foreign aid in 2010, providing them with assistance equal to 1.2 percent of their total GDP. To put it in perspective, it would be as if Pakistan gave the United States $180 billion per year, about the same as our Medicaid budget.[1]

- A survey in June 2011 by Pew Research Center, a nonpartisan Washington-based survey research organization, found that 73 percent of the Pakistanis have an unfavorable view of the United States, while just 14 percent believed that it's a good thing that Osama bin Laden was killed. In fact, 55 percent of the Pakistani people believe that it was a bad thing that he was killed![2]

It's obvious that we are not in sync with the Pakistanis. They don't hold anything against the sadistic mastermind of the 9/11 terror attack that killed three thousand people.

PAKISTAN SHELTERED BIN LADEN

And speaking of bin Laden, is there anyone on the planet who really believes that the Pakistani government, military, and intelligence services didn't realize that public enemy number one was living in an urban area around the corner from their equivalent of West Point?

Yes, there is at least one person—former *New York Times* managing editor Bill Keller. Citing anonymous American sources in his amazingly pro-Pakistan article for the *Times Magazine*, the gullible Keller covers the bin Laden issue as follows:

The Americans who deal with Pakistan believe that General Kayani and the director of the Inter-Services Intelligence Agency, Gen. Ahmed Shuja Pasha, were genuinely surprised and embarrassed that bin Laden was so close by, though the Americans fault the Pakistanis for not looking very hard.[3]

Others who are not as naive and who are familiar with the geographical area and intelligence protocol disagree.

According to the *Christian Science Monitor,* "Ramesh Chopra, a former chief of Indian military

Alrighty then....Now that we are sure that Osama bin Laden is nowhere in Abbottabad, what shall we do for lunch.....

intelligence who was born in Abbottabad, says that any military conducts sweeps of areas and would know its own backyard. For him, it's clear bin Laden was protected by elements of Pakistan's establishment."[4]

And, unlike Keller, Pakistani journalist Mosharraf Zaidi did not swallow hook, line, and sinker the ridiculous Pakistani claims that they were surprised and *shocked* to learn that Obama bin Laden was living around the corner from their elite military school and major military base. After reporting on the story from Abbottabad, he challenged the Pakistanis' story: "The idea that bin Laden got from Tora Bora to that house over the last seven or eight years without a single element of the Pakistani state knowing about it just doesn't ring true. What rings even more hollow is the notion that somehow US military choppers and gunships could fly into Pakistan undetected."[5]

Another Pakistani writer, Tariq Ali, agreed. "The news is that he was in a safe house which is literally next door to the Kakul military academy, one of the most heavily protected areas in the country. And the notion that this was a secret from Pakistan's military intelligence is risible. It's just not believable."[6]

Unless you're the *New York Times*.

So, how do we reconcile this? Our ally and partner in the War on Terror apparently forgot to tell us that the mastermind of 9/11 was alive and well and hiding in plain sight in Pakistan.

And, undoubtedly, bin Laden needed shelter, support, and protection in order to remain hidden from the CIA for ten years. And just who would have been in a position to provide that?

Our allies—the Pakistanis.

It's a big reminder of their duplicitousness, their dishonesty, unreliability, and the exploitive nature of their relationship with the United States.

It gets even worse. After the bin Laden raid, US officials believe, the Pakistanis permitted the Chinese to inspect a modified stealth Black Hawk helicopter that crashed into the compound wall and was left behind.

Navy SEALs, apparently anxious to keep the helicopter's technology secret, had placed explosives in the helicopter, but the tail remained intact.[7] The helicopter was designed to evade and confuse radar, as it successfully did in the raid.[8] The Chinese are major weapons suppliers to Pakistan and giving them access to secret American technology is a shot over the bow to us, supposedly in retaliation for allegedly failing to give them advance notice of the bin Laden raid.

But we made a good decision. Had we told them in advance, there's a good chance that bin Laden would have skipped town.

Our relationship with Pakistan has deteriorated significantly since the US raid on the bin Laden compound. They were insulted that we did not notify them in advance. Insulted? Insulted that we obviously didn't trust them. How could we?

For both sides, it was a turning point in the relationship. But, nonetheless, as James T. Farwell, author of *The Pakistan Cauldron: Conspiracy, Assassination & Instability*, recounts, "The bin Laden attack has had a huge impact on Pakistani politics. From their viewpoint, the attack put them in an untenable posture. Either they did not know bin Laden was present in Pakistan, in which case they were ignorant or incompetent. Or they did, in which case they were complicit. They feel it was another case of American arrogance abusing Pakistani sovereignty."[9]

PAKISTAN BACKS TERROR ATTACKS AGAINST AMERICANS

Pakistan's anti-American activities have been escalating. Pakistan arrested five men for providing assistance to the United States in its hunt for bin Laden, including a doctor who set up a "phony vaccination scheme [in Abbottabad] in the hope of gaining access to the bin Laden compound and getting hard evidence that bin Laden was hiding there."[10]

The Pakistani government's Inter-Services Intelligence (ISI) not only shelters terrorists, it helps them to attack us. US government sources believe that ISI actually helped the Haqqani terrorists who attacked the US embassy and NATO headquarters in Kabul in September 2011, killing sixteen people, including six children.

The Haqqani, an ally of al-Qaeda, is a brutal crime family that US intelligence and military sources consider "the most deadly insurgent group in Afghanistan . . . that has been responsible for hundreds of American deaths."[11]

Former chairman of the Joint Chiefs Admiral Mike Mullen bluntly accused the ISI of aiding the Haqqani in orchestrating the daylong deadly attack. Admiral Mullen told the US Senate, "The Haqqani network . . . acts as a veritable arm of Pakistan's Inter-Services Intelligence Agency."[12]

Mullen, who has played a large role in trying to improve relations with Pakistan, placed the blame for the embassy attack on these terrorists and the ISI. "With ISI support, Haqqani operatives planned and conducted a truck bomb attack [on September 11, 2011], as well as the assault on our embassy," said Adm. Mullen.

He added, "we also have credible intelligence that they were behind the 28 June attack against the

Inter-Continental Hotel in Kabul and a host of other smaller but effective operations."[13]

In 2008, American intelligence operatives had learned that the Haqqani network was behind an attack on the Indian embassy in Kabul that killed fifty-four people, and that they were assisted by ISI. Although US officials confronted ISI, Pakistan refused to shut down the brutal terrorists even though our intelligence operatives had hard evidence of cell phone communications about the attack.[14]

The *New York Times* reported that "according to two American officials, cellphones used by the attackers made calls to suspected ISI operatives before the attack"[15]

In his Senate testimony, Admiral Mullen chastised the Pakistanis for their alliance with the terrorists:

"They may believe that by using these proxies, they are hedging their bets or redressing what they feel is an imbalance in regional power," he said. "But in reality, they have already lost that bet. By exporting violence, they've eroded their internal security and their position in the region. They have undermined their international credibility and threatened their economic well-being."[16]

Shortly after the bin Laden raid, Pakistan began to retaliate against the United States. It expelled 100 special forces and Army trainers and also denied visas to American personnel. Those actions, coupled with the evidence of ongoing complicity with anti-America terrorists, have seriously shaken the already tenuous alliance. And it's definitely getting worse. NPR reported on the troubled state of affairs. "The fragile and troubled relationship between the US and Pakistan is on a deep, downward spiral. Admiral Mike Mullen's comments . . . made public an implication that many officials in Washington and Afghanistan have long voiced only in private—that Pakistan's premier intelligence agency, the ISI, supports insurgent groups, including the Haqqani network . . . His comments signal a more confrontational stance against Pakistan."[17]

The US ambassador to Pakistan, Cameron Munter, added his voice to the public criticism of Pakistan: "The attack that took place in Kabul a few days ago— that was the work of the Haqqani network," Munter told Radio Pakistan. "There is evidence linking the Haqqani network to the Pakistani government. This is something that must stop. We have to make sure that we work together to fight terrorism."

Captain John Kirby, Munter's spokesman, added that his boss believes "that 'elements' of Pakistan's Inter-Services Intelligence agency, known as the ISI, 'directly support' the Haqqani network."[18]

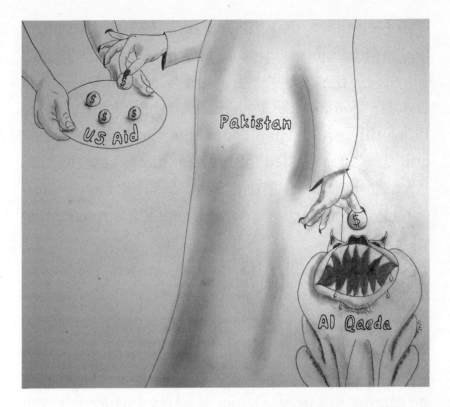

The Pakistani military bristled at Admiral Mullen's comments. General Ashfaq Kayani, Pakistan's army chief, called in his commanders for a special meeting to discuss the security situation. Retired Army Lieutenant General David Barno, a senior fellow at the Center for a New American Security, said that the Pakistani "media people coming out of that [meeting] said that Pakistan intends to defend its borders from incursions from Afghanistan. So I think they're signaling that they're not going to tolerate any US ground intervention certainly into Pakistan."[19]

NPR reports that "Barno says Pakistan considers any ground incursion—any raid by American Special Forces or the like—as crossing a red line, and that the US could face a significant backlash. Among other things, Pakistan could shut down critical land and air routes needed to shuttle military supplies into Afghanistan. Still, Barno says the US has to consider when it reaches a point where it has to take that risk."[20]

But, increasingly, US military leaders are saying that we need to expand our unilateral actions to destroy the Haqqani and al-Qaeda networks without relying on cooperation from Pakistan. The killing of bin Laden illustrates this new focus on unilateralism. Things may be coming to a head. Daniel Markey, a senior fellow at the Council on Foreign Relations, says Mullen's forceful language was striking in its tone and substance. "The implication is that the United States government is saying with one voice that if Pakistan does not end its ties with the Haqqani network, the US will expand its unilateral actions to destroy that network, whether Pakistan likes it or not."[21]

Drone attacks, which have killed more than a dozen top al-Qaeda leaders, have also alienated the Pakistani populace, who see them as a violation of their sovereignty. Many feel the attacks kill innocent civilians.

Farwell says, "Some fear that the attacks are radicalizing elements of the military, opinion leaders, and the middle class, and that Pakistan could reach a tipping point that enables violent Islamists to win control over the state."[22]

Pakistan feels that the United States is forcing it into a civil war by bribing its leaders with foreign aid, assistance they use to line their own pockets and do nothing for the country.[23]

Washington will likely expand its drone strikes in North Waziristan, Pakistan, where the Haqqani network is based, but it could also conduct cross-border raids using US special forces.

Markey surmises that "you could see conventional forces in Afghanistan moved up to the Pakistan border to support cross-border attacks that would probably start out small but could expand. And you could see a variety of other combined efforts that could even include a more extensive bombing campaign that went beyond the use of drones."[24]

Already, there have been two instances of direct military confrontation between NATO and Pakistani forces. In September 2011, the *New York Times* reported that "Pakistani soldiers ambushed their US counterparts in a Pakistani village after seemingly cordial talks in 2007."[25]

Then, in November 2011, US soldiers battled with Pakistani troops across the Afghan border. Each side said the other fired first. Arnaud de Borchgrave, noted expert on the region, said, "The suspicion is that the Pakistanis were harboring the insurgents who first opened fire and then retreated into the army base appropriately named Camp Volcano."[26]

The NATO airstrike on the Pakistani base killed twenty-four of their soldiers. Pakistan retaliated, as it had threatened to do, by "closing two NATO supply routes from Karachi to Afghanistan that supply 30 percent of Afghan war requirements immobilizing hundreds of tanker trucks over two 1,000 mile routes to Kandahar and Kabul."[27]

And now Washington is finally demanding some accountability. This year, the Obama administration suspended, at least temporarily, $1 billion of our military aid to Pakistan because of its failure to effectively fight the War on Terror and its hostile actions against the United States.[28]

Now, both Washington and Islamabad are reassessing their once close relationship. The *New York Times* summarizes the state of play from the American side: "With the United States facing the reality that its broad security partnership with Pakistan is over, American officials are seeking to salvage a more limited counterterrorism alliance that they acknowledge will complicate their ability to launch attacks against extremists and move supplies into Afghanistan."[29]

The *Times* reports that under the coming new relationship, "The United States will be forced to restrict drone strikes, limit the number of its spies and soldiers on the ground and spend more to transport supplies through Pakistan to allied troops in Afghanistan . . . United States aid to Pakistan will also be reduced sharply."[30]

The newspaper quotes a senior US official as saying: "We've closed the chapter on the post-9/11 period."[31]

"THE MOST ANTI-US POPULATION" IN THE WORLD

Pakistan's contempt for America is no secret.

Syndicated columnist and regional expert Arnaud de Borchgrave called Pakistanis "arguably the world's most anti-US population" in the world.[32]

Yet, we give more foreign aid to Pakistan than any country other than Israel, Egypt, Iraq, and Afghanistan. And they hate us for it. What's wrong with this picture? The fact is that we pay more than half of Pakistan's military budget. Now, that's a lot of money that gives them a lot of power. In 2010, we gave the Pakistanis $2.5 billion of military aid,[33] and their total military budget is $5.8 billion.[34] So, our contribution is no small drop in the bucket. And where does it go? Some of it is going to the very terrorists that we are paying to help them attack. Pakistan actually uses our military aid to funnel money to our adversaries behind our back. As a result, we are paying, in effect, for both sides of the war in the region. At the same time that we contribute to NATO through our tax dollars, we're also contributing to the Taliban through our foreign aid to Pakistan!

Our generosity is working against us. While we're there with our money, keeping this otherwise bankrupt state afloat, the Pakistani people hate us, the intelligence service works against us, and the military squanders the aid we give it on corruption while aiding the terrorists. Let's face it: Pakistan is a cesspool of violence, betrayal, terrorist groups, and double-crossing.

So, here's the question: What are we doing there? What are we doing propping up this corrupt, anti-American nation? Ralph Peters, a retired US Army officer who worked with the Pakistan Army and intelligence leadership, sums it up: "(America's) tax dollars are being used to help kill and maim our soldiers, marines and navy corpsmen fighting in Afghanistan. . . . Over the past 10 years, we've given the Pakistanis—primarily their military—over $20 billion in aid. What did we get in return? Our Pakistani allies hid and protected Osama bin Laden; they increased their support to the Afghan Taliban and their partner, the Haqqani terror network; they sponsored repeated terrorist attacks against India; they provided safe havens for terrorists from a 'rainbow coalition' of extremist outfits; and, all the while they purposely whipped up anti-Americanism among the country's 180 million Muslims. Your tax dollars at work."[35]

With friends like them, who needs enemies?

And it's not like they don't need our assistance. Without American aid, Pakistan would collapse. Its finances are a total mess. Thirty-eight percent of its budget goes to pay the interest on its debt, largely to foreigners. Pakistan's debt service for foreign loans now consumes $1.034 billion a year, up from $726 billion last year.[36]

Defense eats up another 18 percent of its total budget, 32 percent if you count pensions for military retirees.[37] (In the United States, by contrast, debt service is about 8 percent of our budget, and defense, including pensions, is another 18 percent.)

This year, the Pakistani government granted its military personnel a 15 percent pay increase.[38] Times are good when Uncle Sam is paying.

Obviously, our virtual financing of the Pakistani military and intelligence operations gives us tremendous leverage, but we won't use it. We've let Pakistan get away with sheltering bin Laden and al-Qaeda leaders and with actually helping terrorists attack us!

And military aid is less than half of the assistance we give Pakistan. We give it another $1.8 billion in economic or civilian assistance including massive funding for disaster relief.[39]

Given our consistent support and our alleged joint antiterrorist goals, one might expect the Pakistani military to be somewhat sensitive to our needs. Instead, it repeatedly bites the hand that feeds it. Farwell explains the Pakistani thinking about the Taliban and al-Qaeda: "Despite bin Laden's presence there, Pakistan has been generally cooperative in fighting al-Qaeda, which they see as comprised of foreigners. They have been more ambivalent about the domestic Taliban. They have seen Pakistani Taliban as fellow countrymen, and they dislike fighting their own citizens. Still, Pakistanis dislike violent extremists. Unfortunately, huge majorities are also hostile to the United States. The Pakistan government wants to defeat violent extremists at home, but key members want to maintain a viable relationship with the Afghan Taliban."[40]

The world views from Washington and Islamabad are light years apart. Politics in Pakistan is characterized by what James T. Farwell calls "a culture of paranoia, betrayal, and assassination." He notes that until Asif Ali Zardari, the current president, "most heads of state were assassinated, forcibly removed, or dismissed."[41] And Zardari himself, of course, became president after his wife, Benazir Bhutto, was assassinated in 2007 during her run for the presidency.

Farwell elaborates: "Because tribal loyalty comes first, the country has a weak national identity. . . . [The reason] their politics are dysfunctional is that for too long the government has responded to the Army and Washington and not Pakistani voters. Because the culture is about power, relationships and political patronage rooted in family, tribe, and clan, political party contests are mainly over who controls patronage, not ideas. The culture is an obstacle to modernization and reform."[42]

Modernization and reform? Far from it. Pakistan gets worse every year. It is a nation threatened with a terrorist takeover, its nuclear arsenal hanging in the balance. Its population vents its anger and frustration against the United States, while the Taliban poses an ever greater threat to its freedom.

With an election looming, Imran Khan, a "charismatic former cricket star turned politician who is

fiercely anti-American, has grabbed the popular imagination recently,"[43] according to the *Miami Herald*.
Khan made headlines on November 6, 2011, when he
addressed a ferocious anti-American tirade to a crowd
of 100,000 people in rival Nawaz Sharif's hometown of
Lahore. Claiming that the United States drone strikes
were killing civilians and that the Pakistani leadership
was participating in the War on Terror only because of
its desire for US aid, he shouted, "Our leaders owned
this war on terror for the sake of dollars. You sold
out the blood of innocent people."[44] Khan argues that
"Pakistan's alliance with the US is the main reason
Pakistan is facing a homegrown Taliban insurgency.
Khan promises to tear up Islamabad's alliance with
Washington and he's made resistance to US drone missile strikes against suspected militants in Pakistan's
tribal areas as one of the cornerstones of his politics."[45]

And Khan's opponent is "another critic of the United
States, former Prime Minister Nawaz Sharif,"[46] whose
provincial government "stopped accepting US aid
money as funds from an 'enemy,' "[47] the *Herald* reports.

Some enemy! We pay for half their military!

While the candidates to succeed him lambaste the
United States, Pakistan's supposedly pro-American
president is totally discredited by his own corruption.
The *Chicago Sun-Times* reports that the "government

of President Asif Ali Zardari, whose party was helped to power in 2008 under a deal with Pakistan's military that was brokered in part by Washington, is sinking in popularity, mired in corruption scandals and tarnished by poor performance in office."[48]

But, in Pakistan, it is not so much public opinion or the civilian elected leadership that is the key power, but the military itself. Carey Showfield, author of the study *Inside the Pakistan Army*, traces the evolution of the Pakistan military from a genteel force to a group of religious crazies.

"During its initial years, the army primarily was comprised of sons of landed families and successful professionals, with almost all prominent families having someone in the forces. Gen. Zia-ul-Haq's Islamisation drive, however, changed that trend, bringing in both officers and jawans [young soldiers] from less affluent and more religious backgrounds. Having lost out to India in three conventional wars since 1947—the third of which severed off erstwhile East Pakistan—Gen Zia's Islamisation programme gave the India-Pakistan rivalry a religious color."[49] And, with that, it promoted Islamist influence in the Pakistan military.

Meanwhile, within Pakistan, there are signs that the regime of President Asif Zardari might be under pressure from the military and ISI. Criticism for his perceived pro-American orientation has been percolating for months. Former foreign minister Shah Qureshi attacked Zardari's national security policies, signaling widespread dissatisfaction with the administration.

In fact, reports are circulating that Pakistan's ambassador to the United States, Husain Haqqani (no relation to the terror group), may have sought to alert American officials to the possibility that a coup d'état was brewing. An American businessman, Mansoor Ijaz, says that Haqqani asked him to deliver a message to the US military to that effect, a request that Ijaz says he believed came from the president.[50] Haqqani resigned as ambassador after the furor erupted on November 22, 2011.

HOW PAKISTAN CAME TO HATE US

Pakistan was founded when India got its independence from Britain in 1947. Since the Pakistani region within the colony of India was mostly Muslim and the rest of India was largely Hindu, the partition seemed logical. Once the two states were created, there was a massive exodus of over twelve million Muslims out of India into Pakistan and a wave of violence engulfed the country, killing up to a million people.

India and Pakistan have been at loggerheads ever since, their relationship aggravated by a dispute over the state of Kashmir, which lies between them. They have fought three wars, all won by India, and tensions continue to mount. India experienced its own version of 9/11 on July 13, 2011, when three coordinated bomb blasts in Mumbai killed six hundred people. Pakistan is widely blamed for the attack.

Throughout the Cold War, India had a socialist government that allied itself with the Soviet Union, despite its pretentions to be one of the leaders of the nonaligned nations. So, the United States backed Pakistan in its conflicts with India, supplying significant military aid. The American relationship with Pakistan warmed further in the 1980s, when the Reagan administration gave a top priority to thwarting the Soviet Union's attempt to take over neighboring Afghanistan. The United States, Pakistan, and the Afghan mujahideen were closely allied in the conflict, which bled the Soviet Union and led to its fall.

During the Cold War, the relationship between Pakistan and the United States was so close that Pakistani military officers regularly trained in the United States and felt a great kinship with their American colleagues.

Afterward, the United States lost interest in Pakistan and in Afghanistan. The Cold War against the Soviets was won and the region no longer was a top priority. The United States ended its ties to the mujahideen, but the Pakistanis continued their close relationship with them and the Taliban, who came to power in the mid-1990s. Greg Bruno and Jayshree Bajoria write that "[ISI] provided the Taliban with advisers and materials in their battles with rival warlords, ensuring a friendly government that controlled most of Afghanistan."[51] The Pakistanis saw the alliance as a way to secure their back door while they focused on their war with India.

Then, the relationship fell apart when Pakistan exploded a nuclear weapon in 1998. India had already exploded its bomb twenty-two years before, with only a pro forma protest from the United States. However, the United States took the Pakistani bomb very seriously. Now two sworn adversaries, India and Pakistan, each had nuclear weapons and the chance that they would use them seemed almost imminent.

Congress voted sanctions on Pakistan after the nuclear explosion, cutting off military and economic aid and kicking the Pakistani military out of US schools.

Meanwhile, as the United States pulled out of Afghanistan after the end of the Cold War, the Taliban in Afghanistan developed a close relationship with al-Qaeda.

When al-Qaeda used Taliban-controlled Afghanistan as a base for its 9/11 attacks on the United States, America and the Taliban became enemies. The United

States invaded Afghanistan and drove the leaders of al-Qaeda and the Afghan Taliban, along with other terrorist groups, across the border into Pakistan. They settled in the region of Pakistan called the Federally Administered Tribal Areas (FATA).[52]

Pakistan pledged to the United States that it would fight the Taliban in Pakistan and help us in Afghanistan. In exchange, the spigot of US aid, closed since the Pakistani nuclear explosion, reopened and massive money gushed forth.

Now, almost one hundred thousand Pakistani troops are deployed along the Afghan border fighting the Taliban, and one thousand of its soldiers have been killed there.

Information from WikiLeaks has exposed the Pakistan army's close relationship with the Taliban. And the discovery that Osama bin Laden was holed up in Abbottabad proved the intimacy of the relationship. While feasting on American military and economic aid, Pakistan was clearly helping al-Qaeda and the Taliban and sheltering bin Laden.

South Asia expert Dennis Kux explains the difference between the world as seen from Washington and from Islamabad. "Washington considers Afghan Taliban and Haqqani Network and the militants led by Gulbuddin Hekmatyar [the leader of the paramilitary group Hezb-e Islami] as terrorists. Pakistan on the other hand considers these groups as useful proxies, to protect itself after the US/NATO forces leave Afghanistan for good."[53]

The *Los Angeles Times* notes that "Pakistani intelligence has long played a double game, seeing a strategic value in tolerating—and sometimes supporting and sheltering—militant groups that it hopes may help it in the future against India or serve as a hedge against potential instability in Afghanistan. This has been a source of frustration to US diplomats and military leaders who view Pakistan as an unreliable ally. . . . Pakistani officials, for their part, have been growing increasingly angry at the American drone strikes that kill civilians, and increasingly reluctant to sacrifice political capital to accommodate the demands of US forces, which they don't trust to sustain a long-term interest in the region; the US withdrawal from Afghanistan is scheduled for 2014."[54]

OUR AID KEEPS PAKISTAN ALIVE

But, even as confrontation with Pakistan looms, we still wallpaper the country with American dollars.

The following table shows the amount of economic and military aid we have given Pakistan since 9/11.

US MILITARY AND ECONOMIC
AID TO PAKISTAN[55]

Year	Economic	Military	Total
2002	$ 937M	$ 1,740M	$ 2,677M
2003	$ 378M	$ 1,760M	$ 2,138M
2004	$ 406M	$ 891M	$ 1,297M
2005	$ 491M	$ 1,397M	$ 1,888M
2006	$ 689M	$ 1,246M	$ 1,935M
2007	$ 689M	$ 1,079M	$ 1,768M
2008	$ 614M	$ 1,378M	$ 1,992M
2009	$1,354M	$ 1,114M	$ 2,468M
2010	$1,867M	$ 2,524M	$ 4,391M
Total	$5,704M	$13,129M	$18,833M

In 2011, US aid to Pakistan was expected to reach $6 billion.

Since World War II, we have given Pakistan $41 billion in aid, both military and economic, adjusted for inflation.[56]

And much of the aid is only very recent. While Bush kept aid to Pakistan somewhat under control, Obama has more than doubled the total assistance, tripling economic aid.

No wonder they hate us!

To protest Pakistan's possible role in the attack on the US embassy and its failure to find bin Laden, the Obama administration withheld one-third of its military aid to Pakistan in 2011. The *Guardian* reports that "the withheld aid includes funding for military equipment and reimbursements for selected Pakistani security expenditures—including a payment of $300M for counterinsurgency programs."[57]

It's not the first time Pakistan has suffered a cut in foreign aid. In the late 1970s, President Carter suspended all except food aid to Pakistan to protest its decision to construct a uranium enrichment facility. And President Bush 41 suspended aid flows in the early 1990s to protest Pakistan's nuclear program.

Of course, vast amounts of US aid are misspent or pocketed by corrupt officials, practically enough to spawn an entire cottage industry.

Since 9/11, the United States has paid for the cost of Pakistan's military operations in the tribal belt along the Afghan border where Taliban and al-Qaeda fighters are hiding out. The *Guardian* recounts how "the US foots the bill for food, fuel, ammunition, and maintenance" for the 100,000 Paki troops engaged in the theater at a cost averaging $80 million per month.[58]

But the newspaper reports that "American officials processing the payments at the US embassy . . . have concluded that Pakistani expense claims have been vastly inflated." One embassy official said, "My back of the envelope guesstimate is that 30 percent of the money they request to be reimbursed was legitimate costs they expended." The rest? He suspected it might have been spent "on F-16 fighter jets or a new house for an army general. Who knows, the roads on Constitution Avenue in Islamabad may have been paved with part of this money."[59] At least half of the US aid of $80 million per month "was thought to have disappeared."[60]

The *New York Times* confirms that "American military officials say the funds [we give the Pakistan army] do not reach the men who need it. That is especially the case for helicopter maintenance and poorly equipped Frontier Corps units." The *Times* reported that "during a recent visit to the border, an American official found members of the Frontier Corps 'standing there in the snow in sandals' . . . Several were wearing World War I–era pith helmets and carrying barely functional Kalashnikov rifles with just 10 rounds of ammunition apiece."[61]

Economic aid is not much more efficient. The BBC reports that "[l]arge sums went on consulting fees and overhead costs and never left US soil."[62] BBC notes that "[a] regular complaint about US aid-funded contractors

is that too much of the money that could be spent building a school or training teachers in the target country
is instead spent on salaries of well-qualified experts
and on overheads such as their offices in the US or
Europe."[63]

Nature has not been kind to Pakistan lately and,
after each disaster, the United States has led the way in
providing relief for the areas most directly hit.

On October 29, 2008, a magnitude 6.4 earthquake
struck southwestern Pakistan, followed by eleven after-
shocks, including one as severe as the quake itself.
There were 166 deaths and 17,500 displaced households. The United States jumped in with $5 million of
quake assistance.[64]

In August and September 2011, heavy monsoon
rains led to 465 deaths and displaced almost 2 million
people, destroying or damaging 1.6 million homes. The
United States stepped up and provided $6.2 million in
disaster aid.[65]

War has caused almost 1 million people to flee
the border area with Afghanistan. The United States
stepped in "to meet displacement-related humanitarian
needs and support sustainable returns to former conflict areas."[66]

In July 2010, heavy rainfall and flooding "affected
up to 1 million people and resulted in as many as 1,100

deaths." The United States provided the funding to dispatch "helicopters and boats to affected provinces to assist with ongoing evacuation efforts and to distribute emergency relief supplies, including tents, blankets, and sleeping mats." We also helped to establish seven camps for displaced families and provided them with food and water.[67]

No wonder they hate us.

ACTION AGENDA

Pakistan has American policy makers befuddled. The best response they can offer to Pakistani outrages is the occasional reduction or suspension of portions of our foreign aid—slaps on the wrist—to try to bring their government and military into line.

The conventional wisdom says that we need each other and that we are stuck with one another in what former Defense Secretary Robert Gates described as a "bad marriage."[68] Neither side can afford a divorce, Washington insiders say.

We need Pakistan precisely because they allow terrorists to slip across the Afghan border into their territory. As a result of this migration, we need to be able to send our drones and special forces in to kill al-Qaeda.

America's homeland security operatives have done their job and the FBI has been very effective in busting terrorist plots before they can materialize. But it is our strikes in Pakistan against al-Qaeda that have been most effective in stopping new attacks on our soil. Our attacks keep the enemy on the defense, scampering from tent to tent, constantly looking up to see if a drone is following them. To keep our troops in Afghanistan, we need the Pakistani supply routes. The alternative is a journey through the north of Afghanistan—only recently open—which involves the always iffy cooperation of Russia and Kazakhstan. (Pakistan has temporarily, we hope, cut off these direct supply routes through its territory in retaliation for our bin Laden raid and for the cross-border incidents in which Pakistani troops were killed).

And Pakistan needs us for our money, which pays for so much of their defense budget. No other alliance offers Pakistan the huge financial resources that flow from the United States. Pakistan would virtually have to cut its military in half without our money, in contrast to India, which has a thriving economy that can support its defense establishment.

China could step into the breach but it might not be able to fill the hole a cutoff in American aid would leave in the Pakistani military budget.

But divorce is not the only option in resolving this bad marriage. There are two key ways to pressure Pakistan and force a change in her conduct and rhetoric:

We could use the Pakistani-Indian feud to our advantage; and

We might scale back our operations in Afghanistan and focus just on al-Qaeda, so we don't need Pakistan as much.

Play the India Card

In 1971, President Richard Nixon and Secretary of State Henry Kissinger changed the fundamental nature of the Cold War by replacing the bilateral rivalry between the United States and the Soviet Union with a three-sided contest by dealing China into the equation. The opening to Beijing permitted the United States to play the Soviets and the Chinese off against one another to our advantage. Whenever Soviet leader Leonid Brezhnev got too outrageous, the United States would set up a high-profile meeting with the Chinese leadership and talk about a rapprochement with them, usually scaring the Soviets into tamer behavior or at least better anger management.

We should do the same thing with India. By opening up the possibility of closer ties with India, and moving away from Pakistan, we can create a competition for our favor and support.

Happy to get out of town, Obama travelled to New Delhi a few days after his disastrous defeat in the elections of 2010. Meeting with Indian Prime Minister Manmohan Singh, he signed deals for $10 billion in US exports to India, backed Indian demands for a permanent seat on the UN Security Council, and removed India from the list of nations to which we cannot export sensitive military and defense technology (where we had placed them after their nuclear blast).[69]

During Obama's visit, India kept dropping hints that it wanted America to become involved in helping it to settle its long-standing feud with Pakistan over Kashmir, and to pressure Pakistan to get tougher on terrorists. Indian expert C. Raja Mohan wrote on foreignpolicy.com that India needed the "United States to pressure the Pakistani army to end its promotion of extremism in Afghanistan and India."[70] Prime Minister Singh said that he foresees no healing in his country's relationship with Pakistan as long as that nation's "terror machine is as active as ever before."[71]

Obtuse as usual, Obama failed to pick up on the hint. He "conceded Pakistan's progress on countering terrorism was slower than desired and stressed that any peace between India and Pakistan would be a result of their bilateral efforts. 'The United States cannot impose a solution to these problems,' Obama said."[72]

President Obama doesn't get it. Nixon would have. The "bilateral efforts" between India and Pakistan aren't producing for either country. But by approaching Pakistani relations from the prism of a three-way relationship that includes India, we can bring real pressure to bear.

The fear that the United States would cut its military help to Pakistan while increasing its assistance to India's army is what would really keep Pakistani generals awake at night. We have been playing Pakistan all wrong. A cut in US military aid would be bad. But an increase in our military aid to India would be major bad news for Pakistan.

The Pakistanis know that our cuts in their military aid are not a serious threat. They know that sooner or later we will have to come across with aid because of our need to kill al-Qaeda operatives hiding in their country. Ironically, it is Pakistan's very willingness to tolerate the presence of these terrorists that gives them a lever to guarantee continued US military aid. They know that we will give them money, if for nothing else than to bribe them to let us kill al-Qaeda on their territory.

But increasing our military aid to India, that's another story. There is nothing to stop the United States from playing the India card (just as Nixon played the China card). If the United States were to help India enhance its military superiority over Pakistan, that would pose a big problem for the ISI and the Pakistani military.

Pakistan is obsessed with India. By contrast, they see their relationship with the Taliban and al-Qaeda, and with us, as just a sideshow.

Former US ambassadors Howard and Teresita Schaffer write that "Pakistan's view of the world begins with the trauma of the 1947 partition of India, and from the chronic insecurity that it engendered. This is the starting point not only for Pakistan's foreign policy, but also for its approach to negotiating with its principal international friends. Pakistan's position as a country one-seventh the size of its giant and, to Pakistanis, hostile neighbor is always at least in the background."[73]

It is all part of Pakistan's inferiority complex. "They feel that the very structure of their history and geography makes them dependent, vulnerable, and discounted. At the same time, national pride and the need to play up the ways in which they believe Pakistan is superior to India are important themes in their dealings with foreigners."[74]

The leaders of Pakistan and India are each fearful of being surrounded on both flanks by adversaries. Pakistan worries that India could expand its influence in Afghanistan and confront her with a threat at both her front and back doors. One of the reasons for Pakistan's flirtation with the Taliban is to use this organization's deep Islamist roots to keep Hindu India at arm's length from Afghanistan. India, on the other hand, worries about a Chinese-Pakistani alliance against it. Having lost a war with China in 1962, New Delhi worries about facing a combination of its two most recent military rivals in the future.

In this environment, there is considerable room for diplomacy and the pressure that it can exert to modify Pakistani behavior.

Two of the three wars India has waged with Pakistan have been over the disputed Himalayan territory of Kashmir, which both claim as their own. Pakistan desperately wants United States help in gaining the upper hand in Kashmir. To bring about such a shift in American foreign policy, Pakistan has been waging a high-stakes game to get American backing for its claims to Kashmir. The Associated Press describes how "Pakistan's spy agency, Inter-Services Intelligence (ISI), directed a clandestine, multimillion dollar effort through a Washington nonprofit group to influence the US position on Kashmir ... Documents filed in federal court describe donations to political campaigns and meetings with White House and State Department officials."[75]

AP reports that Indiana Republican Congressman Dan Burton, the cochairman of the House Pakistan Caucus, "[m]ay have received more than $11,000 in illicit [campaign] contributions"[76] from Pakistani sources. Indeed, the US Justice Department has brought charges against suspected Pakistani agent "Syed Ghulam Nabi Fai for ... trying to influence US officials about Kashmir. He allegedly took his marching orders from an ISI handler ... Fai, a Virginia resident, operated under the close watch of a senior member of the ISI and received as much as $700,000 a year from the government of Pakistan, the court documents said."[77]

Pakistan has even hired a top American lobbying firm, Locke Lord Strategies, to gin up US support for its Kashmir ambitions, paying the firm close to $3 million.[78]

But, the AP reports, "There's little to show for Pakistan's hefty investment of money and time. The US considers Kashmir an issue to be resolved by Pakistan and India and not by policymakers in Washington, a hands-off approach India firmly backs."[79]

On the contrary, Pakistan is worried that the United States will do precisely what we are recommending here, get closer to India as a way of pressuring Pakistan. Dr. Mohammad Samir Hussain writes on foreignpolicyjournal.com that "Pakistan expresses apprehension over the growing India-US ties in general and booming defense and security ties in particular. . . . Pakistan does not want the growing India-US multifaceted strategic relationship to take place because it believes that the growing relationship would undermine its ambition of strengthening defense cooperation with United States that holds the key to deterring India. Without the support of the U.S., it perceives that the existing conventional weapons imbalance would be widened thereby resulting in India achieving its regional hegemony. Also, Pakistan fears losing the United States support that has always come out on its side on the Kashmir issue."[80]

Dr. Hussain details Pakistani fears of what a US-India rapprochement could mean. He says it would "bring down the level of the relationship that Pakistan enjoys with . . . the US, which is the key to the supply of modern technology to Pakistan."[81] He worries that as relations between Pakistan and the United States fray, we will be less willing to pressure India into concessions over Kashmir. He also expresses concern that "the increasing number of multifaceted exercises between the armed forces of India and the US would improve the operational ability and capability of the Indian forces."[82] He even worries that India would begin to draw closer to Israel to get military technology, making common cause against Islamic Pakistan.

Pakistanis worry that "Washington regards India as the more important of the two [India and Pakistan] in ways that disadvantage Pakistan,"[83] write the Schaffers.

They add, "As the Pakistanis are painfully aware, Washington has come to see India as a rising global power and an incipient economic powerhouse, an attractive partner for American strategists and business people. Some influential Americans view it as a useful Asian counterforce to an aggressive China, with which Pakistan has historically enjoyed a warm relationship. The United States and India now sometimes even describe each other as 'natural allies' . . ."[84]

The Schaffers offer a perspective of how the US-Pakistani relationship looks from the other side. American assurances of friendship "have not stilled Pakistani concerns that America will favor India on matters important to Pakistan. Islamabad wants the

United States to deal with it as New Delhi's equal, and reacts sharply to any deviation from this norm. For example, the refusal of the US government to consider a civil nuclear deal with Pakistan similar to the one it negotiated with India is seen as clear evidence that the United States has downgraded its ties with Pakistan, and is often referred to as discrimination against Pakistan."[85]

Unlike the Pakistanis, the Indians like us. As noted, the Pew Research Center found that 73 percent of Pakistanis have an unfavorable view of the United States and, by 69–6, they see the United States as more of an enemy than a partner. (An enemy who gives them $6 billion a year?) But, on the other hand, Pew found that 66 percent of Indians view the United States favorably.[86]

If the United States got closer to India, it would ratify the worst fears of the Pakistanis, particularly those of their military. So let's do it! Every time Pakistan acts to protect terrorists and inhibit our efforts to get at them, let's sign another trade deal with India. We can make an endless number of diplomatic moves to draw closer to India. Let's dole them out, one by one, to punish Pakistan for dissing us.

Pakistan, of course, is not really a democracy. They hold elections but everybody knows that it is the military and the intelligence arm, the ISI, that call the shots.

It is precisely the military who will be most concerned by any moves we make toward India. Each deal for weapons, each dollar of military aid, will send a signal to them that they had better start working with us.

Until now, our response to Pakistani actions we don't like has been to cut our aid to them. That's dumb. Everybody knows that we need a robust Pakistani military to go after the Taliban. We just need to make sure they do it. The way to compel their cooperation is not to cut our aid to them, but to increase our military aid to India. By threatening to help, or offering to withhold aid from their true enemy, we have a tool to discipline the Pakistanis that we now lack.

Now, all we need is a president who has the kind of diplomatic skill Nixon had to implement it. Hint: It's not Obama.

Change Our Objectives in Afghanistan

The other option is to cut our need for Pakistan so we don't have to send them so much money and depend on them so much. After all, why are we giving Pakistan billions in foreign aid? Why do we curry their favor so? The answer is, of course, Afghanistan.

Ever since 9/11, we have made it our mission to destroy al-Qaeda and eliminate its ability to use the Taliban regime that then controlled Afghanistan as the base for its operations.

We have two objectives in Afghanistan:

- Having toppled the Taliban regime, now we are trying to prop up the government we put there in its place.

- And we want to kill as many al-Qaeda in the Pakistan/Afghanistan border area as possible.

Together, these missions require Pakistani cooperation on their side of the border and their assent in supplying our troops in convoys that must pass through their country.

However, if we scale back our mission in Afghanistan, Pakistan becomes less important to us and we no longer need to pay them massive sums of money and hope they help us.

The effort to prop up the corrupt government of President Hamid Karzai is an exercise in nation-building that requires a vast investment of manpower and money. But the attacks, usually by drones, that kill al-Qaeda do not need anything like this level of commitment.

The al-Qaeda terrorists have largely fled to Pakistan. They aren't even in Afghanistan. General Stanley A. McChrystal, our past commander in Afghanistan, told the Senate Foreign Relations Committee recently that there was really no evidence of a significant al-Qaeda presence in Afghanistan.[87] So, it's time to reassess our role there.

Ted Gallen Carpenter, vice president for Defense and Foreign Policy Studies at the CATO Institute (and coauthor of the book *Escaping the "Graveyard of Empires": A Strategy to Exit Afghanistan*), poses the obvious question: "Well, if al Qaeda isn't in Afghanistan, why on Earth are we in Afghanistan? We went there to defeat al Qaeda. If this isn't the arena for al Qaeda anymore, then our mission seems to have no rational purpose whatsoever."[88]

The reason we are so focused on nation-building in Afghanistan stems from the success of the population-centric COIN (Counter Insurgency) Strategy we used in Iraq; we have come to believe that we can defeat terrorists and insurgents by focusing on the population. Celeste Ward, senior defense analyst at RAND, explains that this means "[m]eeting [the people's] needs, establishing governmental legitimacy, developing economies and so on. Indeed, some COIN adherents have even emphasized its potential to 'change entire societies.' "[89]

But, as Ward notes, COIN "assumes that a foreign force such as ours could truly understand, never mind penetrate and manipulate the opinions and loyalties of an ancient tribal people." She bemoans the "conceit inherent in this notion."[90]

The truth is that we don't need to build a nation in Afghanistan to continue the fight against al-Qaeda. Malou Innocent, foreign policy analyst at CATO and the other coauthor of the book *Escaping the "Graveyard of Empires,"* points out that "going after al Qaeda does not require a large-scale, long term military presence."[91]

In an attempt to bring American objectives in Afghanistan back to the realm of the possible, Carpenter says that "[w]hat has happened is we seem to have drifted into an amorphous, open-ended, nation-building mission, one of unlimited scope and unlimited duration. That is a very bad business indeed. Our objective should be to prevent al Qaeda from again using Afghanistan as a reliable sanctuary to plan and execute large-scale attacks against the United States, as it did on 9/11. Now that's a fairly specific, fairly narrow objective. But that's really the core American interest in Afghanistan."[92]

Specifically, Carpenter says, "We don't need to try to transform Afghanistan into a stable, modern, democratic society with a strong central government in Kabul."[93]

Carpenter writes, "We do not need to crush the Taliban to achieve our legitimate objectives regarding al Qaeda. It has been a big mistake of US policymakers to conflate al Qaeda and the Taliban. The former is a foreign terrorist organization with the United States in its crosshairs. The latter is an admittedly repulsive political faction, but it . . . is not a direct security threat to the United States. What has happened over the years is that we have drifted into a war against the Taliban, not primarily against al Qaeda."[94]

And he comes to the conclusion that "we can develop a strategy [that focuses] . . . on disrupting and weakening al Qaeda. We're not going to get some kind of surrender ceremony, or a signed document. Instead, we have to treat the threat posed by al Qaeda as a chronic security problem, but one that can be managed. . . . We don't need a large military footprint to achieve such modest military goals. Small numbers of CIA and Special Forces personnel, to work with cooperative players, should be sufficient."[95]

If we scale back our objectives in Afghanistan to killing al-Qaeda, we should be able to operate with only minimal cooperation from Pakistan. The Taliban might or might not take over Afghanistan if we pull out most of our troops. If they do, we might be able to live and let live with them, accepting their rule over the country in return for a policy of not sheltering al-Qaeda.

If not, we can stay in Afghanistan and the Pakistan border area and kill al-Qaeda with our drones and special forces as long as we like. Neither nation has the ability to make us leave if we decide to stay.

The *New York Times* reports that we are now spending $118.6 billion on the war in Afghanistan as opposed to $14.7 billion in 2003, when Bush began to focus on Iraq instead.[96]

Ultimately, we cannot count on the Pakistanis for anything. If we keep a large military presence in Afghanistan, Pakistan will always have its thumb on our aorta, able to cut off the flow of food and ammunition to our troops. We will continue to have to spend billions in tribute to get Pakistan to let the supplies flow.

Because of this tenuous supply route, and the inherent difficulties in convincing a tribal Afghanistan to accept a corrupt central government, we should pull back our mission there to a focus on antiterrorism directed at al-Qaeda, not anti-insurgency directed at the Taliban.

These two strategies are mutually reinforcing. The less we need Pakistan to support and permit us to supply our troops in Afghanistan, the more Pakistan will feel it has no hold over us. And the more we drift towards India, the more that failure to keep a club over our heads will scare the Pakistani military. By needing Pakistan less, we may acquire more power, not less, over them and their military. Elusiveness might work where mutual dependency has not.

And why are we propping up a corrupt government in Kabul, anyway?

PART FIVE

Afghanistan

LIVES AND MONEY DOWN THE DRAIN

One thousand, eight hundred, and fifty-nine US troops have been killed in Afghanistan since the start of the war there in 2001, including 413 in 2011. The British have lost 393 soldiers and the other members of the coalition, not counting Afghan soldiers, have lost 590 men and women.[1]

Combat Deaths in Afghanistan[2]

Year	US	UK	Other	Total
2001	12	0	0	12
2002	49	3	18	70
2003	48	0	10	58
2004	52	1	7	60
2005	99	1	31	131
2006	98	39	54	191
2007	117	42	73	232
2008	155	51	89	295
2009	317	108	96	521
2010	499	103	109	711
2011	413	45	103	561
Total	**1859**	**393**	**590**	**2842**

Was it worth it? When we read about the horrific corruption in Afghanistan, we begin to doubt it.

In addition to blood, Afghanistan is costing us treasure. The United States gave it $10.9 billion[3] in foreign aid last year. But the Congressional Research Service quotes an Agency for International Development (AID) official saying, "Up to 30% of contracted project costs can be attributed to corruption."[4] With a total of $3 billion in economic aid annually, that would come to the theft of $1 billion, not even counting any money that is stolen from the military aid budget.

THE WORLD'S SECOND-MOST-CORRUPT COUNTRY

The Congressional Research Service explains where the money goes: "Corruption takes many forms, including government officials charging bribes for transporting goods across the border and extorting protection payments. Many analysts view large swaths of the judicial sector and the attorney general's office as corrupt, as evidenced by the lack of prosecutions against high-ranking government officials or warlords accused of being involved in criminal activity or rampant corruption. In other instances, members of the Afghan security forces use their position to demand bribes and extort shipping companies at Afghan borders and airports."[5]

Transparency International, which ranks nations based on their integrity or corruption, says that Afghanistan is the second most corrupt nation on earth, exceeded only by Somalia, which doesn't have a government at the moment. It is tied for 176th place with Myanmar among the world's 178 countries. Certainly, a regime worth defending![6]

American officials, working with the Afghan government, have formulated a novel answer to corruption: Bribe them before the bad guys do. Called *top-up raises*, the US government pays money to Afghan officials to "insulate them from corruption and political interference."[7]

In September 2010, anticorruption investigations and prosecutions, never vigorous in any event, ground to a halt in Afghanistan as "the result of a protracted dispute within the government over the limits of American-backed investigators who have pursued high-ranking Afghans,"[8] the *New York Times* reported.

The *Times* reported that Afghan President Hamid Karzai blew a fuse when US corruption investigators arrested a "top official in [his] government, which by the Afghan president's own account led him to intervene and win the suspect's release from detention."[9]

After the incident, there were no further arrests for corruption for almost two months. Why not? Hint: It wasn't that there wasn't any corruption!

President Karzai takes accusations of corruption very personally for good reason. His government is virtually a full-employment program for his extended family. The *New York Times*, which has taken the lead in exposing Afghan corruption, reports that he makes nepotism a policy of his administration. Ronald E. Neumann, the US ambassador to Afghanistan, says that nepotism is "part of [Karzai's] survival mechanism." He explains: "President Karzai intended to create a support network that could help him survive after the withdrawal of American troops, the same way that another Afghan president, Mohammad Najibullah, survived for years after Soviet troops withdrew in 1989. Karzai is convinced that we are going to abandon him," Neumann said. "What's his answer? To create a web of loyalties and militia commanders and corrupt families all knitted together."[10]

As the *New York Times* revealed, the web of Karzai's family runs very deep:

- Taj Ayubi, who, until recently, "ran a furniture store in Leesburg, Virginia, and before that a thrift shop in Washington," is now Karzai's senior foreign affairs adviser. The *Times* notes that "among Mr. Ayubi's qualifications for his post . . . are ties to President Karzai's extended family. His sister is married to a Karzai, and her sons are now important junior members of the growing Karzai family network in Afghanistan."[11]

- Karzai's brother, Ahmed Wali Karzai, rumored to have been deeply involved in the drug trade, was recently assassinated.[12]

- His other brother, Mahmoud Karzai, now under investigation by American prosecutors, parlayed a $4 million investment into a residential real estate project in Kandahar now worth $900 million.[13]

- The *New York Times* reports, "One of President Karzai's nephews is a top official in the intelligence service, giving him authority over some of Afghanistan's most sensitive security operations. A brother of the president is an official in the agency that issues licenses required for all Afghan corporations; an uncle is now ambassador to Russia."[14]

- The paper reports that "[a]t least six Karzai relatives, including one who just ran for Parliament, operate or are linked to contracting businesses that collect millions ... annually from the American government."[15]

- The *Times* also reports that "American officials say the Karzais and a handful of other well-connected families have benefited from the billions of dollars that the United States has poured into the country since 2001. That money has helped pay the salaries of some Karzais who are government employees, kick-started real estate development and construction projects involving family members and created demand for businesses tied to the Karzais."[16]

Get the picture?

WORLD'S LARGEST PRODUCER OF OPIUM

It doesn't help the fight against corruption that Afghanistan is the world's largest producer of opium. According to two cables obtained from WikiLeaks, "Afghanistan's supply of opium exceeds the world's demand for heroin, with its unsold stock currently totaling 12,400 tons."[17] The Taliban work actively to encourage, and coerce, farmers in southern Afghanistan to grow opium, which they use to finance their war against us.

Karzai, whose brother was linked to the drug trade, has granted early releases to well-connected drug suspects. He also pardoned five border police officers who were caught with 124 kilos of heroin and sentenced to serve almost twenty years in prison. Why? Because they were distantly related "to two individuals who had been martyred during the civil war."[18]

Suspicions about President Karzai's link to the drug trade were intensified when Afghan security forces, according to the *New York Times*, "found an enormous cache of heroin hidden beneath concrete blocks in a tractor-trailer outside Kandahar in 2004." The Afghans impounded the truck only to get a phone call from Karzai's now-deceased brother Ahmed Wali Karzai asking him to release the truck and the drugs. He in turn complied "after getting a phone call from an aide to President Karzai directing him to release the truck."[19]

The Karzais did nothing against the drug dealers. They retaliated, however, against the informant who fingered them, arresting and imprisoning Hajji Aman Kheri, who worked for the CIA. The charges against Kheri, that he had attempted to assassinate Afghanistan's vice president in 2002, were totally bogus. The Afghan Supreme Court ordered him freed for lack of evidence. The *Times* reported that

Kheri had "proved so valuable to the United States that his family had been resettled in Virginia in 2004."[20]

Thomas Schweich, a former senior State Department counter-narcotics official, wrote that drug traffickers were buying off hundreds of police chiefs, judges, and other officials. "Narco-corruption," he said, "went to the top of the Afghan government."[21]

Afghan corruption briefly came into public view in June 2011, when $1 billion disappeared from the Central Bank in Kabul.[22] The Afghan government lost more than $850 million in the bank's collapse. The *New York Times* reported that "while some of that money has been recovered . . . the government will probably have to pay $450 million to $500 million to cover the losses."[23]

Guess which foreign country will probably end up paying for much of that tab!

Neither of the top bank officers implicated in the bank failure nor any of the major shareholders have been prosecuted. These include Karzai's brother and a brother of the first vice president of Afghanistan.[24]

The *New York Times* summed up the corruption nicely, if revoltingly, when it said, "When it comes to governing this violent, fractious land, everything, it seems, has its price."[25]

The newspaper elaborated.

"Want to be a provincial police chief? It will cost you $100,000.

"Want to drive a convoy of trucks loaded with fuel across the country? Be prepared to pay $6,000 per truck, so the police will not tip off the Taliban.

"Need to settle a lawsuit over the ownership of your house? About $25,000, depending on the judge.

" 'It is very shameful, but probably I will pay the bribe,' Mohammed Naim, a young English teacher, said as he stood in front of the Secondary Courthouse in Kabul. His brother had been arrested a week before, and the police were demanding $4,000 for his release."[26]

Then, in a stinging summary, the paper wrote: "Kept afloat by billions of dollars in American and other foreign aid, the government of Afghanistan is shot through with corruption and graft. From the lowliest traffic policeman to the family of President Hamid Karzai himself, the state built on the ruins of the Taliban government seven years ago now often seems to exist for little more than the enrichment of those who run it."[27]

In addition to being a terrible president, there is significant evidence that Karzai is not the choice of the Afghan people.

He claimed victory after the election in August 2009, a contest marred by widespread charges of vote rigging, ballot stuffing, and other election fraud. Under heavy US pressure, Karzai relented and rescinded his claim of victory, agreeing to a runoff election against his chief opponent, Abdullah Abdullah, on November 7, 2009. But, on November 1, Abdullah withdrew from the runoff saying that the election fraud in the balloting would have been so widespread that he had no chance at a victory.

Obama promptly congratulated Karzai and declared him the winner. Some election!

Karzai admits that there was fraud but, in a US television appearance, minimized its extent: "There were irregularities. There must've also been fraud committed, no doubt. But the election was good and fair and worthy of praise, not of scorn, which the election received from the international media. That makes me very unhappy. That rather makes me angry."[28]

Then, in April 2010, Karzai changed his tune and decided that the election fraud was all a foreign plot engineered by the United Nations. In April 2010, he said, "The United Nations office of the deputy [UN representative] had become the focal point for [election] fraud. The fraud was being made from there and organized from there."[29]

ACTION AGENDA

Get out of there!

We were not attacked by the Taliban on September 11, 2001. We were hit by al-Qaeda. True, the Taliban sheltered al-Qaeda and made the attack on us possible. But, with al-Qaeda operatives either dead or in hiding in Pakistan, the rationale for our military intervention in Afghanistan has become overwhelmingly focused on a battle against the Taliban.

As we noted in our earlier chapter on Pakistan, it is just not an essential concomitant of our antiterrorism offensive against al-Qaeda that we keep the Taliban from power in Afghanistan. If the Afghans cannot keep the Taliban from power, or don't want to keep Karzai and his gang in power, that's really their decision. It's up to them.

What is up to us is keeping enough forces in the border area between Pakistan and Afghanistan to hunt down terrorists, just as we do in Yemen, Somalia, and a dozen other countries. If the Taliban ask us to leave, we don't have to oblige them. Our presence will likely be enough of a deterrent to stop the new rulers in Kabul—if there are to be new ones—from getting too cozy with al-Qaeda. Al-Qaeda now comes with a heavy price tag: Half the US military is trying to kill its leaders. Afghanistan's rulers would be foolish to get in a bed that will be the object of a drone strike!

We need to distinguish antiterrorism from anti-insurgency operations. It is one thing to kill al-Qaeda. It is vastly another to engage in nation building, especially with such a corrupt government as Karzai runs wrapped around our neck. We must remember the key lesson of Vietnam: If we do not have a worthy government as our ally, we cannot prevail. In Vietnam, we were trying to keep a corrupt government in power. We failed and will likely fail again in Afghanistan.

Is it worth the almost two thousand American lives we have lost to keep al-Qaeda down? It is. After all, they killed three thousand Americans on September 11.

But, on the other hand, is it worth these lives and all that money to keep Karzai in power?

Hell, no!

There's one other regime the United States keeps in power by sacrificing the lives of our young men and women that reciprocates by screwing us every chance they get—the monarchy in Saudi Arabia.

PART SIX

Saudi Arabia

OUR BARGAIN WITH THE DEVIL

Saudi Arabia is, without a doubt, one of the most evil nations on earth. The authoritarian monarchy is transparently barbaric in its treatment of both its own citizens and foreigners who work there. It infantilizes, discriminates against, and abuses women. Worst of all, it is the central global sponsor and funder of terrorism. The terrorist virus that is spreading throughout the Islamic world incubates in Saudi Arabia.

Saudi Arabia is a monarchy in which only a few people choose the leaders and determine the law. On the rare occasion when a vote is permitted, only men can participate.

For the past fifty years, the United States has been beholden to the Saudis because of their control of over 10 percent of the world's oil production. We've watched our presidents have to kowtow to the Saudi king for decades. Most recently, President Obama bowed deeply on being ushered into his august and royal presence!

But no more! The United States and Canada are now on the verge of becoming the new Saudi Arabia! Our oil production has been soaring and our domestic use shrinking so rapidly that we will be completely independent of Middle East, Venezuelan, or Russian oil within a very few years. And, then, as our production continues to rise, we will become, as we were before World War II, the world's supplier of oil.

And the ability to tell the dictatorial, misogynist Saudis where to go cannot come too soon.

SAUDI HUMAN RIGHTS? NONE!

According to the US State Department, "The Saudi government bases its legitimacy on its interpretation of Sharia (Islamic law) and the 1992 Basic Law."[1] Sharia law is the repressive Islamic code that governs personal behavior such as marriage, divorce, custody, and criminal conduct. "Some interpretations are used to justify cruel punishments such as amputation and stoning as well as unequal treatment of women in inheritance, dress, and independence."[2]

The indigenous laws and customs of a country give us a window into the culture and tolerance of its society. By any such review, the Saudi Arabian regime created and now enforces a harsh, tyrannical atmosphere that fosters human rights violations. In order to fully understand just how oppressive the Saudi Arabian regime is, a review of the State Department's *2010 Human Rights Report* on Saudi Arabia is a good place to start. According to the report, "Saudi Arabia had the following significant human rights problems:

- No right to change the government peacefully;

- Torture and physical abuse;

- Poor prison and detention center conditions;

- Arbitrary arrest and incommunicado detention;

- Denial of fair and public trials and lack of due process in the judicial system;

- Political prisoners;

- Restrictions on civil liberties such as freedoms of speech (including the Internet), assembly, association, movement;

- Severe restrictions on religious freedom;

- Corruption and lack of government transparency;

- Violence against women and a lack of equal rights for women;

- Violations of the rights of children, trafficking in persons;

- Discrimination on the basis of gender, religion, sect, and ethnicity, lack of workers' rights, including the employment sponsorship system, remained a severe problem."[3]

If that doesn't turn your stomach, consider some of the specifics underscored in the report:

- "Judicially sanctioned corporal punishments were carried out. For example, on March 13, the Riyadh Court of Appeals endorsed a verdict sentencing a man accused of sorcery to eight years in prison and 800 lashes after the CPVPV had arrested him for practicing magic and being involved in other activities allegedly contrary to the teachings of Islam."[4]

- "On July 10, the daily newspaper *Arab News* reported that a diabetic prisoner confined to a wheelchair lost his eyesight after being whipped in a prison in Mecca. The prisoner reportedly had been charged with fraud and sentenced to six months in prison and 150 lashes. There was no indication that responsible prison officials were prosecuted."[5]

- "On September 28, the *Saudi Gazette* reported that a court in Qatif sentenced two third-grade students to six months in prison and 120 lashes for stealing examination papers."[6]

- "[T]he government strictly monitored all political activity and took punitive actions, including arrest and detention, against persons who appeared to oppose the government. There were reports from human rights activists of government efforts to monitor or block mobile telephone or Internet usage ahead of planned demonstrations. The government did not respect the privacy of correspondence or communications. Customs officials routinely opened mail and shipments to search for contraband. In some areas MOI informants reported 'seditious ideas,' 'antigovernment activity,' or 'behavior contrary to Islam' in their neighborhoods."

- "Rape is a punishable criminal offense under Sharia with a wide range of penalties from flogging to execution. Generally the government enforced the law based on its interpretation of

Sharia, and *courts punish both the victim and the* perpetrator [*emphasis added*]. The government views marital relations between spouses as contractual and did not recognize spousal rape. By law a female rape victim is at fault for illegal 'mixing of genders' and is punished along with the perpetrator."[7]

- Amnesty International reports that " 'a 27 year old man . . . was sentenced to five years in prison and five hundred lashes for the crime of being a homosexual.' "[8]

But, hey, the news is not all bad. The State Department proudly reports that "unlike in the previous year, there were no judicially sanctioned amputations reported."[9]

Sharia law codifies and encourages rampant discrimination against women in Saudi Arabia. Sarah Stern, editor of the important book *Saudi Arabia and the Global Islamic Terrorist Network*, describes the worst aspects of life for women in Saudi Arabia: "In a Saudi Sharia court, a woman's testimony carries half the weight of a man's. She cannot represent herself in court but must be represented by a male relative. She cannot leave her home without being fully wrapped in the abaya, nor can she drive or vote. If a man wants to divorce a woman all that is necessary is for him to utter the words 'I divorce you in accordance with the laws of Allah.' Religious minorities can be arrested, tortured, and detained without trial."[10]

The country has an indigenous population of 16 million Saudis, but is home to an additional 8.8 million registered foreign expatriates and an estimated 1.5 million illegal immigrants, for a total population of 27 million.[11]

The Saudis are even more vicious to migrant workers living there. Stern reports that "[i]n August, 2010, a Sri Lankan woman alleged that her Saudi employer had hammered 24 nails into her head."[12] Stern notes, "There is absolutely no freedom of assemblage, of the press, of religious minorities, women's rights, and no due process"[13] in Saudi Arabia. On October 26, 2010, the General Court in Qubba imposed a sentence of five hundred lashes and five years in prison on a newspaper correspondent for reporting that Saudi citizens had gathered in front of the electric company to protest higher rates.[14]

THE UNITED STATES PROPS UP SAUDI ARABIA

How does such a kingdom stay in power? Solely and exclusively through the power of the US military and the oil revenues that flow into its coffers from the West.

In 1990, when Saddam Hussein sent Iraqi troops into Kuwait and massed them on the Saudi border, President George H. W. Bush organized a coalition of thirty-four nations who sent almost one million troops to defend the kingdom and roll back the invasion.

We saved Saudi Arabia at the price of the blood of our own soldiers. Two hundred and fifty-eight US soldiers were killed in the Gulf War.[15] But now, the Saudis are the main promoter and funding source for international terrorism. Fifteen of the nineteen 9/11 hijackers were Saudi and 90 percent of the funding for extremist Islamic education globally comes from the kingdom. What a great way to show their gratitude!

Saudi power over the Islamic world, however, comes not only from our petrodollars but also from the moral authority of a government that presides over the most holy sites in the Islamic religion. Mecca, right in the middle of the kingdom, is the epicenter of the religion. Every Muslim must face toward the holy city five times a day during prayers and must make a pilgrimage there during his lifetime.

The US–Saudi relationship began on February 14, 1945, when President Franklin D. Roosevelt sat on the deck of the navy cruiser USS *Quincy*, only eight weeks before his death, and watched the navy destroyer USS *Murphy* steaming across Egypt's Great Bitter Lake toward his ship. Aboard the *Murphy* was Saudi King Abdul Aziz ibn Saud.

The deck of the *Murphy* was "covered with colorful carpets and shaded by an enormous tent of brown canvass." Saud, "a large black-bearded man in Arab robes, his headdress bound with golden cords, was seated on a gilded throne. Around him stood an entourage of fierce-looking, dark-skinned barefoot men in similar attire, each with a sword or dagger bound to his waist by a gold-encrusted belt. On the Murphy's fantail, sheep grazed in a makeshift corral. It was one American witness said 'a spectacle out of the ancient past on the deck of a modern man-of-war.' "[16] Saud himself was a "semi-literate desert potentate whose people know nothing of plumbing or electricity."[17] And now he was going to meet with the president of the United States.

Saud's meeting with FDR on the deck of the *Quincy* lasted five hours. A conference that changed the history of the world. Roosevelt began the meeting by presenting quite a gift to Saud: a DC-3 passenger airplane, specially outfitted with a rotating throne that allowed the king to face Mecca while airborne.[18]

Roosevelt and our military leaders had sought the meeting because they were alarmed at how quickly the war's demand for oil to fuel America's military

machine had exhausted our massive domestic petroleum production. Prior to World War II, the United
States had been the Saudi Arabia of the world, the
main exporter of oil. But now Roosevelt was planning for the day when even our resources would not
suffice to meet our needs. He struck a cosmic deal
with King Saud that remains in force today: The
United States would protect the new Saudi monarchy
(only formed in 1933) and the Saudis would supply
the West with oil.

In the year after the meeting, King Saud authorized
Aramco (Arabian-American Oil Company) to build an
export pipeline from Dhahran to the Mediterranean
coast to expedite delivery to European markets. He
approved an arrangement by which the US Air Force
was allowed to operate the air base at Dhahran that
the Americans had begun building during the war,
and he accepted the deployment of a US military team
assigned to train young Saudis in airfield operations
and maintenance.[19]

The historic partnership had begun.

The US-Saudi relationship has had its ups and
downs. In 1960, Saudi Arabia and Venezuela founded
OPEC—the Organization of the Petroleum Exporting
Countries—in an effort to take control over the pricing
of their principal product. Until then, the price of oil

was set by the Texas Railroad Commission, an elected body in the Lone Star State. Texas's power was based on its dominant role in global oil production.

OPEC now includes Algeria, Angola, Iran, Iraq, Kuwait, Libya, Nigeria, Qatar, Saudi Arabia, the United Arab Emirates, and Venezuela. But it is still Saudi Arabia's show. The kingdom produces more than a third of the group's oil, more than twice as much as the next largest exporter, Iran.

By the '60s and '70s, the United States had become increasingly dependent on imported oil and the exporting nations. In 1973, angry at US support for Israel during the Yom Kippur War, which was started by an unprovoked Arab invasion of Israel, OPEC, led by Saudi Arabia, embargoed oil sales to the West. The dramatic increase in the price of oil demonstrated OPEC's power to set oil prices and its domination has not been challenged since.

Americans chafed under the impact of the Saudi-led run-up in oil prices in the early 1970s and again later in the decade, when the fall of the Shah in Iran triggered a further uptick in prices.

The relationship improved during the 1980s as President Ronald Reagan enlisted the kingdom's help in his economic offensive against the Soviet Union. The Soviet Union was, and Russia still is, the leading producer of oil in the world and oil is its leading export. The Saudis agreed to increase their production of petroleum to bring down the price, crippling Moscow financially and helping to bring down the communist system.

The real test of the US-Saudi relationship came in 1990 when President George H. W. Bush responded to Iraqi dictator Saddam Hussein's invasion of neighboring Kuwait. It seemed that Hussein was about to move on from Kuwait and take on Saudi Arabia. With the world's fourth largest army, the Iraqi move to the Saudi border through Kuwait sent an unmistakable message to the kingdom: You are next.

Bush reacted promptly and fiercely assembling an international coalition of forces from Argentina, Australia, Bahrain, Bangladesh, Belgium, Canada, Denmark, Egypt, France, Greece, Italy, Kuwait, Morocco, Netherlands, New Zealand, Niger, Norway, Oman, Pakistan, Portugal, Qatar, South Korea, Saudi Arabia, Senegal, Sierra Leone, Singapore, Spain, Syria, the United Arab Emirates, the United Kingdom, and the United States itself. US troops comprised 74 percent of the coalition's 956,600 troops that rushed to counter the Iraqi aggression.[20]

While Bush in explaining the reasons for war made much of the need to stop aggression and implement the rule of law, it was clear from the outset that the need to protect Saudi Arabia was very much on his mind. In his speech to Congress, delivered, coincidentally enough, on September 11, 1990, Bush said that within three days after the start of the Iraqi invasion, "One-hundred twenty thousand Iraqi troops with eight-hundred fifty tanks had poured into Kuwait and moved south to threaten Saudi Arabia. It was then that I decided to act to check that aggression."[21]

The United States, literally, saved Saudi Arabia. By sending more than one-half-million young Americans in harm's way, we stopped Saddam from realizing his goal of concentrating the region's oil wealth under his control.

Without this massive and prompt American intervention, there is no doubt that the Saudi monarchy would today be ancient history.

And, to this day, the US government is the reason Saudi Arabia survives. Right after Christmas last year, President Obama put a $30 billion[22] gift under the king's metaphorical tree: F-15 fighters for his air force. Andrew Shapiro, assistant secretary of state for political-military affairs, said, by way of a gift card, "This sale will send a strong message to countries in the region that the United States is committed to stability in the gulf and the broader Middle East. It will enhance Saudi Arabia's ability to deter and defend against external threats to its sovereignty."[23]

Translation: We will protect the Saudis against Iran and the US–Saudi relationship is back in business, as strong as ever. All is forgiven.

And there is a lot to forgive.

THE GLOBAL BANK FOR ISLAMIC TERRORISM

As terrorism has grown throughout the world, the US–Saudi relationship has become more and more of a one-way street. After 9/11, when we learned that fifteen of the nineteen hijackers were Saudi nationals, the tensions became more apparent.

These days, the Saudi monarchy does little to deter, and much to encourage, the terrorists who seek to destroy us—scant compensation for our expenditure of manpower and money to save their kingdom twenty years ago.

A classified memo written by Secretary of State Hillary Clinton, published by WikiLeaks, put the one-way nature of the partnership in stark relief: "Donors in Saudi Arabia constitute the most significant source of funding to Sunni terrorist groups worldwide. It has been an ongoing challenge to persuade Saudi officials to treat terrorist financing emanating from Saudi Arabia as a strategic priority."[24] Priority? The Saudis have made a priority of helping the other side in the war on terror:

- Dr. Rachel Ehrenfeld, one of the world's leading experts on terrorist funding, writes that the "Saudis [have] consistently comprised the largest proportion of foreign forces warring against Americans in Iraq."[25] In 2007, the *New York Times* reported that 41 percent of foreign fighters in Iraq battling US troops were Saudis, "the largest number of fighters listed on the records by far."[26]

- In February 2009, "Abu Ahmed, one of the founders of the Iraqi insurgency who now works with American forces, revealed to Newsweek that he had been bankrolled by Saudi donations."[27]

- In 2006, the AP "reported that millions of Saudi riyals, often collected in the form of *zakat* (compulsory charity), were smuggled to Iraq to pay for missiles and other weapons. . . . in 2006, one Sunni cleric alone had received $25 million from Saudi Arabia, which he used to purchase arms."[28]

- The 9/11 Commission euphemistically wrote that "Saudi Arabia has an uneven record in the fight against terrorism, especially with respect to terrorist financing."[29] And the Congressional Research Service highlighted "Saudi laxity in acting against terrorist groups"[30] in a September 2007 report. In 2009, the State Department International Narcotics Control Strategy report on money laundering identified Saudi Arabia as "continuing to be a significant jurisdictional source for terrorist funding worldwide."[31] And Hillary Clinton wrote (in the WikiLeaks cable) that al-Qaeda, Hamas, and other jihadist groups "raise millions of dollars annually from Saudi sources."[32]

And Saudi money has appeared as an important support for the Taliban's struggle against our forces.

- Afghanistan's financial intelligence unit Fin-Traca reported "in May, 2010 that Saudi contributors have funneled over $1.5 billion to Afghanistan through Pakistan since 2006. Most of the money has entered Afghanistan through Pakistani tribal areas, especially through North Waziristan, which is known as 'al-Qaeda's heartland.' Mohammed Mustafa Massoudi, the director general of US-trained Afghan intelligence in Kabul, said 'Why would anyone want to put such money into Waziristan? Only one reason: terrorism.' "[33]

- undersecretary of the Treasury for terrorism and financial intelligence under Bush 43, Stuart Levey, told ABC News, "If I could somehow snap my fingers and cut off the funding [for terrorism] from one country, it would be Saudi Arabia."[34] Levey testified before the Senate Finance Committee in April 2008: "Saudi Arabia today remains the location from which more money is going to terror groups and the Taliban—Sunni terror groups and the Taliban—than from any other place in the world."[35]

- The Saudis also support Pakistan's Laskhar-e Taiba (LET), the gang behind the Mumbai terror attack in 2008 that killed over two hundred people. "Pakistani police reported in 2009 that the Saudi al-Haramain Foundation—a charitable organization designated as a terrorist sponsor by the US . . . gave $15 million to jihadists, including those responsible for the suicide attacks in Pakistan and the assassination of former Pakistani Prime Minister Benazir Bhutto."[36]

- Dr. Ehrenfeld, who has been targeted by Islamists for revenge for her courageous work against terrorism, writes, "The Saudi-based International Islamic Relief Organization's (IIRO) Philippines branch, which was run until his death in 2007 by Muhammed Ismal Khalifa, Osama bin Laden's brother-in-law, was designated a terrorist sponsor by the US Treasury in August, 2006 'for facilitating fund raising for al Qaeda and affiliated terrorist groups.' "[37]

- A WikiLeaks leaked cable detailed a February 6, 2007, private meeting between US Assistant to the President for Homeland Security and Counterterrorism Francis Fragos Townsend and Saudi Foreign Minister Prince Saud al-Faisal. Townsend asked al-Faisal to stop "the involvement of the Saudi ambassador to the Philippines Muhammad Amin Waly in terrorism facilitation."[38] Townsend noted that Waly had intervened to get the Philippine government to release two IIRO operatives from prison. The Saudis ignored the request and did not recall Waly until two years later.

- Ehrenfeld documents extensive Saudi support for the terrorist group Hamas. "Saudi funding to . . . Hamas has never stopped. In March 2007, Israel notified the US that Hamas leader Ismail Haniyeh transferred a $1 million contribution he received in Saudi Arabia to Hamas' 'armed wing' the Izz el-Deen al-Qassam Brigades . . . Haniyeh told al-Jazeera that he passed the $1 million from a Saudi donor to the 'armed wing' of Hamas."[39]

- In September 2000, the Saudis conducted two telethons to raise money for the families of

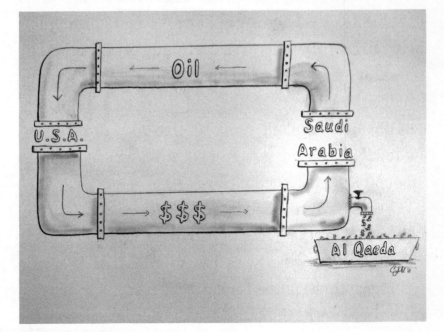

homicide/suicide bombers and of terrorists in Israeli prisons. Saudi Interior Minister Prince Nayef raised $55 million for the relief of the families of these terrorists.

Defenders of the kingdom sometimes try to hide this beneficence to terrorists by proclaiming that the donations are acts of individual charity or generosity, rather than official actions of the monarchy or even the royal family. Dr. Ehrenfeld rebuts this subterfuge: "Saudi Arabia is a theocracy dominated by Wahhabi power figures that . . . control both governmental and nongovernmental sectors of the country. The government/ruling family makes or breaks the wealth of all its subjects. . . . Thus it would be wrong to distinguish between contributions to radical Sunni organizations by the ruling family, the Saudi Government, and wealthy Saudi citizens."[40]

Of course, while it supports terrorism directly and indirectly, the Saudi government still poses in public as an opponent of terrorism.

Domestically, the Saudis do suppress dissent and terrorism for fear that it could lead to the toppling of their monarchy. Particularly as the so-called Arab spring has blown through the region, Saudi Arabia has kept a careful eye on its domestic critics. But internationally, the Saudi pretense of cooperation in the War on Terror is just a façade.

The most dramatic example of Saudi failure to cooperate in the fight against terrorism took place in 1995, when a terrorist bomb ripped through the Saudi apartment complex, Khobar Towers, where American servicemen and women were living. Nineteen Americans lost their lives and almost four hundred were injured.

FBI director Louis Freeh was deeply concerned that the Saudi monarchy would bar American investigators from investigating the attack. The previous year, the Saudis had arrested several men accusing them, some said falsely, of killing five Americans in a terrorist attack in Riyadh. Before the US authorities could question the terrorists, they were beheaded by the Saudis. Dead men tell no tales.

Freeh worried that the Saudis would do the same thing after Khobar Towers. He asked President Clinton to call the Saudi monarch and ask directly to allow FBI agents to examine any suspects that were arrested. Freeh spoke up because he was suspicious that the bombers may have been closer to the Saudi power structure than the kingdom was willing to acknowledge. He wanted to interrogate them to see where the trail led. President Clinton made the phone call, as requested, but did not raise the issue of the suspects. Instead he hit up the king for a donation to his library. A check came soon after. As to the terror suspects, the Saudis did, indeed, bar FBI agents from examining them until former President Bush 41 asked the king for access for old times' sake and got his consent.

The Saudis have been even less forthcoming in other counterterrorism efforts.

For example, when the al-Haramain Foundation (AHF) was designated as a source of terror funding by the US Treasury Department in 2008, the department said, "Today's action targets the entirety of the AHF Organization including its headquarters in Saudi Arabia. Evidence demonstrates that the AHF Organization was involved in providing logistical and financial support to the al Qaeda network and other terrorist organizations."[41] While the Saudis claim to have shut down AHF, the US Government Accountability Office says that it is still active.

Indeed, in 2010, the third largest Saudi bank, the Al Rajhi Bank, refused to comply with a subpoena issued in a terrorist case in the United States involving an AHF operative. The evidence in the trial indicated that he had deposited $150,000 in traveler's checks from the AHF in the bank and that the bank had accepted the deposit.[42] Then the funds vanished, likely going to finance terrorist operations.

WAHHABISM: ISLAMIC
FASCISM, SAUDI-STYLE

The Saudi royal family's commitment to radical Islam is based on its sponsorship of *Wahhabism*, the puritanical strain of Islam founded in the eighteenth century by Sheikh Mohammad ibn Abd al-Wahhab.

The deal between the Wahhabi religious leaders and the Saudi monarchy was fully cemented in 1979, when two events reminded the royal family of their political mortality and the power and revolutionary potential of Islamic fundamentalism. The Saudi king came to realize the truth of Shakespeare's line: "Uneasy lies the head that wears a crown."[43] In that year, the Saudi's fellow king—the Shah of Iran—was toppled by the Ayatollah Khomeini, and an Islamist republic replaced the Iranian monarchy. Closer to home, Islamic fundamentalists took over the Grand Mosque in Mecca, demanding greater fidelity to Muslim principles. Afraid of a domestic uprising, the Saudi monarchy drew closer to Wahhabism and, embracing it, became its leading advocate throughout the world.

Although Saudi Arabia has only 1 percent of the world's Muslims, it funds 90 percent of the outreach to spread jihad throughout the world. And, of course, the faith it preaches is of the puritanical Wahhabi variety.

Lawrence Wright, author of *The Looming Tower*, estimates that the Saudis have spent over $75 billion on global Islamic proselytizing since 1979.[44]

Dr. Sahr Muhammad Hatem, himself a graduate of Saudi Arabia's Wahhabi schools, describes what they are like: "The mentality of each one of us was programmed upon entering the school as a child [to believe] that anyone who is not a Muslim is our enemy; and that the west means enfeeblement, licentiousness, [and a] lack of values. Anyone who escapes this programming in school encounters it at the mosque or through the media or from preachers lurking in every corner."[45]

Hudson Institute scholar Nina Shea explains that the Wahhabi textbooks teach, "along with other noxious lessons, that Jews and Christians are 'enemies' and they dogmatically instruct that it is permissible, even obligatory, to kill various groups of unbelievers."[46]

And the Wahhabists cast a wide net when they target "unbelievers." They include apostates—moderate Muslims—Jews, Christians, Hindu, Buddhists, Shia and Sufi Muslims, homosexuals, and adulterers. Pretty much anyone other than themselves.

Shea writes, "The 'lesson goals' of one of the textbooks have the children list the 'reprehensible' qualities of Jewish people and teaching them that Jews are pigs and apes."[47]

Nor is the impact of Saudi-Wahhabi indoctrination efforts limited to the Third World. The Saudis have donated funds to many major US universities including Harvard ($20 million), Cornell ($10 million), Georgetown ($20 million), and the University of Arkansas ($18 million).[48] The torrent of pro-Palestinian and anti-Israeli propaganda that emanates from our universities and colleges is bought and paid for by the Saudis.

And Harvard pays its Arab donors back with appropriate pro-Palestinian bias through its Center for Middle Eastern Studies. Beneath this innocuous name lurks a hotbed of anti-Israeli and pro-Palestinian propaganda. Steven Stotsky, writing for CAMERA (Committee for Accuracy in Middle East Reporting in America), reveals that the center's director, Paul Beran, is " a dedicated opponent of Israel who publicly pushes the campaign to boycott, divest, and sanction the Jewish State." At a Teach-In and Organizing Conference on December 11, 2005, at Harvard," Stotzky reported that "Beran . . . offered his vision of the BDS [boycott, divest, sanction] movement. Beran advocated 'constructing long-term networks of broad based support for action.' He boasted of successfully forming a coalition with the radical anti-Israel group, Jewish Voice for Peace. In this way, Beran stated, 'it helped the [Palestinian community] to deal more forcefully with the criticism it has and continues to receive from Zionist groups and their ilk.' "[49]

Beran also published a letter in Lebanon's *Daily Star* newspaper on February 6, 2006, accusing Israel's supporters of using threats and influence peddling. Charging that "the town mayor, the pension-fund manager and even elected state representatives were all recruited by pro-Israel groups to urge the council to vote 'no,' [on the divestment resolution]."[50]

The Harvard Center, itself, "pushed the controversial text book, *The Arab World Studies Notebook*, which [Massachusetts] state officials described as 'propaganda' and 'practically proselytizing.' The *Notebook* included such bizarre assertions as the claim Muslims discovered America before Columbus and Iroquois Indian chiefs had Muslim names."[51]

The Saudis get their money's worth from Harvard!

In Britain, the Saudis do even more to influence higher education. "A 2008 report by the British Centre for Social Cohesion indicated that Saudi Arabian and Muslim organizations had poured over $460 million in UK universities. Oxford alone received $39 million for a Centre for Islamic Studies. Cambridge and the London School of Economics are also big recipients of Saudi largesse."[52]

So, when university students demonstrate against Zionism and shed tears for the Palestinian people, they are just reflecting what their schools are paid to teach them. For their funding, the Saudis gain access to the minds of opinion leaders throughout the world, molding their worldview to Islamism, even though it preaches the destruction of the very institutions it funds.

Saudi Arabia also spends billions on mosques throughout the world. Of the 1,300 mosques that were in the United States in 2003, 80 percent received Saudi funding. By now, the number of US mosques has mushroomed to two thousand and it's likely the number funded by the Saudis has increased as well. In Europe, there are six thousand mosques, many funded by the Saudis.[53]

These mosques are generally not peaceful religious institutions. Frank Gaffney's Center for Security Policy studied the US mosques and found that 81 percent were actively teaching jihad as part of their mission, and 60 percent had imams who were actively involved in jihad causes.[54]

In a sense, most of these mosques are really schools for Sharia law (in much the same way those Jewish synagogues are often schools studying Talmudic law). But there is an ocean of difference between the Talmud and Sharia. The Talmud is a peaceful religious document, while Sharia expressly and openly advocates violent jihad to achieve worldwide Muslim domination. These mosques, masquerading as religious places of worship, are really training grounds for terrorists.

In Britain, for example, Tablighi Jamaat, an offshoot of the radical Deoband Islamic Movement, controls half of the mosques in the nation and seventeen of its twenty-six Islamic seminaries, according to a 2007 study by the *Times* of London.[55] The boys at Tablighi Jamaat have been busy lately. They were responsible for bombing the London Underground, an attempted bombing in Spain, and several violent attempted attacks in the United States.

Rachel Ehrenfeld writes that Tablighi Jamaat "serves as a recruiting ground for al Qaeda and other terrorist groups. It also funds the Pakistan-based Harakat ul-Mujahideen, which was designated a terrorist group by the US in 1999 and had ties to the abduction and murder of *Wall Street Journal* reporter Daniel Pearl."[56]

And the organization manages all this out of the mosques it funds in the United Kingdom. These so-called houses of worship are covers for terrorism and jihad, paid for by the Saudis—our friends and allies.

The Saudis were heavily involved in the funding for Abdul Faisal Rauf, the sponsor of the so-called Ground

Zero mosque, a proposed Islamic community center and mosque a few blocks from New York's World Trade Center. Ehrenfeld reports that "Saudi billionaire Prince Alwaleed bin Talal's Kingdom Foundation . . . donated $300,000 to Rauf's American Society for Muslim Advancement."[57] The prince also "lavishly funds Muslim Brotherhood offshoots in the United States such as the Islamic Society of North America."[58]

American politicians, like New York City's Mayor Michael Bloomberg, backed the construction of the Ground Zero mosque in the mistaken belief that freedom of religion was at issue. But any real understanding of what goes on at these mosques makes it clear that they are centers for terrorism, hardly an appropriate activity anywhere in the United States, but particularly abhorrent at Ground Zero.

THE SAUDIS' FINANCIAL JIHAD AGAINST THE WEST

Saudi efforts to spread radical Islam throughout the world are not limited to educational funding or the promotion of terrorism. Beyond the bombs and blood, Saudi Arabia is using its massive financial clout to wage financial jihad by imposing Islamic dictates on global capitalism and banking.

Due to pressure by Saudis and other financial interests linked to the Islamic world, almost every international banking institution has established a Sharia Compliant Fund (SCF). These funds accept deposits from Muslims and pledge to invest them only in purposes that comport with the rules of Sharia law. The UK financial publication *The Banker* says that four of the top twenty Sharia-compliant financial institutions are Saudi.[59]

On the surface, these Sharia Compliant Funds seem benign enough. They preclude investment in the pork industry, pornography, gambling, or alcohol, indulgences prohibited to Muslims. But the restrictions become more problematic when they preclude financing of defense industries that have any involvement with Israel. And they get a lot more dangerous when you realize that they are a vehicle for letting the worst fundamentalist Islamic fascists get control of hundreds of billions of dollars.

Devout Muslims must honor the requirement of *zakat*, the Islamic equivalent of tithing, and donate 2.5 percent of their wealth to charity each year, a huge amount. Sharia Compliant Funds helpfully honor this commitment by dipping into their depositors' funds each year. The radical Islamic clerics who run these funds can decide who gets these charitable donations.

With total Sharia Compliant Fund assets approaching $1 trillion globally, the zakat requirement is a major source of charitable funding in the Islamic community.

But the so-called charities favored by those who sit on Sharia Finance Advisory Boards are not like the United Way or the Red Cross. Hardly. Frank Gaffney, former assistant secretary of defense in the Reagan administration, who founded and heads the Center for Security Policy, reports that "[t]heir favored charities are, by and large, jihadist Islamic organizations." He reminds us, "Three of the largest Muslim charities in the United States were all shut down by the federal government due to their ties to terrorist financing."[60]

When a company that gets money from a Shariah Compliant Fund violates the precepts of Islamic law (as, for example, if a trucking firm financed by an SCF hauled pigs as one of its loads), it is obliged to pay a fine equal to the proceeds of the total investment. The SCF board determines who gets the money, called "purification." And, as with zakat, it often goes to terror-sponsoring organizations. Who are these guys on the SCF boards?

Gaffney explains that "[a] relatively small number of [Islamic] scholars—roughly thirty or so at last count—dominate the Sharia Advisory Boards of most of the West's major financial houses." Gaffney notes, "Given the nature of Sharia and its objectives, affording influence over Western capital and credit flows to these prominent adherents and scholars is extremely troubling. As some of the world's foremost champions of Sharia, they are inevitably leading promoters of jihad."[61]

Here are some of the men who have their hands on the steering wheel for a trillion dollars of Islamist capital.

- Mufti Taqa Usmani was on the SCF board of Dow Jones before he was removed when his extremist views became known. However, he still sits on SCF boards for Swiss RE, Arcapita, UBS-Warburg and HSBC. Usmani is an officer of Deobandi Madrassa, which Gaffney describes as "an academy that indoctrinates boys and young men in one of the most virulent strains of Islamic practice . . . this madrassa is essentially a factory for jihadists reportedly underwritten with funding from Saudi Arabia." Usmani writes that "the purpose of jihad aims at breaking the grandeur of unbelievers and establish that of Muslims." He says that it is the duty of Muslims living in the West to "wage jihad" to "establish the supremacy of Islam."[62]

- Just as bad is Sheikh Yusuf al-Qaradawi. He is the Grand Mufti of the United Arab Emirates and regularly appears on al-Jazeera television. He's the founder of the International Association of Muslim Scholars. He served as the Sharia adviser to the Taqwa Bank until the bank's assets were frozen after US, Jordanian, and Swiss intelligence found that the bank was funding al-Qaeda. Al-Qaradawi has been barred from entering the United States since 1999 and from entering the United Kingdom since 2008. He endorsed homicide bombings, saying, "I consider this type of martyrdom operation as evidence of God's justice . . . he has given the weak a weapon the strong do not have and that is the ability to turn their bodies into bombs as Palestinians do."[63]

Qaradawi is the Sharia adviser of several sovereign wealth funds of Gulf oil states.

But even more important than just the funds the SCFs throw off for dubious charities is their potential to manipulate the entire global capitalist system. As their capacity to steer large amounts of assets grows, their ability to cause mayhem increases proportionately. Financial jihad becomes a real danger to us all, instigated by our good allies in Saudi Arabia. If Sharia takes over the sovereign wealth funds of the Islamic world, it could represent a hefty share of global capital, enough to cause the kind of bubbles that have proven so disastrous for the world's economy.

SAUDI MONEY BUYS JIMMY CARTER AND OTHER INFLUENTIAL AMERICANS

All this information raises the logical question: Where is our government? Why is it not fighting this multi-pronged jihad by our alleged ally? Where is the outrage? The anger?

The fact is that Saudi money has bought off key elements of our civil society and rendered them mute in the face of its jihadist outrages. Perhaps the best example is the corruption of former president Jimmy Carter. Today, Carter is a staunch advocate for the Palestinian cause, blind to its terrorism, and a leading opponent of Israel.

But, back when he was president, Carter wasn't like that at all. After all, he was the impartial broker of the Camp David accords, which bought Israel the only security it has ever known. Without Egypt's population and military might, the remaining Arab states cannot threaten her existence. They can only bleed her gradually through terrorist attacks.

What turned Carter against Israel? Saudi money, including a payoff to the Carter Center from Osama bin Laden's brother!

- The Carter Center has reportedly gotten contributions of upwards of $5 million from Saudi billionaire Prince Alwaleed.[64] He achieved brief fame in the United States when New York Mayor Rudy Guiliani refused his offer of $10 million to help the city rebuild after 9/11. Alwaleed had triggered Rudy's wrath by suggesting that the American policy of support for Israel had brought 9/11 on ourselves.

- In 2001, President Carter travelled to the United Arab Emirates (UAE) to accept a $500,000 honorarium from the Zayed Center for Coordination and Followup, established in 1999 by the Arab League as their think tank. Research by the Anti-Defamation League found that the Zayed Center "regularly published anti-Semitic and conspiracy theory literature and promulgates anti-Americanism and anti-Semitism through its speakers and official publications."[65] These activities include Holocaust denial and a website proclaiming that the 9/11 attacks were "orchestrated by the US military in an effort to blame the attacks on the Muslim world."[66] In fact, in 2002 Carter wrote to the Zayed Center to offer to partner with it and to praise it for promoting "peace, health, and human rights around the world."[67]

- In all, the Carter Center has received over $1 million in support from the UAE.

- Kyle Shideler and Ian Weinglass report that the Carter Center has also received funding from the sultanate of Oman, the Kingdom of Saudi Arabia, Bakr M. bin Laden, Osama's brother for the Saudi bin Laden group, and the Saudi Fund for Development.[68] (Shideler is the senior research fellow at the Endowment for Middle East Truth. Weinglass is a former analyst at the American Center for Democracy.)

With the prestige of the Nobel Peace Prize under his belt, former president Carter speaks with authority on humanitarian causes throughout the world. His aggressive posture toward Israel and his bias toward the Palestinians has inspired millions. Now, it turns out that he was bought and paid for with petrodollars.

Even more pernicious is the Saudi practice of hiring former members of Congress and public officials after they leave office. A prime case in point is former congressman Tom Loeffler (R-TX). In December 2002, the Saudi embassy hired his firm for $840,000 per year to promote their interests. And, in February 2006, it signed another contract with his company for $10 million a year.[69]

Why was Loeffler worth so much? Robert Baer, author of *See No Evil* and *Sleeping with the Devil* (the basis of the motion picture *Syriana*), said that "Loeffler might be as close to the Bush White House, including Dick Cheney, as anyone in Washington."[70] The former congressman served as finance co-chairman on both Bush's 1994 run for governor and his 2000 race for the presidency. And, in 2007, Republican presidential candidate John McCain hired him as his national finance chairman.

As he served Bush and McCain, Tom Loeffler was always mindful of the needs of his Saudi clients. According to Michael Issikoff, writing in *Newsweek*, Loeffler arranged a meeting, which took place on May 17, 2006, among McCain, Loeffler, and Saudi Prince

Turki al-Faisal "to discuss the kingdom of Saudi Arabia and US-Saudi relations."[71]

After Loeffler left the McCain campaign, his employee Susan Nelson took over as finance chairman.

Writing in Sarah Stern's book, *Saudi Arabia and the Global Islamic Terrorist Network*, Shideler and Weinglass summarize the triangular relationship among McCain, Loeffler, and the Saudis: "The cold fact is that McCain owes his nomination and possibly even his personal financial solvency, to the financial prowess of Loeffler and Nelson—two lobbyists who earned millions of dollars from Saudi Arabia. One may safely say that his door as a senator will always be open to them and it would have been had he become president. This may be why the Saudis paid the Loeffler group $1.3 million between June, 2007 and May, 2008."[72]

ACTION AGENDA

Who is giving Saudi Arabia the money to promote terrorism throughout the world? Obviously, we are. Former CIA director R. James Woolsey puts it very well. "If you have any doubt who is paying for [the] indoctrination [funded by the Saudis] just take a few seconds and adjust your car's rear view mirror the next time you stop to fill up. Then look for a moment into your own eyes before you get out of the car to pump gas. Now, you know."[73]

It is especially vital that we free ourselves of global Saudi domination now that revolutions are sweeping the Arab world. King Abdullah bin Abdul-Aziz Al Saud is eighty-seven, and in failing health. In November 2010, the king had Prince Nayef, his heir, chair a cabinet meeting because he himself was unable to do so. Nayef is seventy-seven and suffers from leukemia, diabetes, and osteoporosis. The entire Saudi line of succession is filled with sick old men. The potential for overthrow is obvious.

The Saudis have tried to bribe and bully their people into line. When revolutions broke out in Libya, Tunisia, Egypt, Yemen, Syria, and Bahrain, King Abdullah launched a $37 billion program of new spending on jobless benefits, education, housing subsidies, debt write-offs, and new sporting events. He has also beefed up the once ceremonial Palace Guard to a quarter-million-man elite personal police force, a counterweight to the army.

Should the Saudi monarchy fall, its place would doubtless be taken by the worst of the Islamists. While the Saudis wield their oil weapon with some

discretion, the new rulers would have no such com-
punctions. If Saudi Arabia retains its stranglehold on
global oil supplies, they could fall into the most ruthless of hands.

There is no future in trying to persuade Saudi
Arabia to behave itself. It is the major global sponsor of
terror because that's what its people want it to be. After
lifetimes of indoctrination in Wahhabaism, they are
enthusiastic supporters of Islamist extremism. Their
government is just giving them what they want.

And the evidence of how the so-called Arab spring
has brought to power the Muslim Brotherhood and
Islamist extremists indicates that democracy in the
Arab world simply becomes a means for the worst
regimes to come to power. There is no answer other
than energy independence.

Stop Buying Saudi Oil!

If we become energy independent, the Arab world's
power will collapse. One-third of the GDPs of the Arab
nations comes from the oil sector.[74]

Saudi Arabia is a desert sitting on top of an oil well.
Oil accounts for 75 percent of government revenues, 45
percent of GDP, and 90 percent of its exports.[75] Non-
oil manufacturing generates only 6 percent of the country's jobs.[76]

Take away the world's dependence on Saudi oil and the kingdom will have less political clout than the poorest countries in Africa. The terrorists will starve to death!

We must get free of their oil weapon!

We have been hearing about the need for energy independence ever since the very first OPEC oil embargo in early 1973, but all we have gotten is rhetoric, not action.

Coming Very Soon! US Energy Independence!

But now, a combination of the high price of oil and technological breakthroughs makes energy independence an attainable goal in the very, very near future. The United States and Canada will soon be able to avoid any imports from the Middle East or other hostile countries. Soon after that, we will be able to export oil to Europe and help them become energy independent as well (or dependent on us, not the Saudis, Iranians, and Russians).

The environmentalists have muddled the move toward energy independence by trying to make it synonymous with a switch to renewable resources and cutting our use of oil, coal, and natural gas entirely.

To them, the key issue is the need to avert global climate change by reducing carbon emissions into the atmosphere. And they won't settle for anything less than perfection. To them, it's renewable resources or nothing. For example, they don't like electric cars because they require more power generation. Natural gas won't work because it still emits carbons. Horizontal drilling—called *fracking*—can lead to water and air pollution. Offshore drilling has obvious risks. The Keystone pipeline might leak. Nothing works but windmills and solar panels.

Even from a purely green perspective, electric cars are better than gasoline-powered vehicles. Natural gas fuel is better than diesel. It emits much less carbon. If we generated our electricity from natural gas rather than coal, we would cut carbon emissions dramatically. These solutions may not be perfectly green, but they are good steps forward.

And we can address many of the environmental concerns through safety measures in drilling and shipping energy. But we need to be sure not to make the pursuit of perfection more important than steps we can take now to improve our energy use.

Our pressing national interest requires that we move aggressively to free ourselves of Saudi and Middle Eastern oil. We can't let the pursuit of environmental perfectionism get in the way. We can be energy independent very, very soon if we go for it and don't let ourselves be sidetracked.

Ironically, the Saudis have shown us the way to become independent of their oil. Until recently, they were very careful to keep the price of oil within reason, precisely to avoid driving us to embrace alternate sources of energy. With oil prices moderate, new technologies to pump oil were uneconomical. However, in the past few years, they have been unable to keep the price of oil down, as Chinese and Indian demand for energy has exploded, driving up global petroleum use, even as OPEC's portion of oil exports has shrunk.

Now the price, hovering around $100 per barrel, is high enough to make myriad new technologies economically remunerative. The result has been a dramatic increase in domestic US and Canadian oil production.

US and Canadian Oil Production Is Soaring

North American oil production peaked in 1972, at 11.5 million barrels per day (including 9.5 million barrels from the United States). By 2008, it had dropped to 8 million barrels (with the United States accounting for only a bit more than 5 million of it).[77]

But US and Canadian oil production has come roaring back, spurred by high prices and made possible by new technology. (Meanwhile, Mexican oil production has slumped badly, handicapped by a constitutional prohibition on using foreign investment to acquire new technology for deep-sea drilling.)

The *Houston Chronicle* reports, "US oil production in areas including West Texas' Permian Basin, South Texas' Eagle Ford shale, and North Dakota's Bakken shale will record a rise of a little over 2 million barrels per day from 2010 to 2016, according to data compiled by Bentek Energy, a Colorado firm that tracks energy infrastructure and production projects. Canadian crude production is expected to grow by 971,000 barrels per day during the same period with much of the oil headed for the United States. Combined, the US and Canadian output will top 11.5 million barrels per day, which is even more than their combined peak in 1972."[78]

North Dakota, alone, now produces almost half a million barrels per day, more than the United Arab Emirates. Fargo, North Dakota, may no longer be only known for the movie. It may become the new Dubai!!!

A big part of the increase in domestic oil production is due to fracking, horizontal drilling between one hundred and two hundred feet below the earth's surface in which high-pressure water is used to break up shale deposits and release the oil and gas trapped inside. *Energy Now* reports, "The combination of horizontal drilling and hydraulic fracturing in shale rock formations is opening up previously unrecoverable oil, just as those technologies did for natural gas. It's driving a boom in US energy production and creating bright spots in a tough economy across America."[79]

The United States has the largest shale oil reserves in the world, estimated at 1.5 to 2.6 trillion barrels.[80] That's over a two-hundred-year supply of oil at current US rates of consumption. While not all of it is recoverable with today's technology or economically feasible to mine at today's oil prices, shale gives this nation an ability to achieve energy independence in the very near future.

Environmentalists are, of course, alarmed over the increase in oil production, since it gets in the way of their fantasy of a green utopia—a fossil-fuel-free world in which all power comes from renewable resources. Windmills spin, solar panels bake, and geothermal installations rumble in their promised land, but renewable resources will never fill most of the void left by foreign oil. After a decade or more of effort and massive subsidies, renewables account for only 4 percent of energy generation (up from 2 percent ten years ago).

Environmentalists have several objections to fracking.

- They complain that fracking uses a lot of water. In 2010, the US Environmental Protection

Agency estimated that 70 to 140 billion gallons of water are used to fracture 35,000 wells in the United States each year (about the annual water consumption of two to four million people).[81] While a significant drain on our freshwater resources, this would seem to be a small price to pay for energy independence.

- More serious are environmental concerns about the possibility of contamination of groundwater and air quality around fracking wells. Even though the fracking takes place deep beneath the aquifer, many are worried that chemicals could seep into the water supply. However, a 2004 federal EPA study concluded "that the injection of hydraulic fracturing fluids into CBM [coal bed methane] wells posed minimal threat to underground drinking water sources."[82] Fortunately, in 2005, Congress voted to exempt hydraulic fracturing from any regulation under the federal Safe Drinking Water Act. EPA Administrator Lisa Jackson testified in a Senate hearing, "I'm not aware of any proven case where the fracking process itself has affected water."[83]

- Much of the groundwater contamination that actually takes place does not come from fracking itself but from wastewater stored on the surface after it is used and reused in the fracking operation. Often, the wastewater, and the chemicals in it, are allowed to evaporate into the atmosphere and to fall to earth when it rains. Poorly built pipelines may also leak and contaminate the air and water. Of course, all these problems can be solved by better construction and care in the storage and disposal of wastewater.

- Finally, environmentalists warn of the potential of radioactivity from the shale rock beneath the surface. But the *New York Post* wrote that the Pennsylvania EPA reported "levels [of radiation] at or below the normal occurring in background levels of radioactivity" in seven rivers adjacent to fracking sites that it tested in November and December 2010. The state EPA also said that the levels of radium-226 and -228 were well within federal drinking water standards.[84]

Despite the absence of hard evidence of environmental danger, liberals in New York state, for example, are blocking fracking even as upstate New York rots, losing more jobs and population with each passing year! But North Dakota, Texas, and Pennsylvania

have largely green-lighted fracking and their economies are booming. Rural Pennsylvania, which has the
same topography and population as much of upstate
New York, is thriving because their government allows
fracking while New York's does not.

Another key source of new oil lies offshore in the
Gulf of Mexico and along the Atlantic and Pacific
coasts. *Investor's Business Daily* reports that the United
States has 89 billion barrels offshore in recoverable oil.
Compared with the current domestic production of 8
million barrels per day, the potential of offshore drilling
becomes clear. The paper notes that "we could, in effect,
boost our energy output 50%, and thus our energy independence, by bringing an additional 4 million barrels of
oil to thirsty world markets each and every day."[85]

But from 2002 to 2008, oil production from federal
leases in the Gulf of Mexico dropped from 568 million barrels to 418 million[86] (or about 14 percent of our
domestic oil production). Offshore drilling has gotten
a bad name since the Deepwater Horizon British
Petroleum oil spill in 2010 dumped massive amounts
of oil into the Gulf. But the technology for deepwater
drilling has improved and many of the lessons of the
BP spill have been factored into new designs.

Brazil is leading the way globally in deepwater
drilling. Its semipublic oil company, Petrobras, has

contracted 80 percent of the world's deepwater oil rigs.[87] The potential off the Brazilian coast is dwarfed by the vast reserves that lie in the Gulf of Mexico.

An aggressive policy of approving leases and moving ahead on deepwater oil drilling could trigger a huge increase in US domestic oil production.

Almost as large as the deposits in the Gulf are those that lie off the Atlantic and Pacific coasts of the United States. Long barred to oil companies by federal regulation, the Atlantic coast alone is estimated to have reserves of 7.2 billion barrels of oil.[88]

Many of the acute financial problems of states like California and New Jersey could be solved by allowing drilling off their coasts. Louisiana and Texas profit mightily from severance tax revenues related to their offshore deposits.

Self-destructive as always, the California State Legislature enacted its own ban on offshore drilling in 1994, cutting the state off from a vast source of both jobs and revenue. There are currently twenty-six oil and gas drilling platforms off the Southern California coast and 1,500 active wells (largely grandfathered in before the drilling ban).[89] They have produced more than one billion barrels of oil since the 1960s, but could produce vastly more if allowed.[90] *USA Today* points out that since the massive Santa Barbara oil spill of 1969, these wells have spilled "only 852 barrels of oil, the result of better technology and regulatory vigilance."[91]

By contrast, Louisiana has had offshore drilling since 1947. *USA Today* reports that "about 172 active rigs dot the Gulf of Mexico waters off the coast producing about 79 percent of the oil and 72 percent of the natural gas that comes from drilling off the nation's coastlines. The state gets about $1.5 billion annually in oil and gas revenue, a figure that will grow when it starts receiving part of the oil companies' royalty payments in 2017 under federal law."[92]

Just weeks before the British Petroleum oil spill, President Obama opened large areas of the US coastline to oil drilling for the first time. He ended the moratorium on oil exploration along the East Coast from the northern tip of Delaware to the central coast of Florida, covering 167 million acres of ocean. Exploration from New Jersey northward and along the entire Pacific coast would still be banned.

His announcement came on March 31, 2010, less than two months before the BP oil spill. Responding to public anger about the spill, he announced a moratorium on offshore drilling permits, a ban that he relaxed a year later. But the feds are still loath to issue permits for offshore drilling and oil industry sources complain that it is very hard to get a green light to explore or drill. In fact, the administration maintains a de facto ban on new drilling offshore.

Higher oil prices have made a host of newer technologies economically feasible. One key breakthrough is the use of oil sand technology to extract petroleum. Where wells cannot access the oil from the surface, companies use *oil sand technology*, essentially strip-mining for oil where the surface is cut away to get at the petroleum.

Canada has been the pioneer in oil sands in the Athabasca oil sands of Alberta. Already, they sell about 1.2 million barrels per day from oil sands to the United States, about half of total Canada oil exports to the United States.

To improve our access to oil sands petroleum, the industry is proposing to build the Keystone Pipeline to ship oil sands petroleum from Alberta to refineries in Illinois, Oklahoma, the Gulf Coast, and Texas. Initially, the pipeline will be bring 509,000 more barrels each day of Canadian oil to the United States refineries on the Gulf. Eventually, its capacity will grow to 1.1 million when it is completed.

If we get half a million extra barrels daily through the Keystone Pipeline, it would reduce our need to import oil from our enemies by almost 20 percent.

But, under pressure from rabid environmentalists and needing their help to get reelected, President Obama has vetoed, for now, the construction of the Keystone Pipeline. The environmentalists warn of the potential for leaks and other mishaps. With tens of thousands of miles of pipeline already in use, their concerns seem unrealistic. Their real objection is to the mining of oil sands themselves. Because a form of strip mining is involved, this means of extraction releases more methane into the atmosphere than comes from traditional oil wells. The greenies complain that this adds to global climate change and carbon emissions. Industry sources reply that the total impact on global carbon emissions would be less than one-tenth of 1 percent. And, since oil sands generate massive amounts of natural gas, as well as oil, they offer the possibility of a major shift away from coal in electricity generation, a change that would do vastly more to reduce global climate change than the small extra amount of methane released in the mining process would do to increase it.

Both sides litigated their case before the Obama administration, which put the decision off until after the 2012 election. But Congressional Republicans forced Obama to make a decision and he chose the wrong path.

Imagine what one million extra barrels of oil each day would do for the United States. We now import that amount of oil from Venezuela. As noted in a subsequent chapter of this book, Hugo Chavez, the dictator of that country, is allying himself with Iranian terrorists to mount a serious threat to the United States. As Iran increases its ballistic missile capacity and develops nuclear weapons, its alliance with Venezuela will pose the same existential threat to the United States that the Castro-Soviet alliance did in 1962, precipitating the Cuban Missile Crisis and bringing the United States to the verge of a nuclear war.

But, if we stop buying Chavez's oil and use the oil that comes in over the Keystone pipeline instead, we will deny the Venezuelan dictator the funds he needs to stay in office. (See Venezuela chapter for details.)

The next president must reverse Obama's dreadful decision and build the Keystone Pipeline.

US Oil Use Is Dropping . . . Fast

While American and Canadian oil production has increased and will rise rapidly in the next few years, the United States is using almost one million fewer barrels of oil in 2009 than it did at the start of the decade. (US oil consumption has dropped from 19.6 million barrels per day in 2000[93] to 18.7 million in 2009.)[94]

Gasoline consumption fell from 142.3 billion gallons in 2007 to 138.5 billion in 2010 and it is expected to fall further in 2011.[95]

In the 1990s, the US imported two-thirds of its oil. Now it produces about half of its consumption domestically.[96] High oil prices are doing what four decades of political exhortation and legislative regulation has failed to accomplish, just as the Saudis feared they would!

Energy independence is within reach.

There are a wide variety of strategies we can use to make us independent of oil from noxious nations like Saudi Arabia, Venezuela, Russia, and Ecuador (which is currently under Chavez's control).

A prime one would be to expand dramatically the number of electric cars on the road. Nissan has sold 20,000 electric Leaf cars and Mitsubishi has sold 17,000 electric. The industry is still in its infancy, but more and more companies are bringing out electric models.

There is a lot we can do to reduce further our oil consumption, hastening the day of energy independence. Electric cars are a prime example. They run on a battery that costs only a few thousand dollars. These batteries can propel a car for twenty to forty miles using only one electric charge, usually given overnight. Since three-quarters of American cars travel fewer than forty miles per day, electric-battery-powered vehicles would seem to be a natural fit.

For longer trips, they come with a small internal combustion engine under the hood. Former CIA director F. James Woolsey Jr. explains that their internal combustion engine runs "a small generator when needed to charge the battery as you drive. You can drive electrically most of the time . . . If you are faced with a longer-than-average day's drive, without needing to search for an electric plug away from home, you can drive as far in such a plug-in hybrid as in an ordinary car that has only an internal combustion engine."[97]

Enthusiasm about electric cars cooled a bit recently when the government indicated that two batteries in the Chevy Volt caught fire during crash tests. The New York Times wrote that "G.M. officials have said that the battery's coolant system may have ruptured in crash tests, causing an electrical reaction that could have caused the fires. And the Volt's battery is not shielded from damage by a layer of steel reinforcement, as is the case in the electric-powered Nissan Leaf."[98]

To deal with the problem, GM is switching to a lithium phosphate battery from its current lithium metal oxide device. The lithium phosphate battery, only recently able to be manufactured, lasts longer and is safer. Bloomberg News notes that "the shift in less than two years highlights how quickly the technology is changing for electric and hybrid cars."[99]

Major car manufacturers are planning to introduce as many as thirty electric vehicle models in the next two years using the new lithium phosphate battery. Sacbee.com reports that "mainstream US companies such as FedEx, UPS, Frito-Lay, Staples, and others have placed orders for hundreds of [electric vehicles] over the past year. Early in 2011, GE announced an intended purchase of 25,000 PEVs by 2015, 12,500 of which are Chevy Volt plug-in hybrids."[100]

Even as we increase the number of hybrids and electric cars on the road, traditional gasoline-powered cars are getting more efficient, partially in response to federal legislation mandating higher fuel efficiency (54.5 mpg by 2025). The *Economist* notes that "in Europe, which got strict sooner [than we did in the United States] and where fuel is heavily taxed, petrol and diesel vehicles have become much cleaner. The average new car sold in Britain now does 52.5 miles per gallon, up from 40.6 mpg ten years ago. Even so, says Neville Jackson of the engineering consulting firm Ricardo, 'There remains much scope for improvement: petrol and diesel cars still typically use less than a fifth of the energy stored in their fuel to turn the wheels. Plenty more miles can be squeezed out of each gallon. It is simply a matter of cost.' "[101]

He explains that "to meet a series of deadlines to cut emissions, carmakers are putting into their cheaper models all sorts of gear hitherto mostly seen on pricey high-performance cars: turbochargers and super-chargers (which mean the engine can be smaller and more fuel-efficient), fancy fuel-injection systems and valve trains; grilles with variable aerodynamics, and so on."[102]

The United States can easily absorb the extra drain on its electric grid that would stem from wider use of electric cars. Most of the charging will be done at night during off-peak hours when most electric plants are dormant. And we don't use oil to generate electricity—it accounts for less than 1 percent of our power.

And Natural Gas Is Replacing Coal

Environmentalists worry that increased electric use could worsen global climate change by requiring more coal burning to generate the power. However, the United States has made huge strides in replacing carbon-rich coal with natural gas, which generates a third less carbon, in the production of electric power. Just a few years ago, in 2008, natural gas accounted for 21 percent of electric power.[103] Now it provides 24 percent[104] while the share of power that comes from coal has dropped from 49 percent in 2008[105] to 43 percent today. This trend is likely to continue and even accelerate as more natural gas becomes available.

The real game changer in our foreign energy independence is the rapid, very recent growth of natural gas extraction in the United States. The *Wall Street Journal* reports that "just three years ago, the conventional wisdom was that US natural-gas production was facing permanent decline. US policy makers were resigned to the idea that the country would have to rely more on foreign imports to supply the fuel that heats half of American homes, generates one-fifth of the nation's electricity, and is a key component in plastics, chemicals and fertilizer."[106]

But no more. As the *Journal* notes, "Huge new [natural gas] fields have been found in Texas, Arkansas and Pennsylvania. One industry-backed study estimates the US has more than 2,200 trillion cubic feet of gas waiting to be pumped, enough to satisfy nearly 100 years of current US natural-gas demand." The newspaper adds that "a massive natural-gas discovery in northern Louisiana heralds a big shift in the nation's energy landscape. After an era of declining production, the US is now swimming in natural gas. Even conservative estimates suggest the Louisiana discovery known as the

ELECTRICITY GENERATION IN THE US BY FUEL SOURCE[107]

Coal	43.1%
Natural Gas	24.2%
Nuclear	18.6%
Hydroelectric	8.3%
Renewables	4.9%
Other	0.6%

Haynesville Shale, for the dense rock formation that contains the gas—could hold some 200 trillion cubic feet of natural gas. That's the equivalent of 33 billion barrels of oil, or 18 years' worth of current US oil production. Some industry executives think the field could be several times that size."[108]

Natural gas production has risen steadily even as new reserves are discovered. In 2008, we produced 57.7 billion cubic feet of gas per day. In 2010, the figure rose to 61.8, a 4.4 percent increase. And that rise happened despite a 6 percent drop in Gulf of Mexico production due to the aftereffects of the Deepwater Horizon spill, which shut down operations in the area for some time.[109]

But while natural gas, all of which is produced domestically, is revolutionizing electricity generation, it has had little effect on cars and trucks. To cut gasoline consumption dramatically, we need to replace gasoline with natural gas in powering our motor vehicles in the future.

Between 2008 and 2010, American natural gas extraction rose by one trillion cubic feet—enough to run 12 million cars—about 5 percent of our fleet. David Fessler, an energy and infrastructure expert, estimates that we could "replace 75% of the US vehicle fleet and we're still only talking 15 trillion cubic feet of gas a year."[110]

He notes that "while electric cars might be the ultimate alternative to fossil fuels, switching to natural gas-powered vehicles gets us a long way down the road towards energy independence."[111]

Natural gas tycoon T. Boone Pickens says, "Converting heavy-duty trucks and high-fuel use commercial fleet vehicles to natural gas can reduce our OPEC dependence now while we wait for technology to power the vehicles of tomorrow. . . . Recent unrest in the Middle East underscores the need to take action now."[112]

The key is to start with heavy-duty, long-haul trucks now powered by diesel engines. There are eight million of them in the United States and they consume a total of two million barrels of oil a day, about 10 percent of the nation's demand for oil and more than half of the amount we would need to replace if we were to declare independence from oil imports from Saudi Arabia, Venezuela, Russia, and Ecuador: the suppliers that hate us. But a long-haul truck powered by natural gas can cost almost $200,000 to buy.[113]

At present, only 142,000 of the 250 million vehicles on the road in the United States are powered by natural gas. However, Pickens says that he believes we can increase that number to 1.3 million trucks by 2014. Pickens is pushing legislation to double the subsidies, enacted in 2005, for natural gas vehicles. He wants to increase tax credits for purchase of natural gas cars or light trucks to as high as $12,500 and up to $64,000 for heavy trucks. He would also give filling stations up to $100,000 for converting to offer natural gas at their pumps.[114]

But steep subsidies and tax credits may not even be necessary. Pickens says that the "cost differential between natural gas powered trucks and their diesel versions is fast dissolving and will soon disappear" as more natural gas trucks are produced. Pickens said that a "natural gas powered trash truck that cost $50,000 more than its diesel alternative a few years ago, is now only about $10,000 more." And, Pickens adds, "the natural gas needed to power that truck is $1.50 to $2 per gallon cheaper than diesel today."[115]

Finally, American consumers in the Northeast have been steadily moving away from oil to heat their homes. In 1973, households used 942,000 barrels per day for heat. By 2008, with millions switching to natural gas or electric heat, the consumption had fallen to 309,000 barrels per day.[116] We need to go the rest of the way and eliminate the use of oil heat in the US.

Voilà! Energy Independence!

So, add it up. We can replace 2 million barrels per day by substituting natural gas for diesel trucks. We can drill upwards of 2 million more barrels per day (and Canada can add an extra million) by fully using our offshore resources and expanding our shale drilling. If electric cars come to constitute 10 percent of the cars on the road today, we can save about 1 million barrels of oil per day[117] and switching from oil heat could save about 300,000 barrels per day.

Together, these changes make it possible to declare our energy independence. Good-bye, Saudi Arabia.

Of course, we don't need to be totally independent of oil imports. A lot of our oil comes from countries who are good friends. No problem importing from them.

Here's where we get our oil:

US OIL IMPORTS BY COUNTRY[118]

Friends (or at least not enemies)

Canada	1.9 million barrels per day
Mexico	1.1 million
Nigeria	1 million
Colombia	0.3 million
Iraq	0.4 million
Angola	0.4 million
Brazil	0.3 million
Kuwait	0.2 million
Subtotal	5.6 million

Foes

Saudi Arabia	1.1 million
Venezuela	0.9 million
Ecuador	0.2 million
Russia	0.3 million
Algeria	0.3 million
Subtotal	2.8 million

So our goal should be to replace the 3 million barrels per day that we import from bad guys by increasing production and/or cutting consumption. And, according to current estimates, we should be largely there by 2016!

It's not so easy in Europe, which has to import 9 million barrels of oil per day, largely from the Middle East (about 15 percent) and Russia (about 30 percent).[119] The Continent lacks our resources of shale for fracking and has largely tapped its off shore resources, largely in the North Sea. To help Europe become independent of Saudi oil (and Iranian oil, too), we may need to resume oil shipments to Europe.

The United States has already become a net exporter of energy, for the first time in sixty-two years. In September 2011, the United States exported 3.1 million barrels per day of petroleum products while it imported only 2.2 million.[120] The Conversable Economist website reports, "The US is now a net exporter of oil to Brazil, Mexico, Argentina. While exports and imports will bounce around in the short-run, over the longer run it appears that the US is on track to become an energy exporter of oil, coal, and even natural gas (as technology improves for shipping liquefied natural gas)."[121]

Not only can the United States become independent of Saudi Arabian oil, we can become, again, the new Saudi Arabia for the world, just as we did prior to World War II!

A pipe dream? No way. Amy Myers Jaffe, an energy expert who runs the Baker Institute Energy Forum at Rice University, wrote, "By the 2020s, the capital of energy will likely have shifted back to the Western Hemisphere, where it was prior to the ascendancy of Middle Eastern megasuppliers such as Saudi Arabia and Kuwait."[122]

Won't that be cool! All the rogues of the world, who sustain themselves on our desire for oil, will have to look for a new line of work! Russia, Venezuela, Iran, Saudi Arabia will all lose their power.

Liberals like President Obama love to talk about the need to replace our so-called oil addiction. In the long run, they have a case. But, in the near term, we can drill our way to independence while we promote sensible and easy conservation measures like converting trucks to natural gas, promoting electric cars, and switching from oil heating to natural gas.

Have you noticed the absence of the words *renewable resources* or *sustainable energy* in this chapter? It's deliberate. After a decade or more of touting renewable energy, we now get only a tiny portion of our electricity from renewable sources: wind, geothermal, solar, and everything else combined. The renewable energy sources are so expensive that they cannot compete without major government subsidies, even with oil at $100. The Solyndra scandal, in which the Obama administration gave a half-billion dollars in loan guarantees to a company on the verge of bankruptcy that was backed by one of the president's leading campaign contributors, is an example of what can go wrong when the government tries to defy the market through subsidies.

Ultimately, a form of energy can compete or it can't. No subsidy or loan guarantees can make an uneconomical energy source marketable.

The key is to abandon, or at least postpone until technology has improved, the search for perfection. Natural gas is not a perfect energy source. Its contribution to global warming is more than that of renewable sources. It is far below that of oil and way below coal. We need to promote conservation and switch to domestic oil sources at the same time. Our central goal must be to free ourselves of the domination of the oil export industry by the most heinous actors in the world, a cast led by Saudi Arabia.

One of the big reasons we are getting screwed by the international global community is that its central institution, the United Nations, is totally corrupted. Run by greedy, poor countries whose UN delegations focus on how much they can steal, it has become a center for missing money, corrupt contracts, and kickbacks from suppliers. And, at the center of it all, the United Nations Secretary-General Ban Ki-moon does his best to stamp out any investigation, exposure, or reform of his organization's corrupt ways.

PART SEVEN

The United Nations of Corruption

If you headed a vast international organization with a budget of upwards of $20 billion per year, wouldn't you value an in-house investigator who uncovered more than $1 billion of fraud and corruption in your procurement department? Wouldn't you promote him? Would you fire him?

United Nations Secretary-General Ban Ki-moon doesn't see things that way and neither does the General Assembly. After former federal prosecutor Robert Appleton uncovered twenty significant fraud and corruption schemes as head of the Procurement Task Force in the United Nations' Office of Internal Oversight Services (OIOS), he was rewarded for his diligence by getting fired when the General Assembly—increasingly a group of corrupt nations in on the take themselves—defunded his task force for doing too good a job.

And, when Inga-Britt Ahlenius, the head of the OIOS, tried to promote Appleton and make him her deputy, Ban Ki-moon blocked the appointment. He mustn't want to know about the corruption on his watch.

FOX News reporter George Russell, who has taken the lead in bird-dogging the UN administrative mess, explains that Appleton's "task force was established in 2005 after a FOX News investigation uncovered a major bribery scandal in the UN's multibillion dollar procurement department."[1]

Ahlenius, angry at her inability to get Appleton hired, blasted Ban for "undermining" OIOS and replacing "strong, independent-minded subordinates with a coterie of loyalists on short-term contracts."[2]

The effort by Ban to cover up abuses at the United Nations and close down the only effective investigative agency within his organization is suggestive of widespread corruption at the United Nations.

Perhaps going up to the top!

A FORMER FEDERAL PROSECUTOR DIGS UP CORRUPTION AT THE UNITED NATIONS

Appleton spelled out the pervasiveness of the UN culture of corruption on January 25, 2011, in testimony before the House Foreign Affairs Committee.

"I am often asked why is there no will in the [UN] Organization to pursue [corruption] cases, or address them when misconduct is identified. The short answer is that investigations that uncover fraud and corruption bring bad news, and bad news is not welcome news.

"The approach of the leadership of the [UN] Organization is to minimize such issues, and keep them from public view. The exposure of issues, problems, corruption and fraud, is seen as something that could threaten future funding of donors. Rather than receiving praise for uncovering fraud as a result of intensive oversight, investigators and the Investigation Unit are penalized for doing the right thing, thoroughly investigating fraud and corruption, and reporting on it— wherever it is found.

"However, those in authority in the Organization largely subscribe to this philosophy."[3]

The record of the United Nations under Secretary-General Ban Ki-moon in failing to act on the results of Appleton's investigations is truly appalling.

Appleton told the House committee "the most disappointing aspect of my experience in the [UN] Organization was not with what we found, but the way in which investigations were received, handled and addressed by the UN Administration and the way in which investigations were politicized by certain Member States."[4]

Appleton's procurement investigation task force was set up by former secretary-general Kofi Annan to respond to the massive corruption an investigation by former Federal Reserve Board chairman Paul Volcker found in the UN oil-for-food scandal. With Iraq laboring under sanctions for its failure to heed UN resolutions to allow in weapons inspectors, Iraqi dictator Saddam Hussein appealed to the world body for a limited exemption from the sanctions to provide food and medicine for his people.

Under the aegis of the United Nations, limited sales of Iraqi oil were permitted, with all the revenue to go to humanitarian relief in Iraq. However, the oil money was routinely stolen, paid in bribes to UN officials, and used by Saddam for his military. Gradually, as Saddam pleaded that he needed more money to feed his people, the caps were lifted entirely so all the money could go into the dictator's pocket. Well, not all: The UN diplomats got their share, including the son of the secretary-general.

The ensuing Volcker investigation found literally billions in corruption reaching to the top levels of the UN administration. The United Nations was shaken to its core and donor nations, particularly the United States, demanded action, leading to the creation of Appleton's unit.

Appleton notes that "the Oil-for-Food bribery and fraud scheme, and the [Volcker] investigation, are now distant memories, rarely spoken about in the halls of the UN buildings. Despite one of the largest fraud and corruption schemes in history, important recommendations of the Volcker Committee for addressing fraud and corruption have not been implemented."[5]

He says that things have "unquestionably reverted to pre-Oil-for-Food days," and notes that "there is little capacity [at the UN] to investigate" corruption and "very little will to do so."[6]

Indeed, he points out that "the incentives in the UN are perverted, the support for true investigations and oversight is lacking, and the philosophy of the leadership is to reward inaction rather than action, suppression rather than exposure, and punishment of whistle-blowers and investigators, rather than protection."[7]

Some of the corruption Appleton uncovered boggles the imagination:

- On August 8, 2005, Alexander Yakovlev, the head of the office, "pleaded guilty to federal charges of corruption, wire fraud, and money laundering . . . Federal investigators allege that from 2000 on, Yakovlev [was] transferring bribe money to the head of the United Nations' own budget oversight committee, a Russian named

Vladimir Kuznetsov via the Antigua Overseas Bank in the West Indies. Allegedly the bribe money was in exchange for providing inside information to companies seeking UN contracts."[8]

• Paul Volcker, in the course of his own investigation into oil-for-food corruption at the United Nations, "noted in passing that Yakovlev had received more than $950,000 in bribes from companies that 'collectively won more than $79 million in United Nations contracts and purchase orders.'"[9]

• Sanjaya Bahel, a senior UN procurement official and Nishan Kohli, an agent of a large UN vendor, "were convicted, after a two month trial [pursuant to a prosecution brought by the US attorney for the Southern District of New York based on Appleton's evidence] of engaging in $100 million in fraud, collusion, and bribery in connection with a series of UN contracts."[10] Bahel was sentenced to eight and a half years' imprisonment.

• In one case, "significant sums of money had been stolen by a UN official working in Iraq, and proceeds from a Jordanian bank account had been utilized for the benefit of the official and her family." Appleton "recommended that the privileges and immunities of the staff member be waived, and the matter referred to national authorities with jurisdiction over the matter." Appleton reports that "during the investigation, we were made aware that one national authority had an ongoing criminal case that related to this matter, and that relevant materials in the possession of the UN have not been provided to this authority." But, he concludes sadly, "as far as I am aware, I do not believe any criminal action has been pursued against the individuals involved in this matter."[11]

- Appleton also found tainted contracts for air charter services in Congo, office supplies in Kenya, consulting jobs in Greece, and payroll services at the United Nations' New York headquarters. The payroll scheme involves two American employees who steered $2 million in contracts to private firms in which they had a financial stake. In some of the other cases, UN employees solicited kickbacks to direct deals to specific companies.[12]

THE UNITED NATIONS SOLVES THE PROBLEM BY FIRING THE PROSECUTOR

The most important part of Appleton's story is not the fraud and corruption he uncovered or even how feebly the cases he developed were followed up. The key fact is that his unit was hounded out of existence by UN country delegations and Secretariat bureaucrats who were directly threatened by his findings. Corruption both among member nations and UN employees is so vast and so pervasive that it is the investigators, not the culprits, who are at risk.

Even when Appleton's people confirmed that actual corruption had taken place, "the efforts of [his Procurement Task Force] were opposed by certain Member State delegations that came to the defense of either officials who were nationals, or their companies or citizens."[13]

Not only that, but the UN members and bureaucrats counterattacked and destroyed the Procurement Task Force (PTF) itself, firing its investigators, blackballing them from future UN employment, and sending a message that investigations are not welcome at the United Nations. Appleton writes that "because the PTF undertook several high profile investigations of senior UN officials, diplomats and large value contracts in the jurisdictions of several Member States, the PTF was the subject of criticism and retaliation from the delegations of a few Member States whose senior UN officials, diplomats, companies or citizens were the subject of PTF investigations."[14]

In one of the most incredible episodes, Appleton reports that "prior to the expiration of the PTF [funding] at the end of 2008, the General Assembly, at the behest of one of the Member States that opposed our efforts, commissioned an audit by the UN Board of Auditors of the PTF and its activities. When the Board of Auditors did not find any due process violations or abuses, and further concluded that the PTF's methods and operations were fully compliant with UN rules, regulations and standards . . . no mention was made of these facts by the General Assembly, no apology was offered, and no change in the approach of the opposition occurred."[15]

In fact, those accused of crimes triumphed. Appleton reports that "the hostility to the unique status and independence of the PTF from the Member States that opposed its investigations finally led to the PTF's demise. In 2008, these Member States were able to successfully block further funding of the Unit by the General Assembly, and the PTF was forced to close at the end of 2008."[16]

Up to the last moment, PTF staff worked fever-
ishly[17] to complete five key investigations. They issued
reports right before the PTF doors were slammed shut
by the General Assembly, "including a report on fraud
in Iraq, elections, roads and rebuilding in Afghanistan,
fraud and corruption in the Economic Commission of
Africa in Addis Ababa, and in several matters involving high value contracts for transportation in Africa."[18]
The reports came out but, Appleton concludes, "As far
as I am aware, significant follow up has only been made
in one case, and that was after significant pressure—
including from this Congress."[19]

End of story. The unit, set up to stop further corruption at the United Nations in the wake of the massive oil-for-food scandal, was closed and its functions
transferred to what Appleton calls "a nondescript
unit simply known as 'Unit 5,' which . . . had but a
few investigators and none with serious white collar
fraud experience." The United Nations "refused to
even acknowledge 'fraud' in the title [of Unit 5], and
limited its mandate significantly. At one time, investigators were informed that they were not going to
investigate parties 'external' to the United Nations,
including the tens of thousands of contractors that do
business with the Organization."[20] Isn't that neat? A
unit charged with investigating payoffs from outside

contractors to UN personnel that can't investigate the contractors!

THE UNITED NATIONS CRIPPLES ITS INVESTIGATIVE ARM

The Office of Internal Oversight Services (OIOS) is the weak and withered investigative arm of the United Nations left after the functions of Appleton's Procurement Task Force were transferred into oblivion at Unit 5. Officially charged with auditing, investigating, and evaluating all UN activities under the secretary-general, the OIOS's former US ambassador to the United Nations, John Bolton, complains, is "beholden to those it is responsible for investigating" for financial support.[21]

David M. Walker, the former comptroller general of the United States, said that "UN funding arrangements constrain OIOS's ability to operate independently as mandated by the General Assembly and required by international auditing standards OIOS has adopted." He points out that OIOS "depends on the resources of the funds, programs, and other entities it audits." He explains that "the managers of these programs can deny OIOS permission to perform work or not pay for OIOS services" and concludes that "UN entities could

- U.N. Anti - Corruption Agency -

thus avoid OIOS audits and investigations, and high-risk areas can be and have been excluded from timely examination."[22]

The absurdity of having the investigated pay for their own investigation and of vesting them with the power to curtail or kill the probe is beyond description. But that's how the United Nations works.

Former OIOS chief Inga-Britt Ahlenius, chaffing under Ban's refusal to let her hire Appleton as her deputy after the Procurement Task Force was abolished, noted that the Senior Review Group that did not approve the Appleton appointment was composed of "top UN officials whose departments were likely to be scrutinized by the OIOS."[23]

She also points out that the heads of her department had been able to pick their deputies without any involvement of the secretary-general in the past. FOX News reports that "under a secretary-general's directive issued in 1995 and never modified, no one but the head of the OIOS was supposed to pick the organization's senior staff."[24]

"Never before," Ahlenius told Ban, "had a secretary-general intervened in a matter of appointing staff in the OIOS."[25] But never before had the OIOS taken its mandate to fight corruption at the United Nations seriously.

ANOTHER UN ANTICORRUPTION AGENCY BITES THE DUST

The UN Joint Inspection Unit (JIU), another anti-corruption investigatory unit at the UN, got similar treatment from Ban Ki-moon. The JIU got under the secretary-general's skin by issuing what FOX News described as a "number of wide-ranging reports that have called into question the UN's competence," including harsh criticism of "the UN's $10 billion global procurement system as a mess."[26] No kidding.

The same Senior Review Group that blocked the Appleton appointment in OIOS now struck back, demanding "a bigger say in selecting candidates to become the Unit's powerful executive secretary."[27]

The Investigative Unit protested that "for the previous forty years, staff appointments had been left in the organization's own hands to respect [its] autonomy." The unit's inspectors said they "question not only the fairness of trying to apply a new procedure for selecting its executive secretary, but also the legality of changing a procedure on a fundamental question without at least informing the General Assembly and the staff."[28]

YET ANOTHER ONE GOES DOWN

Ban Ki-moon's propensity for limiting, interfering, and blocking anyone who investigates corruption at the United Nations reached a new height on December 11, 2011, when the judges of the United Nations Dispute Tribunal, a panel that Ban himself had set up two years before, blasted him for obstructing their work.

The tribunal is charged with safeguarding the rights of UN employees, protecting whistle-blowers, and obtaining evidence of corruption. It is unique in that its judges are "deliberately chosen from outside the UN system to help break what has been described as the United Nations' incestuous 'culture of impunity,' which protected corrupt officials and other abusers of authority while punishing whistleblowers and others who bucked the system."[29]

Their criticism of Ban was very harsh. They unanimously charged that the secretary-general was trying to "undermine the integrity and independence" of their court in a bid to crimp their powers.[30]

FOX News reported that the "the judges also charged him with offering a 'misleading and one-sided' account of their judgments to the assembly as part of the attempt to get his way." The judges blasted changes in their operation that Ban proposed, saying that they "raise serious concerns regarding the respect for the rule of law within the Organization," give "power without accountability" to a variety of UN institutions, remove important avenues of legal recourse for UN staffers, and could make the exercise of the court's recently enshrined authority "meaningless."[31]

The changes Ban Ki-moon wants to make will defang the tribunal. Chief among them is that he wants to take away their right to enforce their temporary judgments, called *interlocutory orders* until after they have been appealed to the UN's highest judicial body, the seven-member United Nations Appeals Tribunal.

The judges charged that the change would leave them "toothless, especially when the temporary order granted what the judges call 'interim relief,' for example when ordering the secretariat to cease and desist from an action that judged illegal, invalid or retaliatory."[32]

These interlocutory orders are typically similar to injunctions issued in American courts: decrees from the court when an imminent harm threatens and delay would be injurious to one of the parties. To hold up enforcing such orders until a long appeals process has run its course would be to make them irrelevant. One of the key points at issue is the ability of the tribunal to protect whistle-blowers from being fired. If it cannot block their dismissal until months or years later, long after they have been let go, by the time the appellate court rules, there will be no more whistle-blowing. And that is, doubtless, Ban Ki-moon's objective.

Ban also wants to stop the judges from ordering him or Secretariat to "produce a document or witness in response to charges of unjust treatment."[33] They argue that taking away their ability to enforce such an order would make the court ineffective. After all, what good is a court that can't subpoena witnesses or documents and can't make its judgments stick?

And Ban wants to stop the tribunal from "hearing appeals from some of the United Nations' independent oversight institutions, including the OIOS and the UN Ethics Office,"[34] which protects whistle-blowers.

Shelley Walden, a judicial specialist who has monitored the UN judicial battle, worries that if the changes Ban proposes pass, "then whistleblowers will have no day in court, and little protection." She noted that "the Secretary General has recently claimed that he aims to promote whistleblowing, but his actions don't meet his words."[35]

Ban Ki-moon does not want any whistles blown.

Why not?

He doesn't want people to find out what a mess the UN administrative apparatus is, and how much money it wastes or lets its staff steal. Its management, under the weak leadership of its secretary-general, Ban Ki-moon, is, at best, incompetent and, at worst, a screen for massive fraud and corruption.

MEANWHILE BAN KI-MOON, THE UN SECRETARY-GENERAL, SPENDS THE MONEY WE DONATE FREELY: NO BUDGET CUTS FOR HIM!

This year, the United States will spend at least $7.7 billion on the United Nations and its various agencies: an increase of 21 percent over the $6.35 billion we spent last year, a whopping rise even by Obama administration standards.[36]

And the basic UN budget itself, excluding its various agencies, has more than doubled from $2.6 billion in 2001–2002 to $5.4 billion in 2011–2012.

The current US ambassador to the United Nations for UN Management and Reform, Joseph Torsella, noted, "The average total compensation of UN employees contained in the biennial budget is about $238,000—or $119,000 a year, tax free."[37]

Responding to global financial austerity, Ban Ki-moon announced, with great fanfare, that he had ordered top UN officials to cut their budgets by 3 percent in the face of a financial emergency situation.[38]

But Ban did not announce that he was giving all top UN officials a 3 percent pay hike. That fact was revealed by George Russell of FOX News. Congress reacted angrily, especially since Ban's action comes at a time when President Obama has ordered a two-year pay freeze for all federal employees. Ban turned a deaf ear to the US anger and Torsella vowed to "pursue the rollback during this year's General Assembly session."[39]

The rapidly increasing costs at the UN reflect a culture of opaque record-keeping and corruption that the current secretary-general has done nothing to correct. Indeed, he has made it much worse.

When he was ambassador to the United Nations, John Bolton vigorously attacked this culture of corruption, but, by his own admission, failed. Bolton told the Senate Finance Committee that "to be frank, the overall results [of his reform efforts] have not been particularly encouraging. There has been some movement, but no notable successes so far."[40]

WHERE'S THE MISSING $12.2 BILLION THE UNITED NATIONS WON'T ACCOUNT FOR?

Where does the UN money go? Its agencies won't say.

FOX News reports that "[a]t least two major United Nations development agencies, described as having accumulated some $3.2 billion in cash in 2009, refused to divulge exactly what they spent their program money on, according to a confidential draft report prepared in the summer for the government of Norway and examined by FOX News."[41]

The missing cash was part of a much bigger total of at least $12.2 billion United Nations agencies had in unspent cash in their accounts at the end of 2009.

Norway, one of the United Nations' biggest donors, had commissioned the study by a private consulting firm IDC to "contribute to the understanding of financing flows and current financial planning and budgeting processes" at five selected UN agencies. The investigation was to determine how resources are allocated and where the money goes."[42]

The short answer is that the agencies wouldn't say. The United Nations Population Fund (UNFPA) and its children's fund (UNICEF), according to the Norwegian consultants, failed "grossly" to live up to the "credo of adherence to transparency" that both agencies claim to follow in their work. They cited a third agency, the United Nations High Commission on Refugees, for refusing to provide spending details "particularly recent staff costs."[43]

The UNFPA wouldn't even reveal how much money it spent on wages and salaries, travel, or the hiring of consultants.

The Norwegian consultants said that the lack of an accounting of where cash flows have gone "implies that substantial donor funding is not being used for development purposes."[44]

The study found:

- At UNFPA, the consultants said, about $200 million a year was handed over to various governments and nongovernment organizations in ways that did not let UNFPA auditors examine the accounts. The result: Governments that gave money to UNFPA "have little knowledge regarding the ultimate destiny" of that money, which amounted, the report says, to about 30 percent of the total annual UNFPA programming money disbursed in this fashion.[45]

- UNICEF, formerly one of the most transparent agencies, now is piling up unspent funds. So bloated is its cash bank account that it made $109 million in interest on its holdings in 2008. The consultants report that "officially available information about expenditures remains very limited and fragmented, making it difficult to track use of funds from headquarters down to the ultimate beneficiaries on the ground." It adds that the level of detail in the UNICEF budget "significantly less today than it was five years ago."[46]

UNICEF is run by an American! That's Anthony Lake, Bill Clinton's former national security advisor. He should do better at providing transparency! Do you agree? Let Tony know how you feel!

Tell him to reveal how he spends our money! Fax him at 212-887-7465 or 212-887-7454. Or call him at 212-326-7000. Or write him at:

Tony Lake

Director

UNICEF

3 United Nations Plaza

New York, NY 10017

He'll be delighted to hear from you!

- The United Nations Development Program, the United Nations' main agency for economic development, is especially swimming in cash, with $5 billion on hand and trust funds that "had minimal or no expenditure" for two to four years. The agency put its money, intended for fighting global poverty, in bonds. They may not have spent their money helping anyone in poverty, but the UNDP staffing grew by 29 percent and its personnel costs rose by 80 percent in the past five years.[47]

Former Federal Reserve chairman Paul Volcker, charged with investigating corruption in the Iraq oil-for-food program, spoke of the "culture of inaction" that pervades the United Nations.[48]

Bolton said that "changing that culture and adapting it to modern-day management and accounting norms is no small task, but failure to do so is simply to invite future scandals."[49]

THE UN INFORMATION SYSTEM THAT DOESN'T WORK

As if to make Bolton's point clear, UN Secretary-General Ban Ki-moon has been under heavy fire lately for the collapse of his efforts to update, repair, and streamline the UN information systems. As the Norwegian report makes evident, UN agencies aren't exactly forthcoming about the details of their spending. And, with 1,400 separate information systems, it's not easy to keep track.

So Ban launched the Umoja (Swahili for "unity") Project to replace seven hundred of the information systems and coordinate better with three hundred more. The effort was to cost upwards of $300 million and be finished in 2012. It won't be. In fact, the project is a total mess.

The heads of Umoja quit in the middle of 2011: Paul Van Essche, director of the project, and Ban's undersecretary-general for Management, Angela Kane, the chair of the project steering committee.

The project is now projected not to come on line before 2015, three years late, at a vastly inflated cost.

FOX News reports that "in response to news of the . . . delay, a UN budget oversight committee slammed [Secretary-General] Ban for inattention, slack management, failure to act decisively in the face of the growing fiasco, and overall bad planning for the entire exercise, all part of what it called 'a failure of management' on the project. The committee also said it was 'deeply disturbed and dismayed' by the UN's 'apparent lack of awareness and foreknowledge' about the sputtering status of the project. It further noted that Ban 'makes no attempt to attribute responsibility for the action, or lack thereof, leading to the delay, or to hold anyone to account for this situation.' "[50]

Umoja was started because Ban said that the UN information systems were "at the breaking point, and woefully inadequate for carrying out the increasingly complex, far-reaching operations of the [UN organization.]"[51]

Why the delay in implementing Umoja? Part of the problem lies with the UN's administrative style. Ban recently proudly reported that he had cut the average time it takes to hire a member of the UN staff from one year to a mere seven and one half months!

In implementing Umoja, the UN staff busied itself with endless meetings. Ban's office reports that there were 1,053 meetings involving 1,215 participants that took up about 5,580 days of "staff participation."[52] But still no information system, and there won't be one for three more years, at least!

Of course, the Umoja delays and the lack of budgetary transparency detailed in the Norwegian investigation raise a key question: What are they hiding?

NO WHISTLE-BLOWING AT THE UNITED NATIONS

Ban Ki-moon does not want any whistles blown.

Stung by the accusations of corruption, the UN commissioned a study of its procurement department by the US-based management-consulting firm Deloitte Consulting Services. The results were devastating. The report said that ethics and integrity are "not sufficiently supported by management and is not a conspicuous element of the [department's] culture."[53]

FOX News reports that the study concluded that "UN procurement employees are themselves the only control on the department and that 'significant reliance on people leaves the UN extremely vulnerable to potential fraudulent or corrupt activity and [with] limited means to either prevent or detect such actions.' "[54] This is exactly the kind of fraud that Appleton discovered!

Deloitte said, "There does not appear to be a single, recognized, and well understood Code of Conduct governing ethics and integrity expectations and requirements for [department] employees."[55]

It would be simple to say that Ban Ki-moon is the problem, and that corruption that is so widespread in the UN comes from the top. Kofi Annan, his predecessor, was also accused of covering up corruption, and his own son was implicated in the oil-for-food scandal, much to the embarrassment of the secretary-general.

UN THIRD WORLD NATIONS SUPPORT THE CORRUPTION, AND PROFIT FROM IT

Corruption at the UN comes from the bottom, not from the top. It comes from the member nations of the UN, many of whose governments are themselves deeply mired in corruption. Indeed, some have called such states *kleptocracies*: governments based on stealing.

These governments *support* corruption at the UN. To them, it is the investigators who are evil, not those who are stealing the money. Some even privately speak of theft at the UN as a kind of redistribution of wealth from the rich nations who fund the body to the poor nations that may benefit from the corruption.

Robert Appleton's Procurement Task Force was derailed by the General Assembly itself, not by the unilateral action of Ban Ki-moon. Indeed, Ban himself is really reflecting the will of his constituents, that is, the members of the General Assembly, when he stonewalls corruption investigations and curtails the power of the sleuths.

These corrupt General Assembly nations stonewalled and killed former UN ambassador John Bolton's efforts to clean up the UN and limit its spending. His proposals would all seem obvious. He wanted a mandatory review, after five years, of any UN-mandated program, to subject it to scrutiny and determine if it was still needed. However, the seventy-seven UN member nations, who contribute a total of 12 percent of the UN budget, banded together to block his reforms. They wanted to exclude three-quarters of the mandates from the review. Bolton said, "These countries have made clear their interest in the status quo on this issue, which has resulted in active opposition to any genuine reform."[56]

ACTION AGENDA

Before we turn to the task of how to clean up the United Nations, we need to recognize that its corruption reflects the governing style of globalism. Third

World countries support the Law of the Sea Treaty, IMF, the World Bank, and the International Criminal Court because they confer licenses to steal! For these nations, the function of their UN ambassadors, and their representatives on all these UN bodies, is to swipe as much money as they can: for themselves and their bosses, not for the people of their countries.

It's hard to know where to begin in reforming the United Nations. Robert Appleton, fresh from his experience in uncovering massive corruption in the organization's procurement department, made several important recommendations in his House testimony in 2011.

Appleton said: "There must be a viable legislative framework in the UN that fully punishes financial misconduct, a will and ability to enforce such rules, and a competent judicial mechanism to hear and address cases. Further, the UN Administration must address recommendations for the waiver of privileges and immunities expeditiously, and waive such immunities in appropriate cases so criminal cases may be pursued by the appropriate national authorities. All UN staff, as well as all materials generated and in the possession of the UN, enjoy privileges and immunities—meaning they cannot be subpoenaed, and the UN cannot be compelled to turn them over to external bodies. Only the Secretary General has the authority to waive privileges and immunities of UN staff."[57]

He also testified: "The other structural problem in the United Nations is that oversight lacks true operational, budgetary and structural independence—despite language in resolutions to the contrary. OIOS is dependent upon the UN General Assembly for funding, positions and its mandate and on the Secretariat and Secretary General for selecting senior staff. At any time, the General Assembly can limit, refuse to fund, or end, the oversight body. While independence is stated in its mandate, to a certain degree, this is only theoretical, and not in fact the case. OIOS must have full operational, structural and budgetary independence to be truly independent and an effective oversight body."[58]

How do we get the United Nations to implement these simple, basic recommendations? We use our financial clout. The United States pays for 22 percent of the UN budget, a donation that exceeds $7 billion a year. Nine countries—the United States, Japan, Germany, the United Kingdom, France, Italy, Canada, Spain, and China—pay 75 percent of UN costs.[59]

If there was ever a body where the United States has leverage, it is the United Nations. We can attach conditions to the payment of our dues and make them stick. We can break the culture of corruption and close the Third World candy store that the United Nations has become. All that is lacking is the will to do so in Washington.

Indeed, the real blame for the UN corruption can be laid at the feet of all the recent US administrations. Only President George W. Bush took UN corruption seriously and made a real effort at reform. His nomination of John Bolton as UN ambassador was a real challenge to the go-along, get-along attitude of past US ambassadors.

Bolton was sabotaged by the liberals in the US Senate. Named as a recess appointment, he was never confirmed by the Senate. His path was blocked by Senator George Voinovich (R-OH). The senator objected to Bolton's confrontational style. Huh? At the United Nations, we desperately need a warrior to battle for us and clean things up. Bolton was just such a person. But, since he left, we have been pursuing the same mealy-mouthed approach to UN corruption that we did in the past.

Hopefully, things will change in 2013!

PART EIGHT

The World Bank

THE THIRD WORLD DRUG PUSHER

Like a street-corner drug dealer selling heroin to first-time users, the World Bank pushes loans and grants on Third World countries. The pitches of these two hustlers—one offering drugs and the other pushing loans—is the same: Try it; you'll like it. It will make you feel good! And I'll give it to you for free. And the results are the same: a lifetime of dependency, in the one instance on drugs and in the other on foreign aid and World Bank loans.

The World Bank has helped to create an unchallenged international consensus that more foreign aid and lending to Third World countries is the key to reducing global poverty. It isn't. In fact, the nations that have managed to escape poverty are not the African countries the bank has showered with loans, but Asian states that have done so not by taking aid or loans but by attracting direct foreign investment and selling exports to the West, in particular to the United States.

Aid and loans have done much to keep poor countries impoverished and allow a new colonialism to develop, run from deep in the headquarters of the World Bank.

This new colonialism has a great deal in common with the old colonialism. Both global systems of exploitation empowered and enriched leaders in the poor countries who cooperated with the colonial power. Both offered riches for the bureaucrats who administered the program and each provided massive opportunities for corruption in both the recipient and the donor countries.

AID FEELS SO GOOD TO GIVE, BUT IT DOESN'T WORK

Western countries feel so good about themselves when they provide aid to less-developed countries. Rock stars sing about them. Concerts are held for their benefit. The programs multiply: Live 8, Make Poverty History, the Millennium Challenge Account, Millennium Development Goals, and the Africa Commission. In 2001, British Prime Minister Tony Blair spoke for the global consensus when he said, "The state of Africa is a scar on the conscience of the world."[1]

But look at the record. More than $1 trillion has passed from developed nations to poor countries in the past sixty years. The World Bank, alone, since World War II, has made more than a half trillion in loans and grants to less developed nations. The aid has succeeded in increasing the incomes of dictators, strongmen, military leaders, and tribal chiefs throughout the Third World, and particularly in Africa. But it has done nothing to advance these nations economically.

In fact, the flood of resources into these less-developed nations has created an opportunity for public corruption very similar to the way in which drug revenues have opened the door to such behavior in Latin America or petrodollars have led to decadence in Arab lands or blood has been spilled over diamond mines in southern Africa. The aid has bred corruption in its wake and dependence on more handouts as surely as does drug addiction.

The loans and grants of the World Bank are like pure heroin flowing into the veins of underdeveloped countries. In May 2004, at a hearing before the Senate Committee on Foreign Relations, experts argued that about $100 billion of the $525 billion the World Bank has given in loans intended for development have been misdirected into corruption instead.[2]

But the developed world does so like to give Africa money! It soothes our conscience and seems to square with biblical injunctions to help the poor. However, trade and direct foreign investment do more for the poor in Africa and elsewhere than all the aid in the world.

Indeed, the focus on handouts rather than trade and investment is more theological than economic, appealing to our souls rather than any concrete knowledge based on results and experience of what is best for Africa.

The West has long struck a posture of righteousness as it hands over cash to corrupt African regimes. The condescension goes back to colonial times. In 1899, British poet Rudyard Kipling articulated it well in his famous poem "The White Man's Burden," excerpted here.

TAKE UP THE WHITE MAN'S BURDEN—
The savage wars of peace—
Fill full the mouth of Famine
And bid the sickness cease;
And when your goal is nearest
The end for others sought,
Watch sloth and heathen Folly
Bring all your hopes to nought.

Take up the White Man's burden—
And reap his old reward:
The blame of those ye better,
The hate of those ye guard—
The cry of hosts ye humour
(Ah, slowly!) toward the light:—
"Why brought he us from bondage,
Our loved Egyptian night?"[3]

The more the aid is wasted, the more the self-pity of which Kipling writes is in evidence. And if the aid does not put Africa on a self-sustaining basis, as trade and investment would do, so what? We can keep giving aid and feeling good about ourselves at the same time! And, if, after all, "Sloth and heathen folly bring all your hopes to nought," so what? Just try the same thing all over again!

The problem is that trade, which can really enrich poor nations, puts American workers out of jobs. It rewards rich industrialists who, by our standards, pay their workers a pittance. It seems to foster income inequality and appeals to our worst fears of unbridled capitalism. Direct foreign investment also smacks of money making. Profit, not social good, is always the criterion, something that has limited appeal for soothing our consciences.

TRADE AND INVESTMENT ARE HOW TO END POVERTY

Trade and direct foreign investment work. Boy do they work!

Through these two strategies, not through grants or loans, we have come very close to eliminating extreme poverty on earth. Since 1990, the percentage of people who live in poverty, according to the World Bank, has fallen from 41 percent to 25 percent,[4] a reduction of 40 percent in twenty years!

Most of those who have made it out of poverty live in China and India, nations that have prospered from big increases in trade, manufacturing, outsourcing, and foreign investment. But of the $525 billion in World Bank guaranteed loans since its founding, only 17 percent has gone to China or India, where 80 percent of the poverty reduction has taken place.[5] In fact, China, which alone is home to more than half of those on earth who have escaped poverty since 1990, has gotten only 7 percent of the bank's financing.[6]

Before that, the poverty reductions were concentrated in the Asian tiger countries: Taiwan, South Korea, Singapore, and Malaysia. In more recent times, low-cost production countries like Vietnam have profited from spurts of economic growth. Neither Taiwan nor Singapore has gotten any significant World Bank financing. South Korea has gotten 3 percent of its largesse, Thailand 2 percent, Malaysia less than 1 percent and Vietnam .5 percent. The vast bulk of World Bank financing, more than three-quarters of it, has gone to nations that have had very little, if any, reduction in poverty.

Foreign investment has proven a very effective way to reduce poverty.

Even in Africa, despite its low levels of direct foreign investment, private economic growth, in fact, is bringing down the poverty rate. As high as 66 percent in 1998, it has dropped to 50 percent in sub-Saharan Africa, thanks to real economic growth. Roelef Horne, a portfolio manager for the Mackenzie Universal Africa & Middle East Class mutual fund, says, "For the last eight years, [Africa] has been outpacing the rest of the world in economic growth." He added: "When you say that to people, they sit up and look at it differently."[7]

Indeed, *Financial Post Magazine* "paints a much different picture of Africa—one that has enjoyed years of strong economic growth . . . While real GDP stagnates in the developed world, many African economies are firing on all cylinders with growth of 6% to 7% annually. Stock market returns over the past three years have followed suit: 47% in Zambia, 67% in Mauritius, 155% in Malawi."[8]

Horne believes that the investment opportunities in Africa are akin to those in Latin America in the '80s. "Because there is not yet a lot of external capital there, there are very nice opportunities."[9]

After its GDP growth fell from 6 percent a year to only 2 percent, as the recession of 2007 to 2009 gripped the world, the African economy has bounced back smartly, to a 5.5 percent annual growth rate over the past two years, almost three points higher than in the developed world. Who should be lending to whom?

AFRICAN GDP GROWTH[10]

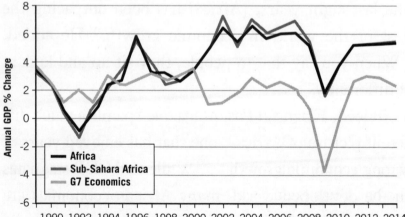

Brady Yauch, writing at probeinternational.org, suggests that economic growth and the amount of foreign aid are at least not connected, and possibly inversely proportional. "Economic figures show that, despite claims by the World Bank and other institutions, that aid is necessary, many poor countries' economies grew as aid funds dropped. In the last 15 years, as the amount of Official Development Assistance (DA) has declined or stagnated to countries in Africa, economic growth has remained positive and outperformed the advanced economies of the G7. And, according to the World Bank itself, the incidence of poverty in sub-Saharan Africa has been steadily decreasing during that time period."[11]

Much of Africa's economic revival has come from higher commodity prices, spurred by increased demand from the newly industrializing countries like China and India. Its inflation is low, its growth rate is impressive, and about half of the continent now lives in countries that hold regular, democratic elections.

George Will reminds us, "The World Bank's initial job was to finance reconstruction in Europe [but] the Marshall Plan rendered that task superfluous." So, the bank has been recast as a vehicle for the economic growth of less-developed nations through direct loans. As Will notes, "The idea was to lend to governments [in less developed nations] that were creditworthy but had no access to rich-country capital markets."[12]

But, as Adam Lerrick, a professor of economics at Carnegie Mellon University, points out, "Now we live in a world where there are huge global capital markets where, if anything, investors are too willing to invest in developing countries."[13]

Africa doesn't get nearly as much direct foreign investment as it could profitably use, and that is why it is still the global center of poverty.

Compare sub-Saharan Africa with Latin America. Sub-Saharan Africa gets only $410 per person in direct foreign investment while Latin America gets $2,145 per person.[14] And, partially as a result, sub-Saharan Africa has a poverty rate of 51 percent, while Latin America's is only 8 percent.[15]

COMPARISON OF SUB-SAHARAN AFRICA AND LATIN AMERICA[16]

Foreign Direct Investment		Population	Per Capita Investment	Poverty %
Africa	$ 313B[17]	763.M	$ 410	51%
Latin America	$1,180B[18]	550.M	$2,145	8%

LATIN AMERICA FOREIGN DIRECT INVESTMENT[19]

Brazil	$ 349 billion
Mexico	328
Chile	136
Argentina	87
Colombia	85
Peru	43
Venezuela	38
Dominican Republic	19
Panama	15
Costa Rica	14
Ecuador	12
Jamaica	9
Bahamas	8
El Salvador	8
Guatemala	7
Bolivia	5
Uruguay	5
Honduras	4
Nicaragua	3
Paraguay	2
Antigua	2
Guyana	1
Total:	$ 1,180 billion

SUB-SAHARAN AFRICAN DIRECT FOREIGN INVESTMENT[20]

Angola	$ 92 billion
South Africa	83
Nigeria	67
Equatorial Guinea	11
Tanzania	6
Ivory Coast	6
Zambia	5
Chad	5
Congo	4
Cameroon	4
Ghana	4
Ethiopia	4
Namibia	4
Mozambique	3
Uganda	3
Liberia	2
Mauritania	2
Madagascar	2
Congo (formerly Zaire)	2
Zimbabwe	1
Mali	1
Botswana	1
Mauritius	1
Total:	$313 billion

When you compare the direct foreign investment in the nations in each area, Latin America's advantage becomes obvious.

Africa's poverty is persistent because of a lack of investment, not a shortage of charity.

The basic question is: How can countries escape from poverty? The left's answer is always more foreign aid, World Bank lending, and humanitarian relief. However, the evidence is that the only effective strategy for alleviating poverty is though economic growth, and, in particular, through foreign investment and trade.

In fact, the World Bank has seen a recent sharp drop in its lending even as direct foreign investment in poor countries is rising. In 2010, the bank made $26.7 billion in new loan commitments, compared with $44.2 billion in 2009,[21] putting in stark relief the key question: Do we need it?

Which brings us back to the question George Will has asked: Is lending the best way for the World Bank to help? To help answer his own question, he quotes Nancy Birdsall, a former World Banker who runs a Washington think tank called the Center for Global Development. She says that "lending and grantmaking at the country level should not be the end-all and be-all" for the bank. Instead, she argues that the bank "should be the vehicle for advice and constant rebuilding of the bank's knowledge."[22] Among other things, Birdsall recommends a reduction in the bank's staff of ten thousand!

Some say that foreign aid is not only not helping, but is actually hurting the chances poor countries have to climb out of poverty.

Dambisa Moyo, author of the incredibly important book *Dead Aid: Why Aid Is Not Working and How There Is a Better Way for Africa*, says that "aid means governments don't have to rely on their citizens for public revenues, making them unaccountable spendthrifts." She says, "Western donor countries should phase out state-to-state aid money."[23]

Moyo says that aid and loans replace real economic growth. The strategies for maximizing aid replace those for increasing economic growth. She says that "in Africa particularly, if foreign aid slows, then government leaders will be forced to pursue programs and initiatives that foster economic growth and stability. They will have to establish domestic tax regimes and in the process, account to their people."[24] Being head of an African country will no longer just be a license to live high off World Bank loans and American foreign aid.

Moyo, an African woman from Zambia who studied at Harvard, earned a doctorate in economics at Oxford, and worked at the World Bank, poses the challenging question: "Has more than \$1 trillion in development aid to Africa over the last several decades made the African people better off?"

Her answer is a resounding "No. In fact," she says, "across the globe the recipients of this aid are worse off; much worse off. Aid has helped make the poor poorer and growth slower . . . The notion that aid can alleviate systemic poverty and has done so is a myth. Millions in Africa are poorer because of aid. Aid has been, and continues to be, an unmitigated political, economic, and humanitarian disaster for most parts of the developing world."[25]

In fact, there is a direct correlation between foreign aid and a *lack* of economic growth! Moyo points out that "the most aid-dependent countries have exhibited an average annual growth rate of *minus* 0.2 percent. Between 1970 and 1998, when aid flows to Africa were at their peak, the poverty rate actually rose from 11 percent to a staggering 66 percent."[26]

Moyo's case is, essentially, that putting such massive funding at the disposal of African governments is just an invitation to corruption. She argues, "The receipt of concessional (nonemergency) loans and grants has much the same effect in Africa as the possession of a valuable natural resource: it's a kind of curse because it encourages corruption and conflict, while at the same time discouraging free enterprise."[27]

In the West, we are used to relatively minor public corruption. Once in a while, some mayor or governor is brought away in handcuffs or caught on a wiretap trying to sell appointments to public office. Massive campaign contributions by special interests buy favorable votes on legislation. But, relative to the size of our economy, corruption is a minor problem. In Africa, it is the single biggest problem, the largest diversion of resources from the needs of the people.

For example, Zaire's President Mobutu Sese Seko "is estimated to have stolen a sum equivalent to the entire external debt of his country: $5 billion."[28]

Nigerian President Sani Abacha was also alleged to have stolen about $5 billion from his country and deposited it in his Swiss bank accounts. After an international stink, $700 million of the stolen money was returned to Nigeria.[29]

In Uganda in the 1990s, corruption was so extensive that only 20 percent of the aid intended for education ever reached its destination.[30]

Zambia's current president, Levy Mwanawasa, says that his predecessor Frederick Chiluba, who served from 1991 to 2002, stole $80 million from his impoverished nation.[31]

In the midst of a famine that imperiled the lives of thousands of people in Malawi, grain consignments, sent as foreign aid, went missing and, coincidentally, a top Malawian official at the state-run grain marketing board who was to testify in two corruption cases mysteriously disappeared.[32]

In 2006, BBC News wrote that $1.5 billion was transferred out of Kenya by the family and associates of former Kenyan leader Daniel arap Moi.[33]

Moyo argues that "the provision of loans and grants on relatively easy terms encourages this kind of [corruption] as surely as the existence of copious oil reserves or diamond mines. Not only is aid easy to steal, as it is usually provided directly to African governments, but it also makes control over government worth fighting for. And, most importantly, the influx of aid can undermine domestic savings and investment."[34]

It is worth probing the case Moyo makes against foreign aid and World Bank lending in more detail.

She says it encourages civil war, a plague that has left Africa bleeding and suffering. Forty million Africans have died in civil wars in the past fifty years. Moyo explains: "In a cash-strapped/resource poor environment, the presence of aid, in whatever form, increases the size of the pie that different factions can fight over."[35] The more money there is in the pot, the more control over it is worth fighting for.

She argues that loans and grants siphon off talented people into a national scramble to get their hands on the money. Men and women who might otherwise create new businesses and jobs are instead lured into the hunt for aid, an irresistible prize that lures them away from productive employment in the private sector. She says World Bank loans and foreign aid weakens countries by "removing pressures to reform inefficient policies and institutions."[36]

Corruption is not just a violation of our civic sense of right and wrong. It is a major factor, some say the single most important factor, in inhibiting economic growth.

Since 1995, Transparency International has published a Corruption Perceptions Index, using surveys of businesspeople to assess the integrity of the nations in which they work. International economist Graf Lambsdorff found that a one-point improvement (on a scale of one to ten) in a country's corruption score was correlated with an increase of productivity of 4 percent of GDP.[37]

Another economist, Joel Kurtzman, found that for each one-point drop in transparency, there was a $1,000 decrease in personal income.[38]

So, the World Bank loans and grants, by fostering corruption, actually undo the economic growth they are meant to ignite, spreading the poverty they are designed to vanquish.

With all this evidence, why is the international community so focused on loans and grants to Africa and other undeveloped countries?

The foreign aid establishment employs hundreds of thousands of people, not in Africa, but in the developed nations that make the grants and loans. The World Bank employs ten thousand. The IMF five thousand. Moyo estimates that other UN agencies focused on aid issues employ another five thousand and registered NGOs (nongovernmental organizations) have another twenty-five thousand people working on aid. In all, she says there are "around 500,000 people [working on aid]. Sometimes they make loans, sometimes they give grants, but they are all in the business of aid."[39]

The left claims that, if economic development is left to the private sector, the economic inequalities in the poor countries will just be exacerbated. Critical of China and India for their income inequality amid economic development, they worry that the same story will repeat itself in other impoverished regions of the world.

Would that it did! The economic successes of China, India, and a host of other Asian countries (and, increasingly, Brazil) are truly inspiring, and they have offered a way out of poverty for almost one billion people.

From 1981 through 2005, the percentage of China's vast population living in poverty has fallen from 81 percent to 16 percent.[40] In India, 40 million people join the middle class every year. Marvin J. Cetron, founder of Forecasting International, writes than an estimated 300 million Indians now live middle-class lives, one-third of whom have emerged from poverty in the past decade. At the current rate of growth, he estimates that a majority of India's population will be middle class by 2015.[41]

While economic growth reduces poverty, it clearly accentuates income inequality, so the left doesn't like it. Sometimes our liberal friends seem to want everyone to be equally poor!

Instead of aid and grants, Moyo proposes four vehicles to replace foreign aid and World Bank loans to governments:

- She urges poor countries to "access the international bond markets and take advantage of the falling yields paid by sovereign borrowers."[42] African bonds are practically a safe investment next to the sovereign debts of countries like

Greece, Italy, Spain, and Portugal (in some cases their former colonial masters).

- The African governments should promote "large-scale direct investment in infrastructure,"[43] as China has done.

- Africa should "press for genuine free trade in agricultural products, which means that the United States, the European Union, and Japan must scrap the various subsidies they pay to their farmers, enabling African countries to increase their earnings from primary product exports."[44]

- "They should encourage financial intermediation. Specifically, they need to foster the spread of microfinance institutions of the sort that have flourished in Asia and Latin America. They should also follow the Peruvian economist Hernando de Soto's advice and grant the inhabitants of shanty towns secure legal title to their homes so that these can be used as collateral. And they should make it cheaper to send remittances back home."[45]

Moyo bids us remember that thirty years ago Malawi, Burundi, and Burkina Faso (all African nations) had per capita incomes greater than China. "Foreign direct investment and rapidly growing exports, not aid, have been the key to China's economic miracle. Africa needs to learn from Asia."[46]

If corruption were a central obstacle to economic development, it would seem that the World Bank would focus its efforts on reducing it in underdeveloped countries. Instead, however, the record of corruption at the World Bank itself and in its lending programs indicates that, quite to the contrary, it is helping to spread this epidemic.

President George W. Bush raised international hackles when to reform the bank he appointed former deputy secretary of defense Paul Wolfowitz to be the World Bank president. (By custom, since the IMF and the World Bank were founded in 1944 at an international conference in Bretton Woods, New Hampshire, the head of the former body is European while the leader of the bank is appointed by the American president.)

Bush appointed Wolfowitz in 2005, at about the same time he named John Bolton US ambassador to the United Nations. Together, these appointments signaled a desire to get tough with Third World corruption and to overhaul the global system of diplomacy and aid.

If all hell broke loose when Bush appointed the assertive and outspoken Bolton, the global community really had a fit when he nominated Wolfowitz.

Wolfowitz had achieved fame among domestic conservatives and notoriety on the left by his strong advocacy of the Iraq War and support for toppling Saddam Hussein. A so-called neoconservative, Wolfowitz worked closely with Vice President Dick Cheney and Defense Secretary Don Rumsfeld on prosecuting the war and its aftermath.

At the World Bank, his tenure was just as stormy. He introduced a novel idea into bank circles: There should be no corruption in meting out bank loans and in how the recipients spend the money. His crusading style uncovered dozens of instances of chicanery at both ends of the lending cycle, prompting a housecleaning at the bank and a cutoff of lending to nations like Cambodia, the Republic of Congo, India, Kenya, and others, all on the grounds of corruption.

He so rattled the culture of the World Bank that he earned the animus of its long-term staff. They accused him of arrogance, excessive travel, headline hunting, failure to consult the board, and disregarding input from the staff.

All the criticisms had some merit, but they were not the reason Wolfowitz came under fire. It was his crusade against corruption that they feared. The liberals at the World Bank, already hostile to Wolfowitz for his support of the Iraq War, came to feel personally and institutionally threatened by his emphasis on cleaning house.

Wolfowitz gave them an opportunity to strike back when he had an affair with Shaha Riza, a bank employee whom the late Christopher Hitchens praised for her efforts to support "civil-society activists in the Palestinian territories, in Iran, in the Gulf, and elsewhere."[47]

Wolfowitz disclosed the relationship to the bank's ethics committee and, according to George Will, "The in-house ethicists told him she should be moved to another agency and given a raise for her troubles."[48] Wolfowitz got her a job at the US State Department with a pay raise of $47,000, an amount he computed based on what her pay would have been had she stayed with the bank. His critics jumped on the story and used it to force him out as bank president.

To replace Wolfowitz, Bush named Robert Zoellick, whom he had previously appointed as US trade representative. Zoellick has been a disappointment, making sure he doesn't ruffle the feathers of the bank bureaucracy, mindful of what happened to Wolfowitz when he did.

Why was Wolfowitz forced out? The *Wall Street Journal* harbors dark suspicions: "Mr. Wolfowitz was removed from the bank in a bureaucrats' coup via a made-up scandal, the real purpose of which was to undermine an anti-corruption agenda that threatened the bank's zero-accountability, self-dealing culture."[49]

When Suzanne Rich Folsom, Wolfowitz's deputy at the bank in charge of the anticorruption unit, resigned six months after Zoellick took over, alarm bells went off. The ever-vigilant *Wall Street Journal* had warned previously that the same long knives that got Wolfowitz would be out after Folsom. Months before she quit, the *Journal* wrote that "sources inside and outside the [World] Bank tell us that a follow-up to the putsch against Mr. Wolfowitz is being engineered by Managing Director Graeme Wheeler and Staff Association Chair Alison Cave against Suzanne Rich Folsom."[50]

The *Journal* gave voice to suspicions that Folsom was being forced out as a result of an investigation of an Indian health project where she found bid-rigging and bribery. Her investigation led Wolfowitz to cancel all World Bank loans to India in 2005 "despite fierce protests from the project's managers." The *Journal* noted that Wheeler "has been lobbying the bank's executive directors to place Ms. Folsom on administrative leave" and to "radically" diminish her responsibilities.[51] Her apparent crime was to expose corruption in the $570 million loan program to India.

The scandal concerned the procurement of medicines as part of the World Bank's Reproductive and Child Health I project (RCH 1). The program was dispensing drugs that were substandard and syringes that failed to meet international standards. Charming.

Folsom's Institutional Integrity unit found that "RCH 1 was subject to systematic fraud and corruption through i) bribery of the Procurement Support Agencies and government officials; ii) falsification of performance certificates; iii) collusion among bidders; and iv) coercion of companies by cartel members and PSA officials." Folsom said that "multiple witnesses admitted to bribing government officials, including ministers, in an effort to secure the award of Bank-funded contracts." The anticorruption unit said the fraud led to "substantial losses" into the tens of millions or more. And it called into question the integrity of the entire $2 billion program of loans to India.[52]

Things got so bad at the bank that Praful Patel, its vice president for the South Asia region, who had run the loan program to India, retired in advance of the mandatory retirement age of sixty-two. The *Wall Street Journal* editorialized that "Zoellick would have sent a stronger signal that such performance won't be tolerated had he fired Mr. Patel rather than allowing him to slink out the back door." But, the *Journal* noted ruefully that "at the World Bank, the main deeds that are punished are good ones."[53]

One of the most graphic illustrations of the bank's refusal to take corruption seriously came when it released a report on April 21, 2008, that uncovered "sufficient evidence to substantiate allegations of fraud, corruption, and disallowed expenses" in the $100 million loan program to the Democratic Republic of Congo. That disclosure did not stop the bank from lending Congo more money! The *Wall Street Journal* reported that "the very next day, April 22, the bank announced that it had approved an additional $50 million grant" for the same program in the Congo![54]

The *Wall Street Journal* complains, in its editorials, of a "shove-the-money-out-the-door mentality"[55] at the bank where grants and loans are made without proper planning or precautions to stop it from being gobbled up by corruption.

Moyo explains: "For most developmental organizations, successful lending is measured almost entirely by the size of the donor's lending portfolio and not by how much of the aid is actually used for its intended purpose."[56] As the end of the fiscal year approaches, money burns a hole in the accounts of those in charge of meting it out. "Any non-distributed amounts increase the likelihood that their subsequent aid programs will be slashed. With the added corollary, of course, that their own organizational standing is placed in jeopardy."[57]

There's another reason money flows so freely out the door of the World Bank—without new lending, the recipient countries might not be able to repay their past loans! Moyo notes that "[t]his circular logic is exactly what keeps the aid merry-go-round humming."[58]

The bank makes loans to everybody, whether they need it or not. The *Wall Street Journal* asks: "Why does the bank continue to lend to China, a country that has foreign-currency reserves in excess of $1 trillion? Why lend to Mexico or Brazil, two countries that can easily obtain credit in the private market?"[59]

The *Journal* points out that the bank's lending is often without regard to whether or not the loan can ever be repaid. They write: "The system by which the bank's executive directors approve loans is also geared to handing out money regardless of the intrinsic merits of the projects it funds. Between 1996 and 2003, fewer than half of the bank's 598 projects in Africa were judged to be 'sustainable'—and that's according to the bank's generous self-assessment. Fewer projects, with better oversight and follow-up, could help turn that depressing record around."[60]

In an editorial, the *Wall Street Journal* railed against the World Bank's "dysfunctional institutional culture— the way it winks at corruption, punishes dissent, and applies rules selectively to protect its hefty salaries and perquisites."[61]

And are they hefty! Counting salary, pension contributions by the bank, and other benefits, Zoellick made $700,000 in 2009.

Here are the total compensation packages of the top World Bank staffers:

COMPENSATION OF WORLD BANK STAFF[62]

Robert B. Zoellick, President	$700,986
Ngozi N. Okonjo-Iweala, Managing Director	$506,471
Graeme Wheeler, Managing Director	$511,517
Vincenzo La Via, CFO	$488,300
Lars Thunell, Exec. VP	$476,500
Juan Jose Daboub, Managing Director	$476,500
Anne-Marie Leroy, Sr. VP and General Counsel	$462,054
Izumi Kobayashi, Exec. VP	$459,818
Marwan Muasher, Sr. VP	$448,152
Vinod Thomas, Director General	$473,196
Yifu Lin, Sr. VP and Chief Economist	$418,188

In addition, executive directors earn $230,000 plus pension and fringe benefits and alternate executive directors make $200,000 plus pension and benefits.[63] The bank is the third largest employer in the Washington, D.C., area! Its total administrative budget is $2.2 billion.[64]

Despite his inability to control corruption at the Bank, Zoellick is free with advice for the rest of the world.

It was Zoellick that got the ball rolling toward expanding the G-7 into a more global body. In October 2008, he called for a "new multilateralism" and urged that the G-7 be expanded to become the G-14, calling for the inclusion of China, Russia, Saudi Arabia, Brazil, India, Mexico, and South Africa. Eventually, when global leaders took him up on his suggestion, six other nations got into the act and the G-20 came to be.

And it was Zoellick, an American, who suggested that the IMF run the new international organization, increasing European power over the world's economy. He said that the G-14 group of nations "instead of becoming merely a . . . new 'steering group' would have a more flexible makeup and coordinate more actively with public and private institutions." Like the IMF. Zoellick said, "the IMF, backed by the steering group, can offer more options, including pegs linked to currency baskets or commodities."[65]

So, the idea for a G-20 group of nations policed and coordinated by the IMF, which, as noted, is leading toward global control by European central bankers, originated from a former neoconservative refugee from the Bush Administration!

Zoellick was even less helpful to the interests of his native land when he suggested that "America's days as an unchallenged economic superpower might be numbered." He said that the "dollar was likely to lose its favored position as the euro and the Chinese renminbi assume bigger roles." He said, "The United States would be mistaken to take for granted the dollar's place as the world's predominant currency. Looking forward, there will increasingly be other options to the dollar."[66]

Other options? Really? Like the euro, which is now teetering on the verge as southern Europe finds that it can't pay its debts? Or the renminbi that Beijing frantically manipulates to keep it undervalued so that they can rip us off by selling us cheaper products and costing us jobs?

Mr. Zoellick, an abject failure at policing his own institution, should keep such helpful comments to himself.

ACTION AGENDA

The United States has vast power over the World Bank. It should use its authority to lead the institution in radically different paths.

The next president must not hesitate to fly right into the teeth of the culture of corruption that permeates the institution. Perhaps a new Paul Wolfowitz can't be found, but the president should look for an aggressive crusader who will battle the bureaucracy to curb its institutional corruption.

But the change must encompass more than just housecleaning. The World Bank needs to replace its culture of philanthropy with one of entrepreneurship. It should operate on the philosophy that trade and investment, not aid, is the key to Third World development. Handouts accomplish nothing but feeding corruption in the developing country.

The world needs a World Bank. But not a supercharity that passes out funds and does nothing to solve the basic problems of poverty in the Third World.

But the failures at the World Bank, both its apparent inability to run its lending without corruption and the failure of these loans to lessen poverty, raises a key question about the utility of the American program of foreign aid.

PART NINE

Foreign Aid: Biting the Hand That Feeds Them

If loans and grants from the World Bank are so useless and even counterproductive, why does the United States give away vast amounts of foreign aid? In fact, why have we increased our foreign aid spending by 48 percent under the Obama administration?[1]

The same question that plagues the World Bank development aid program must also be directed at the United States program: Does the aid do any good?

The United States gave away $58 billion in foreign aid to more than sixty-nine countries in 2009.[2] Thirty-four billion was in economic aid and $11 billion was in military assistance. Add $13 billion in assistance from other government agencies.[3]

How much of a strain does foreign aid put on our financial resources? Apostles of conventional wisdom are quick to point out that $58 billion is a drop in the bucket of $3.7 trillion of total government spending this year. However, strip away spending on entitlements and defense and the true picture emerges. Apart from the military and other budgets, the $34 billion we spend on economic aid through the State Department and the Agency for International Development (AID) represents about 5 percent of our total nondefense discretionary spending, a very hefty commitment of our increasingly limited resources!

Even when we confronted fiscal Armageddon during 2011 with its debt limit brinksmanship, foreign aid survived without cuts. The total we give away this year comes to $5 billion more than we spent last year! (Lawmakers cut $6 billion from State Department and AID funding for foreign assistance but then added $11 billion for war-related aid in Afghanistan and Iraq for a net increase of $5 billion—about the only sector in the US budget that actually rose this fiscal year!)[4]

Especially bewildering is the number of countries that get significant foreign aid from the United States. Obviously, the big recipients are the countries in play in the War on Terror: Afghanistan, Pakistan, Iraq, Israel, and Egypt. But, all told, forty-three countries get more than $100 million a year in aid from us:

COUNTRIES GETTING MORE THAN $100 MILLION IN FOREIGN AID[5]

Afghanistan	$8,700 million
Bangladesh	$ 172
Bolivia	$ 101
Chad	$ 222

Colombia	$ 895 (incl $57 military)
Congo (formerly Zaire)	$ 349 (incl $23 military)
Egypt	$1,800 (incl $1.3 billion military)
El Salvador	$ 156 (incl $11 military)
Ethiopia	$ 940
Georgia	$ 622 (incl $13 military)
Ghana	$ 175
Guatemala	$ 141
Haiti	$ 369
India	$ 133
Indonesia	$ 226
Iraq	$2,300
Israel	$2,400 (almost all military)
Jordan	$ 816 (incl $238 military)
Kenya	$ 918
Kosovo	$ 136
Liberia	$ 225 (incl $52 military)
Malawi	$ 135
Mali	$ 222
Mexico	$ 499 (incl $34 military)
Micronesia	$ 108
Morocco	$ 244
Mozambique	$ 325
Namibia	$ 396
Nigeria	$ 501
Pakistan	$2,500 (incl $1,100 military)
Peru	$ 149
Philippines	$ 185 (incl $30 military)
Russia	$ 479 (incl $83 military)
Rwanda	$ 170
Senegal	$ 144
South Africa	$ 571

Sudan	$1,200(incl $39 military)
Tanzania	$ 377
Uganda	$ 474
Ukraine	$ 167
West Bank/Gaza	$1,039
Zambia	$ 292
Zimbabwe	$ 286

COUNTRIES THAT GET OUR AID DON'T NEED OR DESERVE IT

Why do we give away such massive amounts of aid, especially to our sworn enemies like the Palestinians on the West Bank and in Gaza?

What will the Palestinian Authority and Hamas do with the $1 billion in foreign aid we give them every year? At best, they will use it to deliver services to their people so they can free their other resources to fund terrorist attacks on Israel. At worst, the money will go directly into their terror-sponsoring apparatus.

Who among us can possibly forget the scenes of jubilation on the West Bank and in Gaza that greeted the news of the 9/11 attacks on the United States? The parades? The machine guns fired into the air in hysterical celebration over thousands of dead Americans? One wonders which of us would be happy knowing that it was our tax money, personally, that went to the terrorists of the West Bank and Gaza?

"Excuse me miss.....We understand that the US is giving out foreign aid???"

The State Department says it is using our foreign aid as a lever to modify the Palestinians' conduct and keep them at the negotiating table with Israel. Specifically, they cite the Palestinian Authority's threat to seek admission to the United Nations General Assembly as an observer. If they get this status, it would mean the end of their bilateral negotiations with Israel and, we are threatening, a cutoff of our foreign aid.

All this skirts the more basic question: Why are we giving any foreign aid at all to our sworn enemies on the West Bank and in Gaza? And, if it is to gain leverage, what precisely have we accomplished with all that money? They still fire rockets into Israel and remain committed to its destruction.

Why do we give $12.9 million in foreign aid to China, a nation with more than $1 trillion of foreign currency reserves? And why did the Obama administration request $20 million for Castro's Cuba?[6] Can't these folks stop giving away our money?

Many of our aid recipients are able to access vast oil reserves, prompting one to wonder why they need our money. With Nigeria pumping 2.5 million barrels of oil a day[7] (generating revenues of about $90 billion a year) why do they need a half billion from us? Why does Mexico, with a growing economy and plenty of domestic resources (to say nothing of about $50 billion in oil revenues annually), need a half billion of our money?

In fact, we are giving hundreds of millions in foreign aid to countries that lend us money! The Congressional Research Service reports that in fiscal year 2010, the United States gave a total of $1.4 billion to sixteen foreign counties that held at least $10 billion each in Treasury securities. The list includes China, Brazil, Russia, India, Mexico, and Egypt. (China holds $1.1 trillion of our bonds. Brazil has $194 billion. Russia holds $128 billion. India owns $40 billion, Mexico $28 billion, and Egypt $15 billion in Treasury debt.)[8]

Senator Tom Coburn (R-OK) makes the key point: "If countries can afford to buy our debt, perhaps they can afford to fund assistance programs on their own. At the same time, when we borrow from countries we are supposedly helping to develop, we put off hard budget choices here at home." Coburn adds that the situation "creates co-dependency and financial risk at home and abroad."[9]

Giving foreign aid to countries we ask to lend us money reminds us of the famous O. Henry story "Two Thanksgiving Day Gentlemen," in which a rich man invites a beggar to his home for Thanksgiving dinner every year. After several decades, the beggar, inspired by the rich man's example, works his way up and becomes quite wealthy himself. At the same time, the rich man is impoverished by the stock market crash. But each changes into his appropriate costume every year—rags for the former beggar and an expensive suit for his once-wealthy patron to reenact the Thanksgiving Day ritual, neither admitting to the change in his status to the other! Then, the sad Thanksgiving comes when each man enters the hospital after the dinner—the formerly rich man due to starvation because he spent his limited funds buying food for his formerly poor friend, and the once poor man for overeating in order to satisfy the desires of his buddy.[10]

The United States is, by far, the main provider of foreign aid in the world. The almost $60 billion we gave away last year is far ahead of France, which was in second place at $13 billion, Germany at $12 billion, the United Kingdom at $12 billion, and Japan at $10 billion.[11]

Even so, the United States comes in for a bath of criticism from the global community for not giving enough! The liberals of the world have adopted a standard that would require each country to give seven-tenths of 1 percent of its GDP annually in foreign economic assistance. Even at our high current levels of foreign aid spending, the United States falls way short of this standard, giving only four-tenths of 1 percent of our GDP in aid. Don't feel bad: The only countries to reach this standard of purity are Sweden, Norway, Luxembourg, Denmark, and the Netherlands.[12]

THE UNITED STATES LEADS THE GLOBAL FIGHT AGAINST POVERTY BY LETTING IN IMPORTS

But when it comes to trade, not aid, the United States is still the engine whose consumer spending is pulling the world out of poverty. In 2010, the United States imported $2 trillion in goods from the rest of the world, about one-sixth of the total of $12 trillion in global imports. We may spend less than one-half of 1 percent of our economy on aid to other countries, but we spend 15 percent of our personal income buying their products—a much surer way to eradicate their poverty, and, at least in the case of our massive trade deficit with China, to make ourselves poor in the process.

Far more significant than the foreign aid budget was the law Congress passed in the last year of the Clinton administration allowing African textiles into the United States without import duties or quotas. The result has been an explosion in textile imports from sub-Saharan African, which has done far more to reduce poverty than all the foreign aid we could ever send.

In 2010, the United States imported $66.3 billion from sub-Saharan African (not counting oil) under the African Growth and Opportunity Act, up from $50 billion in 2007.[13]

Think about what that $66 billion of sales to the United States means to those countries! The GDP of sub-Saharan Africa was $1.1 trillion in 2010.[14] Thus, our purchases of their textile exports accounted for almost 7 percent of their total GDP, which is a huge leg up in the battle to emerge from poverty. This vast increase in American imports from Africa, far more than the relatively minor amounts of aid or lending, is the key reason poverty has dropped in Africa from 66 percent in 1998 to 50 percent in 2009.

Trade, not aid, is the key to African development.

FOREIGN AID DOESN'T HELP

Well-meaning idealists still press for more and more foreign aid. Without considering the dismal track record of almost $1 trillion in global aid since World War II, they see these outlays as critical to the global fight against poverty. They love to quote John F. Kennedy's eloquent justification of these outlays in his 1961 inaugural address:

> To those peoples in the huts and villages of half the globe struggling to break the bonds of mass misery, we pledge our best efforts to help them help themselves, for whatever period is required—not because the Communists may be doing it, not because we seek their votes, but because it is right. If a free society cannot help the many who are poor, it cannot save the few who are rich.[15]

But, for all these soaring words, the fact remains that there is no correlation between the massive outlays of foreign aid we have been making for decades now and any reduction in global poverty. The countries that have made real progress in breaking out of poverty—China, India, Vietnam, Malaysia, South Korea, Taiwan, and Singapore—have done it by selling us goods and services, not by raking in our foreign aid.

Those nations who have been getting massive infusions of aid all along, like Kenya, South Africa, Haiti, Nigeria, and Ethiopia, have almost nothing to show for it in economic growth or in any decline in poverty. Indeed, the observations of Dambisa Moyo, author of *Dead Aid: Why Aid Is Not Working and There Is a Better Way for Africa*, which are recounted in the previous chapter, suggest that direct aid has a negative effect and actually encourages poverty and societal dysfunction.

US foreign aid has not proven to be an effective way to reduce poverty. Since 1980, the United States has given more than $503 billion (in inflation-adjusted money) in development assistance to poor countries. (This sum does not include military aid or humanitarian relief for natural disasters). And it hasn't done much good.

Of the ninety-seven countries that got development aid from the United States between 1980 and 2009:

- Twenty-three had a net decline in per capita GDP over the period.

- Twenty-seven had only growth of less than 1 percent.

- Forty-four had growth of an average of 1 to 4 percent per year.

- Only four had real economic growth of 5 percent or more. They were Bosnia, Serbia, Cambodia, and Botswana.

The Heritage Foundation reports that for a poor country to reach lower-middle-income status, it must have a growth rate of 5 percent for over twenty-five years, a standard that ninety-four of our ninety-eight aid recipients have failed to reach. But our solution is just to pour in more foreign aid!

If anything, US development assistance is more prone to being used to subsidize Third World corruption than are the funds of the World Bank. Much of the World Bank spending at least goes to specific projects, even though they are often rife with corruption. Most US direct aid goes government-to-government, where there is a virtual certainty that it will go into some dictator's Swiss bank account.

According to one estimate, nearly half of the money Africa gets in foreign aid leaves the continent every year. A lot of it winds up in the bank accounts of African dictators and generals.

In fact, most of our foreign aid goes to very corrupt governments. Transparency International measures perceived corruption in each country in the world and rates them on a scale of one (the most corrupt) to ten (the most honest).

Of the forty-one nations (excluding Israel and the West Bank/Gaza) that get more than $100 million in annual US foreign aid, 58 percent goes to countries that rank among the bottom thirty in the world in honesty according to their Transparency International Corruption Perceptions Index, which lists 184 nations. Here are the ten nations, where corruption is perceived to flourish, that got a combined $16 billion a year in foreign aid in 2009:

THE DIRTY TEN

Transparency	Ranking	Foreign Aid
Afghanistan	180.	$8,700 million
Sudan	177.	$1,200 million
Iraq	175.	$2,300 million
Haiti	175.	$369 million
Chad	168.	$222 million
Kenya	154.	$918 million
Congo (formerly Zaire)	154.	$349 million
Zimbabwe	154.	$286 million
Pakistan	134.	$1,800 million
Ukraine	152.	$167 million

To give these countries money is to throw it away. Their governments are too corrupt to put it to any good use and there is no point in subsidizing them. They make a mockery of our self-righteousness in dispensing aid. We speak of helping the people who "live in the huts and villages across the globe" and their leaders laugh like hell as they pocket our millions.

So, why do we do it?

DO WE BUY INFLUENCE WITH OUR FOREIGN AID? NOT REALLY

The fact is that our foreign aid budget is not about fighting poverty but about winning friends for the United States. Despite JFK's statement that we do not give countries aid because "we seek their votes," getting their support for our foreign policy objectives is a key motivation for our generosity. Foreign aid is often more about diplomacy than economics.

Certainly the massive amounts we give Israel ($26 billion from 1999 to 2006) and Egypt ($16.7 billion over the same period) is to honor President Jimmy Carter's commitments to them at the Camp David summit. Carter essentially bought peace between Egypt and Israel by promising massive, ongoing foreign aid to both nations. And Uncle Sam has kept that promise. Does it make any sense to continue to give Egypt $1.8 billion in aid every year? With its government arresting American citizens who came there to promote democracy, that's a good question. As Egypt moves to repudiate its peace agreement with Israel—impelled by its Muslim Brotherhood parliamentary majority—we should cut off the aid that was attached to the agreement. Egypt is becoming our enemy and we should not be showering it with aid.

We aid Afghanistan and Pakistan because of our efforts to keep al-Qaeda and the Taliban at bay, and pump billions into Iraq to quell the insurgency that erupted when we overthrew Saddam Hussein.

We give Ukraine $167 million and Georgia $622 million to help them live independently of Russia, particularly after the Russian invasion of Georgia.

Some of our foreign aid is related to our efforts to stop the cultivation, processing, and importation into the United States of narcotics and other drugs such as the $895 million a year we give to Colombia and the $101 million to Bolivia.

There is no strategic purpose in our massive aid to most of the Third World countries that receive it. We have no pressing strategic needs in Kenya ($918 million a year), Congo ($349 million), Mozambique ($325 million), Namibia ($396 million), Nigeria ($501 million), South Africa ($571 million), Tanzania ($377 million),

Uganda ($474 million), Zambia ($292 million), or Zimbabwe ($280 million). So, if our aid isn't effective in fighting poverty, does it buy us influence?

The best way to tell is to track how countries that get our aid vote in the United Nations. The Heritage Foundation has tallied the data, focusing on non-consensus votes in the General Assembly body from 1999 to 2006.

The results are a disaster!

According to the Heritage Foundation, 95 percent of our aid recipients (including all but two of the thirty largest) voted against us in the United Nations a majority of the time.[16]

Worse, of the top thirty aid recipients nineteen voted against our position 75 percent of the time or more![17]

They bite the hand that feeds them.

The following chart, from the Heritage Foundation, shows the total amount of aid each country has gotten from the US taxpayer from 1999–2006 and the percentage of the time they voted with us in the UN.[18]

Total Aid (1999–2006)		% Support US
Iraq	$ 31,000M	8% (under Saddam)
Israel	$ 26,000	91%
Egypt	$ 16,700	13%
Afghanistan	$ 10,700	11%

Russia	$ 8,400	26%
Colombia	$ 6,400	19%
Jordan	$ 5,400	14%
Pakistan	$ 4,400	14%
Sudan	$ 3,100	14%
Ethiopia	$ 3,100	19%
Indonesia	$ 2,400	17%
Serbia	$ 2,200	43%
Peru	$ 2,200	27%
India	$ 1,800	19%
Bolivia	$ 1,700	23%
Philippines	$ 2,000	20%
Georgia	$ 1,500	45%
Kenya	$ 1,500	19%
Ukraine	$ 1,400	38%
Haiti	$ 1,100	20%
Armenia	$ 1,100	26%
Bosnia	$ 1,100	51%
Mozambique	$ 1,000	17%
Bangladesh	$ 1,000	18%
Nigeria	$ 1,000	20%
South Africa	$ 1,000	18%
Uzbekistan	$ 900	31%
North Korea	$ 900	6%
Honduras	$ 900	28%

So, foreign aid doesn't help the poor, it feeds corruption, and it does not induce political loyalty in its recipients. It does nothing to promote integrity and may actually retard the process of development.

THE COUNTRIES THAT GET OUR AID HATE US

Does the billions we give in foreign aid at least make us friends in other countries? Does it at least generate friendly vibes in those who depend on it? Not on your life.

The House Foreign Affairs Committee reports that American popularity has fallen off a cliff despite our billions in aid.

In 2006, people in twenty of the twenty-six countries polled felt more negatively than positively about the United States. These dismal ratings were a sharp drop from only four years before. In 2002, the people in thirty-five of the forty-two countries polled by the Pew Research Center gave the United States a higher favorable than unfavorable rating.[19]

Certainly, our massive aid to Egypt has done nothing to buy us good will there. An August 2011 survey by polling organization Zogby International found that the United States had a 5 percent favorability rating among the Egyptian public, lower than it had during the Bush 43 presidency.[20]

Nor has our extensive aid to Jordan, arguably the most pro-American Arab country, done anything for our popularity there. Despite annual aid of almost $1 billion, Zogby found that only 15 percent of Jordanians had favorable opinions of the United States, down from 35 percent in 2002.[21]

In Indonesia, America's popularity dropped 45 points between 1999 and 2006, despite our gift of $226 million in annual aid. In Morocco we fell 51 points despite $244 million in aid.[22]

Latin Americans have a negative view of the American government (33 percent favorable and 45 percent unfavorable), despite more than $2 billion in annual foreign aid.[23]

Dr. Steven Kull, director of the Program on International Policy Attitudes at the University of Maryland, says it's the worst he's ever seen. "There has really been no time for which we have data that shows the broad level of dissatisfaction with US foreign policy that we find today. This is definitely unique. We have never seen numbers this low."[24]

Dr. Andrew Kohut, president of the Pew Research Center, adds that "certainly over this 25-year period, this is a low point [in US favorability ratings]."[25]

Many people had hoped that with Barack Obama's election, America's image would improve throughout the world. President Obama has focused especially on changing the perception of the United States in the Islamic world. In his seminal speech in Cairo early in his term, Obama tried to debunk the idea that the United States was at war with Islam and, throughout his term, he has done all he could to assuage Islamic sensibilities. No longer does the White House use the word *Islamic* in describing terrorists and it often goes out of its way to even avoid speaking of the War on Terror.

Data shows that his efforts haven't helped at all. America's ratings in Arab countries have been in free fall during his presidency. Even his identification with the Arab spring revolutions in Egypt, Libya, Tunisia, Yemen, and other Islamic countries has done nothing to improve the negative perceptions of the United States. Obama's public-relations offensive in the Arab world must be rated a dismal failure.

What about foreign aid? Even the 50 percent increase in foreign development assistance that Obama passed has done nothing to improve America's image abroad. The same nations that take the most of our aid hate us the most.

Notably, in the thirty-one-page report of the House Foreign Affairs Committee, which examined every aspect of America's image abroad, including foreign policy, ratings of our leaders, and the perception of our unilateralism, does not mention foreign aid. It didn't even occur to the authors of the study that the distribution of over $50 billion a year to other countries should have any impact at all on their opinions of us! It is just their entitlement!

Dr. Tawfik Hamid, the author of *Inside Jihad: Understanding and Confronting Radical Islam*, has some interesting ideas on how to use foreign assistance to improve American popularity.

Hamid notes that "[d]espite the billions of dollars that the United States has spent in aid to many Muslim countries, its image in many of these countries continues to be profoundly negative. The 'winning hearts and minds' strategy simply is not working."[26]

He reminds us that most media in the corrupt dictatorships that get the bulk of our aid are controlled by the government. Why not require that the government receiving our aid publicize our work through their media? He adds that such an effort might also curtail radical Muslim propaganda over the airwaves.

He also recommends that we spend money on specific infrastructure programs that can be linked in the popular mind with the American aid that paid for them.

For example, he writes that "Japan and France create highly visible projects that significantly help improve their image . . . When you visit Cairo, people on the street refer to 'the French and Japanese hospitals' yet you cannot find an equivalent prominent American hospital that people refer to. The visibility of such projects is an important factor in improving the image of any country."[27]

ACTION AGENDA

There is an alternative to foreign aid: overseas investment. The Overseas Private Investment Corporation (OPIC, as distinct from OPEC!) is a US government agency that promotes private investment in other countries to help them develop and encourage them to buy American products and services, creating jobs in the United States as well.

OPIC is the junior partner to the Agency for International Development (AID). OPIC made $2.3 billion in new commitments in 2010,[28] a pittance compared to the massive foreign aid spending.

But OPIC commitments are a vast improvement over foreign aid. First, they don't cost taxpayers anything! OPIC finances its operation by charging market rates for its services and capital. It can provide direct financing, consulting services, or insure loans against political risk.

Its operations have been markedly successful. OPIC has generated $74 billion in US exports and claims to support 274,000 American jobs in the process.[29]

OPIC is, by anyone's definition, a win-win agency. It provides capital for needed projects in the developing world and investment and export opportunities for American firms, particularly for small businesses. As OPIC put it in its 2010 annual report: "For US small businesses that want to compete in emerging markets overseas . . . OPIC removes obstacles and opens opportunities by offering eligible small businesses affordable project financing and political risk insurance not available in the private markets."[30] Their projects are diverse and a lot less prone to corruption than government-to-government grants in aid. Here are some examples of OPIC's good work:

- OPIC financed a solar photovoltaic plant in Punjab state, India, that provides power to 4,000 rural homes by providing capital from California-based US investors.

- Boston-based investors are providing mortgage loans for homes in Ghana. Their operation is one of only two mortgage financing sources in the country. So far, they have written 545 mortgages worth more than $26 million.

- In Tbilisi, Georgia, $10 million in OPIC financing will help an American company to build four residential apartment buildings with 328 units.[31]

Small potatoes? Surely. But an attractive alternative to giving corrupt dictators billions to pocket or squirrel away in Switzerland. And it operates at no cost to the taxpayer.

Fundamentally, we need to get away from the very idea that handouts are the way to reduce poverty. We need to realize that catalyzing capitalism is the way to do it effectively. OPIC and the US program of encouraging imports from Africa are both good examples of how to use government to promote real development and growth in emerging markets.

But the lesson of China, India, Malaysia, South Korea, Singapore, Taiwan, and, increasingly of Vietnam, Thailand, and Bangladesh is that to reduce poverty, government basically needs to get out of the way and let private capital do its job. While our foreign aid establishment, with its hundreds of thousands of bureaucrats and tens of billions in funding, labors away like a superfoundation, giving away money with little purpose, private investors are turning around poverty-stricken countries throughout Africa and the rest of the Third World.

Their work may not look much like Mother Teresa's efforts in Calcutta, but it is doing the job in a way that philanthropy would never be able to match.

PART TEN

In Our Backyard: The Chavez-Ahmadinejad Alliance

The Cold War reached its apogee in 1962, when the Soviet Union tried to put missiles in Cuba, a move that would have brought all major American cities within range of their nuclear weapons. The United States and the Soviets dueled at the brink of a global nuclear war, coming closer to the total destruction of life on this planet than we have ever been. Is history repeating itself as Iran develops nuclear weapons and seems to be interested in basing them, along with their ballistic missiles, in Hugo Chavez's Venezuela? As Karl Marx once said, "History repeats itself, first as tragedy, second as farce."[1]

History may be about to repeat itself, but whether it will be as tragedy or farce, we don't yet know.

In a maneuver to get around America's flank, Iranian dictator Mahmoud Ahmadinejad and Venezuelan strongman Hugo Chavez have formed an alliance with annoying, but possibly very dangerous, implications for the United States. We are accustomed to regarding the rantings and ravings of the likes of Castro and Chavez with detachment and, sometimes, even amusement.

But when uranium, missiles, drones, nuclear weapons, cocaine, and assassinations are involved, we need to take them much more seriously. As Ahmadinejad said in a 2009 radio broadcast, "When the western countries were trying to isolate Iran, we went to the US backyard."[2]

IRAN AND VENEZUELA: A MARRIAGE MADE IN HELL

Consider the record:

- Iran is selling drones to Chavez. The *Wall Street Journal* reports that "Venezuela purchased 10 Iranian Mojaher 2 drones in a $29 million deal with a company owned by the Revolutionary Guard in 2007 that included training, advisers and an assembly plant, according to documents presented by the Defense Ministry to Venezuela's Congress in March and made public by Venezuela's El Nacional newspaper."[3]

- Iran is developing terrorist bases in Latin America for forays against the United States. A declassified Pentagon analysis on Iran's military power released to the US Congress in April 2010 says

Al Qods, an elite branch of the Iranian military, has had "an increased presence in Latin America, particularly Venezuela."[4]

- Iran is pouring money into Latin America to expand its terror operations there. It has earmarked $4.5 billion in is 2011 budget, according to New York's *Daily News,* "to strengthen its influence and operations in Latin America." The *News* reports that "Hezbollah's primary base of activity in Latin America is in the remote triborder area of Argentina, Paraguay, and Brazil."[5] The RAND Corporation identifies this as the "most important center for financing Islamic terrorism outside the Middle East."[6] A 2009 RAND report calculated that the terrorists net $20 million annually from illicit activity such as drug trafficking.[7] The *New York Times* described "the direct involvement of high-level Hezbollah officials in the South American drug trade."[8]

- Iranian assassins are operating on US soil from bases in Latin America. Two officers from Al Qods have been indicted for trying to hire a hit man from a Mexican drug cartel to assassinate the Saudi Arabian ambassador to the United

States while he was eating in a Washington restaurant.

- Venezuela did some Christmas shopping for Iran when it tried to help Iran get around the UN arms embargo by selling 18,000 Iranian HK2002 automatic rifles to the Uruguayan armed forces in 2007. The scam was discovered by an opposition congressman in Uruguay, and a Uruguayan navy ship, poised to load the weapons, had to return empty.[9]

- The *Journal* reports that "various European newspaper reports this year said Iran was planning to base medium range Shahab 3 missiles in Venezuela and that Mr. Chávez had leased military facilities to Tehran."[10]

- Israel's ex-foreign minister Danny Ayalon accused Venezuela and Bolivia (which Chavez controls) "of supplying uranium to Iran, which lacks domestic sources of the radioactive mineral needed to make nuclear power and which Bolivia has in large quantities. Bolivia has 16 major uranium deposits, according to international mining surveys, including one conducted in 2006 by the Canadian company Mega Uranium Ltd."[11] In

2010, Iran's mining and industry minister Akbar Mehravani visited Bolivia, presumably to further the deal.

- In 2008, the Bush administration blacklisted branches of Iran's Export Development Bank in Venezuela, charging that "binational funds" managed by the bank were being used to launder money to circumvent UN sanctions against Iran's nuclear program.[12]

- Links have grown stronger between Chavez and Iran-backed Hezbollah. A Lebanese-born Venezuelan diplomat, Ghazi Nasr al Din, was named in a US Treasury Department investigation in 2008 as a "facilitator and fundraiser" for Hezbollah. The *Wall Street Journal* reported that "Mr. Al Din was serving as chargé d'affairs at the Venezuelan Embassy in Damascus and director of political affairs at the embassy in Beirut. . . . The Treasury Department banned him as well as another Venezuelan-based Syrian businessman from conducting business in the US or with US citizens."[13]

- Venezuela and Iran have signed seventy deals worth at least $17 billion of joint ventures in recent years. Ahmadinejad has visited Venezuela four times. The deals focus on "energy, construction, and fisheries, and including a factory to assemble cars and tractors under the brand name 'Veniran,'" according to the *Wall Street Journal.*[14]

To ferry weapons and God knows what else from Iran to Venezuela, the two nations have started regular direct flights between Caracas and Tehran. One current US intelligence officer told the *Daily Beast,* "we worry about these flights because they are not checked at the airports and often times they have no passengers other than the crew. What is in the cargo?"[15]

Cynthia Arnson, the director of the Latin American Program at the Woodrow Wilson Center, said, "Venezuela is the port of entry for Iran in Latin America. Hugo Chavez has rolled out the red carpet and facilitated relations between Iran and other governments in the region."[16]

CHAVEZ'S EMPIRE IN LATIN AMERICA

And Chavez's influence in Latin America is quite far-reaching. His miniempire includes Bolivia, Ecuador, and Nicaragua. He has also spread his tentacles to Peru and Argentina.

In Bolivia, he sponsored the candidacy of Evo Morales, who was elected president in 2006. Using Venezuelan money, Morales won by appealing to the disenfranchised Indians who live in the country's highlands. Since then, Chavez's money has kept him in power and made him highly popular at home. Morales ran pledging to end cooperation with US antidrug cultivation programs, and he has kept his promise. Speaking up for coca growers in Bolivia, Morales has made defying the DEA a centerpiece of his administration.

In nearby Ecuador, Chavez elected Rafael Correra president in 2006. Ecuador has since joined itself at the hip to Chavez, using its oil wealth to subsidize their regimes and, like Morales, win backing from the previously unrepresented Indians in the Ecuadorian highlands.

Chavez also has his hooks into America's old friend Daniel Ortega, the once and now again current president of Nicaragua. You've got to hand it to Ortega. He robbed the country blind and then won back the presidency in a largely free election. When Lincoln said, "You can fool some of the people all the time," he must have had Nicaragua in mind.

Beyond his closely held empire—Venezuela, Bolivia, Ecuador, and Nicaragua—Chavez has increasingly close relations with a host of other Latin American countries. He has bought and paid for a close relationship with Argentina, lending it $2.5 billion in 2005 alone, when the International Monetary Fund cut off the country because it reneged on its debt payments.[17]

Then, Chavez went the extra mile and sent a suitcase containing $800,000 in cash to Christina Kirschner, Argentina's president.[18] The suitcase was intercepted by American customs agents in Miami, but it's the thought that counts.

In Peru, Chavez has sponsored, in the past, the new president, Ollanta Humala. Humala lost the election in 2006, despite strong support from Chavez. In 2011, he seemed to keep his distance from the Venezuelan dictator and, this time, won. How independent he will stay remains to be seen.

Chavez uses his oil wealth to cozy up to Uruguay as well, and he welcomed the recent election of leftist candidate Jose Albert Munica Cordano in 2011.

With close ties to Brazil, Chavez is cooking up his own regional empire, centered around his oil wealth and dedicated to bringing down the United States.

Standing against him, almost alone, is Colombia, which, thanks to massive US military aid, has subdued its Marxist rebels and driven out much of its drug trade. Chavez is always trying to destabilize Colombia and has been caught arming and funding the guerillas during the civil war.

Chavez is making Latin America an anti-American zone right near our shores.

IRANIAN-VENEZUELAN CYBERATTACKS ON THE UNITED STATES?

We have a rare opportunity to see the Iran-Venezuela terrorist network at work through a neat piece of espionage conducted by Juan Carlos Munoz Ledo, an instructor at Mexico's Autonomous National University. Munoz Ledo had been approached by a fellow professor in 2006 as part of a cyberterror plot against the United States, which was being organized out of the Cuban embassy in Mexico City, involving Iranian and Venezuelan operatives. As he pretended to cooperate in the project, Munoz Ledo taped their meetings.

He caught on tape a session in 2007 with Mohamed Hassan Ghadiri, then the Iranian ambassador to Mexico. According to frontpage.com, "They discussed a plot to hack into American computer systems at nuclear power plants, the White House, the CIA, the FBI, the NSA, and other critical sites from Mexico. A 'digital bomb' would be implanted that would be 'worse than the World Trade Center.' The footage of Ghadiri shows his excitement over the plot."[19]

Then Munoz Ledo, with the cameras still rolling, met with Liva Acosta, the cultural attaché of the Venezuelan embassy in Mexico City. "Like Ghadiri she was interested in the cyberplot. She promised to put any information they provide into the hands of Hugo Chavez. She was particularly pleased when the team claimed it could access the computers of nuclear power plants, specifically Florida's Turkey Point and Arkansas' Nuclear One."[20]

Interviewed by the *Daily Beast*, Ledo "said he and other students were asked to attack the mainframes and computers associated with government agencies and major businesses in the United States."[21]

Munoz Ledo's film also "revealed . . . the involvement of Iran and Venezuela" in the failed terrorist attack against New York's JFK Airport in 2007.[22]

The US-based Spanish language network Univision broadcast the film. Good for them!

CHAVEZ VIOLATES UN SANCTIONS AGAINST IRAN

Iran's greatest vulnerability is its need to import more than half the gasoline it uses to power its cars and trucks. Despite the country's vast oil reserves, international sanctions have stopped it from building enough plants to refine the oil to produce fuel.

But Chavez is coming to their rescue! The *Wall Street Journal* reported that "[t]he Venezuelan state-owned oil monopoly, known as PdVSA, has been selling 'reformate'—used to upgrade the quality of gasoline—to Iran in violations of the Comprehensive Iran Sanctions Accountability and Divestment Act (CISADA) of 2010."[23]

Chavez admits to selling Iran 20,000 barrels of gasoline in 2009, but denies selling them any since the 2010 sanctions were imposed. But the US government isn't buying his story. On May 25, 2011, the US imposed sanctions against PdVSA for selling gasoline to Iran.

Blocking gasoline sales to Iran was the key idea behind the new CISADA sanctions. The *Wall Street Journal* reports that "CISADA has been working to discourage businesses and governments from providing [Iran] gasoline or the means of refining it." But evidence indicates that PdVSA "shipped chemicals used in the production of fuel to Iran in December [2010]. One two-page order form, on PdVSA letterhead, shows cargo originating in Bullenbay, Curacao, destined for the port of Fujairah in the United Arab Emirates. The National Iranian Oil Company is the buyer. There is also a bill of lading."[24]

THE IRANIAN THREAT COMES TO OUR BACKYARD

Looming on the horizon, of course, is the fear that if Iran develops a nuclear weapon, as now appears increasingly likely, the nightmare of the Cuban Missile Crisis of 1962 could resurface. Iran's missiles are quite capable of reaching Israel but could not threaten, as yet, the United States. Chavez could provide a base for them that would put their weapons within reach of many major American cities.

We are used to worrying that Iranian missiles, with nuclear warheads, could be used to wipe out Israel, but the ties between Iran and Venezuela threaten to bring their weapons within range of American cities.

Even short of such brinksmanship, Chavez, working with the narcoterrorists, Hezbollah, and Iran, could conspire to commit acts of terrorism, cyber or even nuclear, against the United States. Our leading defense against Islamic terror is, after all, the distances involved and their lack of access to our country. But, with the proximity of Venezuela to the United States and the obviously porous border we maintain with Mexico, the chances for domestic terrorism increase. And, especially, the opportunities for the use of weapons of mass destruction.

We got a chilling foretaste of what Iran might do when rebels toppled Libyan strongman Muammar Gaddafi. On November 20, 2011, the *Washington Post* reported that Iran might have supplied Gaddafi's government "with hundreds of special artillery shells for chemical weapons that Libya kept secret for decades." The *Post* reported that "the shells, which Libya filled with highly toxic mustard agent, were uncovered . . . by revolutionary fighters at two sites in central Libya."[25]

A US intelligence official said, " 'We are pretty sure we know' the shells were custom-designed and produced in Iran for Libya."[26]

If Iran supplies its allies with such military hardware, could such munitions be going to Venezuela from Iran in the daily flights between Tehran and Caracas? Reports that the planes are often empty and that the cargo is never inspected at either end raise serious concerns.

We don't need to let Iran threaten us, through Chavez, in our backyard.

ACTION AGENDA

It would be very simple to close down Chavez and put a dent in the plans of his Iranian allies by simply stopping our purchase of his oil (we buy about one million barrels per day from Venezuela, which constitutes more than half of their international sales).

The *Wall Street Journal* explains that Chavez would have difficulty selling his oil if we didn't buy it. "To get top dollar for its heavy oil, Venezuela must send it to specially equipped refineries on the US Gulf Coast. Otherwise it has to be sold elsewhere, in faraway markets not prepared to handle it. That means the price will be cut to adjust for transportation and higher refining costs. For a military government that relies on oil revenue to buy its legitimacy, this will not be a welcome development."[27]

We, on the other hand, have plenty of options. We could stop buying a million barrels of Venezuela's oil a day and wait him out as he starves to death. We could easily replace Chavez' oil by tapping our 727 million barrel Strategic Petroleum Reserve.

Or, with our rapid progress in generating new oil production by fracking and offshore drilling, we could obviate the need for Venezuelan oil (see chapter on Saudi Arabia).

As noted, US and Canadian oil production is expected to rise by three million barrels in the next three years. Combined with conservation—we are using one million fewer barrels per day than we did in

2000—we can easily get free of dependence on Hugo Chavez and his oil. Once the oil revenues stop flowing, so will Chavez's largesse to his people, and his popularity, already waning as crime skyrockets, will sink to the vanishing point. Will the military stay loyal to a bankrupt Chavez? Not very likely.

But, instead of action, all we are getting from Obama is rhetoric designed to hurt Chavez's feelings (and, more charitably, to decrease his popularity in Venezuela). Obama has criticized Chavez, stating that his "actions, which have restricted the universal rights of the Venezuelan people, threatened basic democratic values and failed to contribute to the security in the region."[28]

Obama added, in December 2011: "In Venezuela, we have been deeply concerned to see action taken to restrict the freedom of the press, and to erode the separation of powers that is necessary for democracy to thrive. In all countries of the region, we want to see elections that are free and fair."[29]

Obama said, "It's unfortunate that the Venezuelan government is often more interested in revisiting the ideological battles of the past than looking forward to the future."[30]

Obama criticized Chavez's flirtations with Ahmadinejad and Castro: "I would argue . . . that the

Venezuelan government's ties to Iran and Cuba have not served the interests of Venezuela or the Venezuelan people."[31]

"Ultimately, it is up to the Venezuelan people to determine what they gain from a relationship with a country that violates universal human rights and is isolated from much of the world," Obama said. "Here in the Americas, we take Iranian activities, including in Venezuela, very seriously and we will continue to monitor them closely."[32]

But it will take more than words to undermine Chavez. We have got to hit him where he is vulnerable: oil. The black gold that is the source of his power can be the key to his defeat.

The United States must begin to take Venezuela seriously. Were it not for the likelihood of Iranian nuclear weapons and the emerging close relations between Chavez and Ahmadinejad, we would not need to be nearly this concerned. But we can't disregard the very real possibility that an Iranian-Venezuelan alliance could pose a mortal threat to America. No longer would Chavez be a global clown whose only impact is to take control of some mountainous Latin American countries with large indigenous populations. Now he would represent a vital corridor for the introduction of nuclear and other weapons of mass destruction into our hemisphere—exactly what we could not tolerate from Castro's Cuba.

The one thing we do not need to do is to continue to do business with Chavez, keep him in power, and subsidize his deepening relationship with Iran and their demonstrated willingness to strike us on US soil. It's time to end our complaisance and act.

PART ELEVEN

The Enemy Within

FOREIGN GOVERNMENTS LOBBYING FOR SPECIAL FAVORS

The previous chapters in this book paint a revolting picture of how the United States is routinely exploited by other nations and by bureaucratic international organizations. Those stories, however, beg the fundamental question: How do they get away with it? Why don't our elected officials stand up for us? Why, for example, do they permit China to drag our economy down? Why are we so dependent on Saudi Arabia? Why are we gulled by Pakistan? Why do we hand out foreign aid to corrupt regimes that hate us?

The answer is, in part, that there is a dedicated corps of lobbyists for each of these foreign countries that works ceaselessly to influence the decisions of the American government, even if it means screwing the United States.

To make matters even worse, these lobbyists are often the very people whom we originally elected to lead us and pass laws to protect us. Now in retirement from public office, they pass through the revolving door and work against our interests, dancing to the tune of the often corrupt nations that pay them.

Former congressmen are highly sought-after lobbyists. They're the first choice of many special interests. During the consideration of the Dodd-Frank bill on financial services, more than seventy former members were hired as lobbyists. And it's not just American companies who chase after them. Foreign governments love them, too. No unemployment problems for former members of Congress.

Lobbyists have their own microeconomy in Washington. There's plenty of work for them.

We all know that special interests have been running the show in our nation's capital for years. That's no surprise. American corporations and unions have the right to be heard by their elected representatives. And they make sure they are.

But, more and more, it's not just American voices who maneuver to get special favors from Congress, the White House, and federal agencies. Over the past decade, there has been a proliferation of foreign governments and businesses hiring high-priced Washington lobbyists to get what they want from the officials we elect.

Whether it's more foreign aid that adds to our deficit, or preferential trade deals that cost Americans their

THE ENEMY WITHIN · 487

1

jobs, or special tax treatment that drains our coffers, or government and military contracts that enrich them at our expense, these foreigners, who have no right to be heard in Washington, pay millions to DC lobbyists to get what they want.

The foreign governments fully understand that they need an experienced hand to do their bidding in the United States. They've learned that there's nothing coincidental, nothing serendipitous, nothing spontaneous about the way that decisions are made in the federal government. Every word, every comma, every definition is precisely planned. Nothing happens by chance. Foreign aid allocations don't just land in the foreign aid bill. For the most part, they're individually bought and paid for.

That's the way things work in Washington. The only way.

That's why foreign lobbying is such a growing and lucrative business.

According to *Roll Call*, "130 countries spent about $460 million on lobbying Congress and promoting their interests before the Executive Branch in 2010."[1]

One hundred thirty countries with foreign lobbyists! There only are one hundred eighty in the world. Almost every country on the planet now has a highly paid lobbyist plying the Washington waters for special favors . . . all at our expense! And many countries have boatloads of lobbyists: some visible on the surface and others hidden beneath, peddling their influence in stealth.

And with the lobbying business contracting because of both the recession and the disappearance of the lucrative earmark business, the largest lobbying firms are actively seeking to replace domestic clients with foreign ones. Never mind that they may be selling out the United States, often acting against our interest and helping foreigners screw us.

They're just doing their jobs—and they want to do much more.

The Podesta Group, a lobbying firm headed by the brother of President Clinton's former chief of staff, recently hired Frank Lowenstein, former staff director for the Senate Foreign Relations Committee, to help build a consulting business with multinational corporations and expand their foreign client base.

The firm has been rapidly increasing its revenue from foreign clients.

In this economic climate, foreign governments and foreign businesses are the emerging markets for Washington's lobbyists. Just think about all those unrepresented countries out there.

WHY DON'T WE PROHIBIT FOREIGN LOBBYING?

Why don't we just prohibit any foreign entity from paying any US lobbying firm to do its bidding?

Why don't we prohibit any American from accepting payments to influence any government action?

It makes sense.

What happened to diplomatic channels? Aren't they the traditional way that foreign countries communicated their needs to the United States? No longer.

Now countries are sidestepping the diplomatic process and going right to the decision makers through their hired guns. Why don't we make them let their embassy staff convey their government's positions to ours? That's what they're there for, isn't it? Let's ban foreign companies or countries from hiring lobbyists.

It would certainly be naïve to assume that these lobbyists for foreign governments rely on eloquence, facts, and persuasion to convince our elected officials to do the bidding of their overseas clients. No way. Lobbyists routinely make campaign contributions to the members of Congress who have the power to help their foreign clients. They wallpaper Congress with these donations to get special access and specific favors. That's the way the game is played.

The Podesta Group, for example, like most other successful lobbying firms, has contributed over $1.6 million to federal candidates since 2000, and bundled another half million for various leadership committees and a few legislators, according to InfluenceExplorer. com. Senate Majority Leader Harry Reid was one of the firm's favorites; the Podesta Group has collected $123,500.[2] That'll open some doors.

And there's nothing illegal about it. But when members get contributions from lobbyists that are representing foreign entities, it can get more complicated. It might lead to special favors.

That's why we have strict laws that prohibit the donation of foreign funds to federal campaigns. And the reason for that is that we don't want foreign governments to influence our electoral process. So why should we let them influence any other part of our government?

In 1996, the nation was convulsed by the revelation that President Clinton's reelection campaign had received significant illegal campaign contributions from sources tied to the Chinese government. The investigation by then-Senator Fred Thompson (R-TN) demonstrated that, while the donations were nominally made by American citizens, the source of the money was foreign. Particularly galling was a donation from the monks at a Buddhist monastery who were so affluent that they each gave the maximum allowable donation to the Clinton-Gore campaign.

So, we tightened the campaign finance laws to keep those foreign contributions out. But occasionally they still sneak in.

In July 2011, two American citizens of Pakistani descent were indicted for secretly trying to influence US policy on Pakistani issues without registering with the Justice Department. The pair was also charged

with contributing $100,000 per year to federal cam-
paigns through straw donors. The source of the money
for the $4 million twenty-year project was Pakistan's
Inter-Services Intelligence, ISI. The illegal contributions went to Republican Dan Burton and Democrats
Jim Moran, Gregory Meeks, and Dennis Kucinich, all
of whom denied any knowledge.[3]

So, taking money from foreign governments is a
big no-no in American politics. It was clear from the
Chinese case that even if you laundered the funds by
giving them to an American citizen to donate to the
campaign, you were still in violation of campaign
finance laws.

However, now foreign governments hire American
lobbyists and can get their cash indirectly into the
hands of pliant American congressmen. Here's how it
could happen: A foreign government or corporation
pays a lobbying firm; the lobbying firm employees
then contribute to the members of Congress who are
most important to their client; the member then delivers for the client.

And, of course, there's no problem with that; it's not
illegal because there would be no foreign money contributed. The foreign money became US money once it
reached the lobbying firm. If it were then contributed to
a campaign, it would be US money, not foreign money.

This kind of potential problem is just one more reason to get rid of lobbyists for foreign concerns.

Of course, foreign embassies and diplomats can't do that. That's a good reason to end foreign lobbying.

That would be a major reform.

So, let's close down the foreign lobbying business once and for all.

They're not doing us any good.

In fact, they're wasting the time of our elected representatives, who are only too willing to meet with the top lobbyists who hand out campaign contributions. If we stop this, it would free up a lot of time for the people whom we elect to actually spend time serving us.

When he worked in the Clinton White House, Dick proposed to the president that he issue an executive order banning any contact between foreign lobbyists and executive branch officials. He knew that Congress would never ban foreign lobbying—too many of them wanted to go into the business after leaving office—but such an executive order would make it virtually impossible for foreign lobbyists to operate.

The president was very positive about the proposal and circulated it to his foreign policy advisers. They went nuts. Before their eyes, they could see the lucrative futures they had planned for themselves going up in smoke. They collectively killed the idea. But it's still a damn good one.

However, the main reason to ban foreign lobbying is that these skilled practitioners of the political art are very good at advancing their clients' interests even when it means real harm to ours.

THE NEW CAREER PATH: FROM CONGRESSIONAL LEADER TO LOBBYIST

The latest trend in the world of special interests is to hire former members of Congress as lobbyists, especially those who have been in leadership positions. Who would know better the arcane world of legislation? Former Congressional leaders bring experience, invaluable relationships, and, in some instances, raw political power to their clients. Some of the people they lobby may have owed the former leaders for their positions. Thus, the former Speakers and majority leaders have a lot to offer. And charge a lot for it.

It's one thing when these leaders, who used to write our laws, hire on to work for their fellow American citizens and their companies. It is quite another when they contract their services out to foreign governments, sometimes against the best interests of the United States.

Since it has now become de rigueur for Congressional leaders to retire to lobbying firms, it raises the question of whether legislative leaders give any preferential treatment to lobbying firms or their clients who might be potential employers in the near future, particularly when their clients are foreign governments.

It's a legitimate concern because the trend of hiring legislative leaders as lobbyists is growing.

Since 1977, with only one exception (Bill Frist), every single retired Senate majority leader—George Mitchell, Robert Dole, Trent Lott, and Tom Daschle—has gone through the revolving door on Capitol Hill that goes from the Congress to a lobbying firm. And many of them represent foreign governments.

And it's not just former senators who have crossed over to the dark side. The House leadership has joined the party, too. Former Speaker of the House Dennis Hastert and his son have been lobbyists. His predecessor as speaker, Newt Gingrich, has never been a registered lobbyist, but eyebrows were raised when he disclosed that he had earned over $40 million by consulting[4] with businesses and industries that have issues before the government. And, of course, he was paid $1.6 million to advise Freddie Mac,[5] the bankrupt quasigovernment agency. Newt insists that his work was carefully crafted so as not to be lobbying at all.

His critics don't buy that and categorize his work as lobbying.

Newt's successor as Speaker was to have been Congressman Bob Livingston, longtime chairman of the House Appropriations Committee. But, before he took office, he became enmeshed in a scandal over his marital infidelities and resigned, opening the door for Dennis Hastert to succeed Newt.

No matter, both Livingston and Hastert ended up in the same place: as lobbyists. And Livingston has represented lots of foreign countries, including Libya, Turkey, and Egypt.

On the Democratic side, former House majority leader Dick Gephardt immediately joined the lobbying team at DLA Piper when he left Congress in 2004. Now he has his own lobbying firm, the Gephardt Group.

DLA Piper has been a popular landing place for former Congressional leaders.

Former Republican leader Dick Armey also found a home there until he was asked to leave. His sin? He gave voice to his own opinions on a matter of principle—a no-no in the world of lobbying—when he publicly opposed the position of several DLA Piper pharmaceutical clients during the health-care debate, making them a bit unhappy.

After he left office as Democratic Senate majority leader, former senator George Mitchell followed the well-trod path to DLA Piper, where he oversaw its lobbying efforts for Dubai, the UAE, and Turkey. Then he went in the other direction, resigning as a lobbyist to become President Obama's special envoy to the Middle East.

Former Democratic Senate majority leader Tom Daschle joined DLA Piper recently after a stint at another lobbying firm, Alston & Bird. Like Gingrich, Daschle insists that he is not a lobbyist, although he admits to advising" corporate clients, particularly in the health-care field.

Former Republican majority leader Bob Dole has lobbied for the Taiwan government for years at Alston & Bird.

Former Senate majority leader Trent Lott initially teamed up with former Louisiana senator John Breaux when he decided to retire. Since then, both senators have joined Patton, Boggs, the megalobbying firm. In 2010, Patton, Boggs topped the list of foreign lobbyists, representing fifteen countries and earning $3.4 million in the first half of 2010. The firm's clients included China, Korea, Cyprus, Albania, Cameroon, Ecuador, and Sri Lanka.

Lobbying is a lucrative business for these former public servants.

One of Hastert's clients, tobacco company Lorillard, paid his firm Dickstein, Shapiro over $2 million during the first nine months of 2011.

And the rest of the elite leadership group is raking it in, too.

According to the *New York Times*, "Lobbyists and several executives at financial firms that employ them, none of whom would agree to be named, said that former members of Congress and staff members were in high demand because they brought invaluable expertise and access on federal matters.

"'Hiring a well-connected staffer can run a firm something like $300,000 to $600,000 a year, and for a member of Congress, it's anywhere from $1 million to $3 million,' said Craig Holman of Public Citizen. 'The only businesses that can really afford that are those that are very wealthy, but clearly these companies are getting their money's worth.'"[6]

Sometimes the former leaders are hired by countries with questionable goals.

FORMER HOUSE LEADER BOB LIVINGSTON LOBBIED FOR LIBYA'S MUAMMAR GADDAFI

Libya, an overt sponsor of terrorism, ruled for decades by the deranged dictator Muammar Gaddafi, engaged the services of former House majority leader Robert

Livingston in 2008 and 2009. Gaddafi was, of course, toppled and killed in 2011.

Did it not occur to Bob Livingston that he should not be representing the interests of one of the most brutal, anti-American regimes in the world? Or was the $360,000 fee that Gaddafi paid just too enticing?

Livingston seems to have had no qualms at all. He pulled out all the stops to help Gaddafi, using his long-term relationships in Congress on the dictator's behalf.

Unlike some other foreign lobbyists, you get your money's worth with Bob Livingston.

Livingston and his firm, the Livingston Group, made an astounding 881 contacts on behalf of the Libyan government with members of Congress, key committee staffs, the chief of staff to the secretary of state, the State Department's assistant secretary for legislation, and lots of others. Livingston's tireless work to get Gaddafi's point of view across to the elite opinion leaders earned him big bucks.

It pays to be an ex-leader of the House if you'll flack for anyone.

Those who welcomed the Livingston Group lobbyists and spent time with them to hear the dictator's representative explain his client's position included the following members of Congress:

Senators

Carl Levin (D-MI)   Jim DeMint (R-SC)

Judd Gregg (R-NH)

U.S. Representatives

John Boehner (R-OH)	John Conyers (D-MI)
Jesse Jackson Jr. (D-IL)	Robert Scott (D-VA)
Nita Lowey (D-NY)	Ben Chandler (D-KY)
Jim Moran (D-VA)	Howard Coble (R-NC)
Ike Skelton (D-MO)	Thaddeus McCotter (R-MI)
Ralph Regula (R-OH)	Norm Dicks (D-WA)
Solomon Ortiz (D-TX)	Rodney Alexander (R-LA)
John Murtha (D-PA)	Edolphus Towns (D-NY)
Barbara Lee (D-CA)	Louise Slaughter (D-NY)
Adam Schiff (D-CA)	Candice Miller (R-MI)
James Clyburn (D-SC)	Gene Green (D-TX)
Alcee Hastings (D-FL)	David Hobson (R-OH)
Donald Payne (D-NJ)	Dan Burton (R-IN)
Jim Saxton (R-NJ)	Jo Ann Emerson (R-MO)
Nick Rahall (D-WV)	Jack Kingston (R-GA)
Joe Wilson (R-SC)	Alan Mollohan (D-WV)
Bill Young (R-FL)	Maurice Hinchey (D-NY)
John Culberson (R-TX)	Sam Farr (D-CA)

The firm also met with Nancy Pelosi's policy adviser, spoke by phone with Admiral Brent Scowcroft, former national security advisor to the president, and met or spoke with or emailed hundreds of others, including Congressional staff members, State and Defense department personnel, and other lobbyists.

These folks worked hard for their pay!

Apparently, it wasn't very difficult to get appointments to see so many members on behalf of one of the most brutal rulers in the world. A former chairman of the House Ways and Means Committee is doubtless owed a lot of favors.

Then there's the large number of campaign contributions that Livingston showered on members of Congress. Since he started lobbying in 2000, he has given a whopping $2,799,849 to Congressional candidates and political committees.[7]

The Livingston Group also worked for Gaddafi's favorite charity, the Gaddafi International Charity and Development Foundation. The firm's disclosure reports indicate meetings with democracy groups to discuss—and this is *not* a joke—human rights and democracy initiatives in Libya.

That must have been a short discussion.

Although the United States resumed diplomatic relations with Libya in late 2007, it is useful to review the the long history of state-sponsored terrorism and the consistent denial of human rights in Libya that led to the termination of relations. We have to realize just how bad Gaddafi was to understand how appalling it was that he was able to retain the former chairman of the House Appropriations Committee, and almost the Speaker of the House, to do his bidding.

According to the Council on Foreign Relations, "Qaddafi established terrorist training camps on Libyan soil, provided terrorist groups with arms, and offered safe haven to terrorists . . . Among the groups aided by Qaddafi were the Irish Republican Army, Spain's ETA, Italy's Red Brigades, and Palestinian groups such as the Palestine Liberation Organization. Libya was also suspected of attempting to assassinate the leaders of Chad, Egypt, Saudi Arabia, Sudan, Tunisia, and Zaire (now Democratic Republic of Congo)."[8]

That's quite a resume—even for a dictator.

From 1979 until 2007, the United States brought economic and political pressure on Libya because of this strong support of terrorists. Sanctions began shortly after the United States designated Libya a state sponsor of terrorism in 1979. A defining moment in the bilateral relationship occurred in 1981, when Libya opened fire on two US military planes that were on routine flights over the Mediterranean in the Gulf of Sidra.

In 1982, the United States refused to permit Libyan oil to be imported. and shortly afterward, placed an embargo on all exports from the United States to Libya except food and medicine.

In 1986, Ronald Reagan ordered an air strike on Libya in retaliation for a terrorist attack on a discotheque in Berlin that killed three Americans and disabled twenty-nine people.

The US air strike killed sixty Libyans. At the time, Gaddafi showed reporters the dead body of an infant girl and claimed that it was his adopted daughter, Hana. In 2011, after the death of Gaddafi, numerous foreign newspapers reported that she was alive and practicing medicine.

Gaddafi's most horrific act was the bombing of Pan Am Flight 103 over Lockerbie, Scotland, in 1988, killing all 243 passengers. A three-year investigation by authorities in Scotland and the FBI implicated Libya. A Libyan intelligence officer and citizen, Abdelbaset al-Megrahi, was indicted and charged with murder.

Gaddafi originally refused to cooperate, but, in 1999, reeling from the effects of US and UN sanctions, Megrahi was turned over to the Scottish police.

That was beginning of the process that brought Libya back into diplomatic relations with the United States. Through secret channels, Libya eventually agreed to provide $2.7 billion to compensate the victims of Lockerbie,[9] to give up nuclear weapons, and to renounce terrorism. It was an amazing turnabout, hastened by both the effects of the economic sanctions and by the ouster of Iraq's Saddam Hussein; Gaddafi read the handwriting on the wall.

Megrahi was convicted and spent eight and a half years in prison until he was released for compassionate reasons, involving prostate cancer that was so advanced that he was only expected to live another three months. He returned to Libya in a private plane owned by Gaddafi, accompanied by the dictator's son. On his arrival, hundreds of people greeted him at the airport, welcoming him home as if he were a hero.

That was too much for even Bob Livingston and he cancelled the Gaddafi contract. Two years later, Megrahi was still alive.

Our own State Department has had a lot to say about human rights in Libya and, not surprising, it's definitely a very different message about conditions there than the one spun by the Livingston Group.

In 2009, one of the the years during which Livingston was flacking for Libya, the US State Department Annual Report on Human Rights in Libya found abominable conditions.

Here are some excerpts:

- The Great Socialist People's Libyan Arab Jamahiriya is an authoritarian regime.

- The government's human rights record remained poor.

- Citizens did not have the right to change their government.

- Continuing problems include reported disappearances, torture, arbitrary arrest, lengthy pretrial and sometimes incommunicado detention, official impunity, and poor prison conditions.

- Denial of fair public trial by an independent judiciary, political prisoners and detainees, and the lack of judicial recourse for alleged human rights violations were also problems.

- The government instituted new restrictions on media freedom and continued to restrict freedom of speech (including Internet and academic freedom). It continued to impede the freedom of assembly, freedom of association, and civil liberties.

- The government did not fully protect the rights of migrants, asylum seekers, and refugees, and in some cases participated in their abuse. Other problems included restrictions on freedom of religion; corruption and lack of transparency; discrimination against women, ethnic minorities, and foreign workers; trafficking in persons; and restriction of labor rights.

Perhaps no one told Livingston that there was no democracy at all and very few human rights in Libya.

Livingston was not alone in coming to Libya's aid. A former assistant secretary of defense under Ronald Reagan was happy to help out the dictator, too.

RICHARD PERLE, FORMER UNDERSECRETARY OF DEFENSE, MAY HAVE FLACKED FOR GADDAFI, TOO

According to *Politico*'s Laura Rozen, Richard Perle, an undersecretary of defense during the Reagan administration and chairman of the Defense Policy Board under Donald Rumsfeld during the George W. Bush administration, was paid to help out Libya, too.

Perle was hired as a consultant to the Monitor Group, a Cambridge, Massachusetts, consulting firm that was paid $3 million by Gaddafi.[10] Monitor denies that it, or any of its consultants, ever lobbied, but internal documents directly contradict this claim.

According to Monitor's own report of its activities, the group was actively lobbying for Libya: "At a critical time when the United States was debating its recognition of Libya, Monitor met with senior officials in the United States government to share its perspectives on Libya," the company's 2007 Phase I executive summary states. "In coordination with the client Monitor briefed officials and various agencies of the United States government. Monitor continues to advocate on Libya's behalf with a range of leading individuals. Many of these individuals have indicated a willingness to engage with Libya and visit in the future."[11]

These included "Richard Perle . . . an American political advisor and lobbyist."[12]

Monitor's 2007 Phase I Libya project summary states, "Perle made two visits to Libya (22–24 March and 23–25 July 2006) and met with Qadhafi on both occasions. He briefed Vice President Dick Cheney on his visits to Libya."[13]

Why did Perle meet with Cheney if he wasn't representing Libya or conveying a message for Gaddafi?

It sure sounds like Monitor was engaged in lobbying and public relations in the United States on behalf of Gaddafi. But Monitor went one step further. Not only were they seemingly representing Gaddafi before the US government, but they also sought to directly influence American public opinion to spin Gaddafi's image to make him more acceptable.

Now, that was taking on a big job.

According to *Politico*, Monitor would "continue the cultivation of an elite group of influence makers to help improve Libya's global image and reputation, etc.—a highly involved program that 'is a mission of several years.'"[14]

Propagandizing on behalf of a foreign country requires registration and full disclosure, but neither Monitor nor Perle registered as Libya's agent under the Foreign Agents Registration Act.

Maybe they wanted to keep their help to Gaddafi secret.

That's certainly understandable.

US COMPANIES LOBBIED TO PROTECT GADDAFI'S ASSETS FROM BEING SEIZED BY TERROR VICTIMS

As part of his effort to get US economic sanctions lifted against his country, Gaddafi agreed to provide compensation to the families of those he had killed in the Lockerbie bombing.

Once Libya started paying the Lockerbie victims, other victims of its state-sponsored terrorism apparently came demanding payment.

New Jersey Senator Frank Lautenberg pushed for a bill to make it easier for plaintiffs in terrorism lawsuits to seize foreign-government-owned assets from state sponsors of terrorism.

According to Paul Blumenthal, the insightful columnist for the Sunlight Foundation, the Lautenberg Amendment "proved problematic for companies that had already entered into business arrangements with Libya as the government had not finished making payments to plaintiffs in the Lockerbie bombing case."[15]

Worried that the amendment would jeopardize their ability to do business in Libya, Gaddafi told the American companies with licensing agreements in Libya to fix the problem.

Blumenthal reveals that "cables show that the Libyan government told the US oil companies that 'it [the danger posed by the Lautenberg Amendment] is "their problem" to solve, and has begun requiring US and other companies to conduct all operations in non-dollar denominations.' "[16] This meant that the companies would have to face the consequences of any future settlements that occurred under the Lautenberg Amendment.

That galvanized the American companies into action seeking repeal of the Lautenberg Amendment. Fifteen companies, including every major oil company, lobbied the federal government to keep Libyan markets open and to insulate Gaddafi and the Libyan government from claims of victims of terrorism in order to protect their investments in Libya.

Based on a review of lobbying filings by the Sunlight Foundation, the following companies actively lobbied on the Libyan issues: ExxonMobil, BP, ConocoPhillips, Chevron, Marathon Oil, Occidental Petroleum, Shell, and Hess Corporation, along with Boeing, Caterpillar, Dow Chemical, Fluor Corporation, Halliburton, Motorola, and Raytheon.

"For the large part of 2008, the fifteen companies lobbying then focused on the repeal of the Lautenberg amendment. On August 4, 2008, they were successful. The resolution, known as the Libyan Claims Resolution Act, exempted Libya from the Lautenberg amendment barring the seizure of its assets to assist the victims of the other four Libyan terrorist attacks. On August 14, 2008, the United States approved a $1.8 billion settlement for the victims and the companies no longer faced the possibility of asset forfeiture."[17]

Gaddafi is gone, but the new leaders in Libya, the transitional government, made sure to keep a lobbyist in Washington. In one of its first official acts, it retained the Harbour Group to help it gain recognition from the United States and to unfreeze the assets of the Libyan government. Harbour is not charging a fee . . . yet.

DICK GEPHARDT, POPULIST CRUSADER . . . UNTIL HE GETS PAID OFF

In 2003, House Democratic minority leader Dick Gephardt sponsored a Congressional resolution on the Armenian Genocide. It called on the president to "ensure that the foreign policy of the United States reflects appropriate understanding and sensitivity concerning issues related to human rights, ethnic cleansing, and genocide documented in the United States record relating to the Armenian Genocide. . . ."[18]

After he left the House, this same Dick Gephardt, now working as a highly paid lobbyist for Turkey, succeeded in killing the resolution he had sponsored!

That's the way it works in Washington.

In 1915, there were 2.5 million Armenians living in the Turkish-controlled Ottoman Empire. By 1923, only 1 million were left alive. The other 1.5 million had been murdered by the Turkish government.[19]

According to the Knights of Vartan Armenian Research Center at the University of Michigan–Dearborn: "The Armenians were called from their homes, told they would be relocated, and then marched off to concentration camps in the desert . . . where they would starve and thirst to death in the burning sun. On the march, often they would be denied food and water, and many were brutalized and killed by their 'guards' or by 'marauders.' " In one area, the Turks "loaded Armenians on barges and sank them out at sea."[20]

To this day, the Turkish government denies that there was any Armenian Genocide.

The House resolution was an effort to move Turkey to do so. And Gephardt was right in the middle of it.

According to the *New Republic*, Armenian-American activists considered Gephardt to be a friend and were shocked to see him turn on them. The magazine reported, "A few years ago, he was a working-class populist who cast himself as a tribune of the underdog—including the Armenians."[21]

In 1998, the magazine noted, "Gephardt attended a memorial event hosted by the Armenian National Committee of America at which, according to a spokeswoman for the group, he spoke about the importance of recognizing the [Armenian] genocide."[22]

Two years later, Gephardt was one of three House Democrats who co-signed a letter to then-House Speaker Dennis Hastert urging him to schedule an immediate vote on the genocide resolution. "We implore you," the letter read. "Armenian-Americans have waited long enough for Congress to recognize the horrible genocide."[23]

That was before the Turkish government paid him to switch sides. In 2007, Turkey retained the lobbying firm of DLA Piper and its lobbyist Dick Gephardt for a fee of $100,000 per month to defeat his own Armenian resolution.[24] The contract with Turkey was unusual in one aspect. It hired Gephardt not only to oppose the genocide resolution, but to prevent debate on anything that harms Turkey's reputation. Only a former majority leader would offer this.

The contract particularly outraged the Armenian National Committee of America (ANCA). In a 2007 press release, the organization publicly castigated Gephardt:

"These new Department of Justice filings reveal just how deeply Dick Gephardt has sunk, compromising his integrity by turning against a human rights issue he energetically supported as an elected member of Congress. . . . We are especially troubled by the provision in the contract that seeks to export Turkey's Criminal Code Article 301 to the United States by requiring DLA Piper to prevent even 'debate' on issues Turkey considers harmful to its image. This requirement, which falls far outside the American democratic tradition, is, sadly, entirely consistent with [the] Turkish government's efforts to suppress freedom of expression by criminalizing speech that 'insults Turkishness.' "[25]

When Gephardt left DLA Piper to set up his own firm, Turkey left with him. And they've gotten a real bargain—he only charges them $70,000 a month.

Dick Gephardt is the ultimate Washington insider. He doesn't really know any other way of life. Elected to the US House of Representatives from St. Louis in 1976, he served fourteen terms. He's spent more than half his life as a legislator, Democratic Party leader, and lobbyist. He's spent the past thirty-five years in the rarefied bubble of Washington's elite power center.

Along the way, he was always reaching up for the next rung. In 1988, Gephardt ran for Democratic Party nomination for president, backed by major unions, in large part because of his strong opposition to free-trade agreements, but his campaign never really took off and he placed way behind Michael Dukakis.

Now that has to have been a humbling experience. After his loss, Gephardt came back to Washington and moved way up the ladder. The next year, 1989, he was elected House majority leader, the second most important position in that body. He continued in that position until the Democrats lost the House in 1994. From then on, he was the House minority leader.

His role as majority leader ultimately laid the groundwork for his popularity as a lobbyist. It is the role of the majority leader to determine which bills are going to go to the floor. Members introduce hundreds of bills each year, but very few of them ever see the light of day.

As part of his job, Gephardt had to work with rank-and-file members every day. For new members, he was a teacher, mentor, and cheerleader. For longtime members, he opened the gates. All of this led to close personal relationships, the kind that makes members welcome him back when he comes to see them on behalf of his clients. It's certainly paid off.

The Gephardt Group's website provides a subtle hint that the former leader is still the one to go to because of his connection to so many members of Congress, noting that "Mr. Gephardt was a colleague in the House to 49 currently serving US Senators and members of the Executive Branch."[26]

(Translation: Dick Gephardt can get in to see anyone. He is truly well connected. In fact, if you think about it, he was probably instrumental in appointing some of these folks to the very committees that are now considering your legislation. Hire him.)

Gephardt keeps up his friendships. In 2009, when his firm represented Turkey, he and his lobbying colleagues contributed over $100,000 to congressional campaigns.

And Gephardt is impeccably discreet, even if it means that he does not properly comply with the Foreign Agents Registration Act, which requires disclosure of persons contacted in the course of foreign lobbying. While his staff reported hundreds of contacts by naming the person that they met with, emailed, or phoned, Gephardt's disclosure report gives us only a small clue as to the identity of the very few members he met with.

For example, Gephardt discloses that on February 12, 2009, he met with "Rep D-NY, Member of Congress," as well as "Rep D-Va," to discuss "US-Turkey Relations; Transcaucasus Relations," but he keeps the name of the member whom he meets with secret. He just doesn't provide it. He also met with "Rep. D-Va, Member of Congress," along with the "Turkish Ambassador . . . to discuss US-Turkey relations and Transcaucasus."

Wonder whom he met with?

During the 1988 presidential race, the Dukakis campaign produced a devastating television ad against Gephardt. As a figure somersaulted across a black line across the screen, a voice said: "Congressman Dick Gephardt has flip-flopped on a lot of issues. He's been both for and against raising the minimum wage. For and against freezing social security benefits. Congressman

Gephardt acts tough toward big corporations but takes their PAC money. Mike Dukakis refuses PAC money, opposes Reaganomics and supports a strong minimum wage and social security. You know where Mike Dukakis stands. But Congressman Gephardt, he's still up in the air."[27]

And Gephardt is still flipping and flopping. You can't teach an old dog new tricks.

Besides his change of heart on the Armenian Genocide resolution, he's switched his position on China.

DICK GEPHARDT, CHINA'S NEW BEST FRIEND

As a congressman, Gephardt was vehemently against giving favored nation status to China and expanding its trade opportunities with the United States. He also opposed the North American Free Trade Agreement (NAFTA).

In opposing the bill to grant normal trading relations with China, Gephardt passionately insisted that "[t]here is nothing 'free' about our trade with China,"[28] and that free trade with China will mean that Americans buy more toys made in prison camps run by the Chinese army.

But that was before he was paid off to switch sides. Now, those days are over.

As a board member of Amerilink Telecom, an American distributor of products made by the Chinese telecommunications company Huawei Technologies, Gephardt has changed his tune.

And Huawei is no ordinary company.

The second-largest telecom equipment company in the world and the pride of the Chinese government, Huawei has been trying for years to enter the US markets. Several years ago, it attempted to invest in 3Com, but the Committee on Foreign Investment in the United States (CFIUS) refused to give a green light to the deal because of national security concerns and the company's relationship to the People's Liberation Army. Huawei then tried to invest in Motorola, but was thwarted again.

After that, the company took things into their own hands. Instead of seeking permission from CFIUS, they simply went ahead and acquired technology from 3 Leaf Systems, a California company. The committee learned of the transaction and invited them to submit a request. Huawei took the position that the committee had no jurisdiction, since Huawei had only bought technology, not assets. CFIUS ordered Huawei to divest. After initially refusing to do so, Huawei walked away from the deal.

However, the company, founded by a general in the People's Liberation Army, is desperate to get into the US markets.

In 2010, eight senators wrote to the Treasury Department raising national security concerns about Huawei's bid to sell equipment to Sprint Nextel, fearing that the Chinese might be able to monitor American communications. The senators were also upset about evidence suggesting that Huawei had sold products to Saddam Hussein and had a relationship with Iran.

In December 2011, Huawei promised to curtail its sales in Iran, "where the company provides services to government-controlled telecom operators, following reports that Iranian police were using mobile-network technology to track down and arrest dissidents."[29]

But now, Huawei has apparently come up with a new strategy for acceptance in the United States. In September 2011, Amerilink Telecom, Huawei's American distributor, announced the appointment of Richard Gephardt and James Wolfensohn, former president of the World Bank, to its board.

By setting up an American distributor with an American name, and appointing the two prominent Washington insiders to its American board, Huawei has begun a campaign to clean up its image.

And Dick Gephardt, who touts his devotion to human rights on his website, is no longer concerned about the brutal generals or human rights conditions in China.

There's no problem there when you're getting paid.

SOMETIMES, FOREIGN LOBBYISTS ARE WORKING AGAINST OUR INTERESTS

Foreign lobbyists—that is, American citizens representing foreign countries—often don't stop to think, or care, about the needs of their own country in their hurry to do their clients' bidding.

For example, the Patton Boggs lobbying/law firm, one of the biggest, signed on with South Korea to get the US-Korea Free Trade Agreement ratified. The helpful attorneys at Patton Boggs laid out a strategy, in incredible detail, of their view of how to get the Senate to approve the long-sought agreement.

And they filed it with the Justice Department with their foreign agent registration.

Then they threw in a bonus. In addition to mapping out the steps to get the Senate okay, they gratuitously told South Korea that the United States might have violated its commitments to the World Trade Organization when Congress explicitly banned the payment of any stimulus money to foreign contractors or suppliers. How helpful! The firm was basically accusing the United States of violating trade agreements and pointing it out to their foreign client. By raising an issue over which they had not been retained, they gave anti-US ammunition to Korea.

In his letter of agreement to the chairman of the state-sponsored Korea International Trade Association, Thomas Hale Boggs, the legendary lawyer and lobbyist, proposed a strategy that included opposing "Buy America" provisions in US legislation.

In counseling the Korean trade organization, Boggs cited the World Trade Organization's Government Procurement Agreement (GPA), which prohibits discrimination against nonlocal businesses by governments. Boggs criticized the US "Buy America" policy and suggested it violated the agreement.

"As the Republic of Korea and the United States are both signatories to the World Trade Organization Government Procurement Agreement (WTO GPA), products made by KITA [Korean International Trade Association] members should be on an equal footing as American items considered for U.S. government procurements."[30] Boggs pointed out that that American firms would be getting priority in the allocation of US tax dollars: "Nevertheless, as suggested by the clear language issued by the G-20 leaders in London, U.S. procurement officials are usually taking the politically easy step and buying U.S.-made goods, even when they are of inferior quality."[31] Boggs singled out the stimulus legislation, designed to jump-start the American economy, and suggested that its "Buy America" provision violated the WTO and "cast a long shadow over United States international trade policy, including trade agreements with Korea."[32]

So Patton Boggs, like so many Americans who represent foreign powers, was putting client first, country second; money first, America's needs second.

Regrettably, they're not the only ones.

ACTION AGENDA

The next president should ask Congress to pass a law banning lobbying on behalf of foreign nations or corporations. But will it pass?

Fat chance! With so many members of Congress, and all of the leadership, eager to cash in once they leave office by representing foreign countries, especially rich ones, there is no way on earth that they'll close down that lucrative retirement opportunity.

However, the next president can do what Dick urged Clinton to do: Sign an executive order banning executive branch employees from having any contact with a lobbyist representing a foreign country. If they can't get in to see the State Department or the trade representative or the head of AID or the National Security Council or the Defense Department, what good can a lobbyist do for his client?

An executive order like that would close down foreign lobbying in a heartbeat and bring Americans one step closer to controlling their own government!

Conclusion

As he emerged from the Constitutional Convention, a woman approached Benjamin Franklin and asked, "Well, Doctor, what have we got, a Republic or a Monarchy?"

Franklin's answer echoes through to this day: "A Republic, madame, if you can keep it."[1]

Indeed. Keeping the republic we were bequeathed by our fathers and mothers is the hardest part about being an American. We constantly have to repel threats to our freedom and keep vigilant against those who would undermine it.

In this book, we've visited many of these threats, both foreign and domestic.

We've talked about how China is waging a unilateral war against us . . . and how our elected leaders are doing nothing to defend our interests. But if the next president stood his ground and defended our interests, China would have no choice but to back down.

In Pakistan, we face an ally who is making a habit of betraying us, even as it accepts our aid. And, in Afghanistan, we are sacrificing lives to defend one of the most awful governments in the world. If the next president used diplomacy to play India off against Pakistan, and revised our mission in Afghanistan to fighting terrorists, not sustaining the government in power, we could set things right.

We turn a blind eye as Saudi Arabia uses our petro-dollars to fund our terrorist foes. But if our next president put aside environmental perfectionism, he could ensure that we would be energy independent and can treat the Saudis as the enemies they are.

And, in Venezuela, we face a foe who is giving Iran a Western Hemisphere base of power, threatening us at our doorstep. But if the next president focused on domestic energy sources, we could stop buying Chavez's oil and he would fade from the scene.

However, the major threats we face are not from foreign nations but from international organizations that would deny us our hard-won sovereignty and replace democratic control of our institutions with control by bureaucrats and self-selected experts.

If the next president drew a line in the sand and told the IMF to stop trying to run our economy and fought to keep the dollar as the international currency, we would go far to ensuring our control of our economic destiny.

And if he firmly refused to join the International Criminal Court or to sign the Law of the Sea Treaty or to enforce Agenda 21, he would do much to stop autocratic globalists from determining our destiny.

We need to tell the United Nations that it will get no more money from us until it cleans up its corruption.

We have to slice our foreign aid budget and our contribution to the World Bank and expand opportunities for direct foreign investment in poor countries to alleviate poverty.

And if the next president outlaws foreign lobbying, he will help rid us of this plague of corruption that infests our legislative process.

It's a formidable agenda, but the interesting thing is how simple it is. Each step can be taken quite easily. We have all the leverage and constitutional power that we need. We need not wage wars or invade any nation. We don't need massive new spending. We don't even need new programs. We just need a president who fights for us.

And, hopefully, in 2013 we'll get one!

Notes

INTRODUCTION

1. In 2009 and 2010: Alex Knott, "Lobbying by Foreign Countries Decreases," RollCall.com, September 14, 2011, http://www.rollcall.com/issues/57_29/Lobbying_by_Foreign_Countries_Decreases-208745-1.html?zkMobileView=true.
2. A July 2011 poll: "National Survey of 1,000 Likely Voters," TheHill.com, July 28, 2011, http://thehill.com/images/stories/news/2011/08_august/crosstabs072811.pdf.
3. Percentage of Likely Voters: Ibid.
4. A February 2011 Gallup poll: Lydia Saad, "China Surges in Americans' Views of Top World Economy," Gallup.com, February 14, 2011, http://www.gallup.com/poll/146099/china-surgesamericans-views-top-world-economy.aspx.
5. July 28, 2011, poll: "National Survey of 1,000 Likely Voters."

6. 17 percent of Americans believe: "New Low: 17% Say U.S. Government has Consent of the Governed," RasmussenReports.com, August 7, 2011, http://www.rasmussenreports.com/content/view/full/42520.

PART ONE

1. "regulation by do-gooders" . . . "soft tyranny": Mark R. Levin, *Liberty and Tyranny: A Conservative Manifesto* (New York: Threshold Editions, 2009).
2. "The Obama Administration's": Marion Smith, "An Inconvenient Founding: America's Principles Applied to the ICC," Heritage.org, February 18, 2010, http://www.heritage.org/research/reports/2010/02/an-inconvenient-founding-americas-principles-applied-to-the-icc.
3. "sent the vice president": Warren Ellis, "The Position," Forbes.com, October 15, 2007, http://www.forbes.com/2007/10/13/warren-ellis-fiction-tech-future07-cx_we_1015position.html.
4. "taking away the punch": "William McChesney Martin," Wikipedia.org, http://en.wikipedia.org/wiki/William_McChesney_Martin.
5. "Can you give me": Alexander Cockburn, "Rick Perry: One Lucky Son-of-a-Bitch," CounterPunch.org, August 19–21, 2011, http://www.counterpunch.org/2011/08/19/rick-perry-one-lucky-son-of-a-bitch/.
6. 80 percent of the global: Larissa Epatko, "5 Things to Know About the G20 Summit," PBS.org, November 3, 2011, http://www.pbs.org/newshour/rundown/2011/11/g20-primer.html.

7. "Brazil and other": Ian Katz and Sandrine Rastello, "IMF Seeks Funds for European Debt Crisis as U.S. Stands Back," BusinessWeek.com, December 14, 2011, http://www.businessweek.com/news/2011 -12-14/imf-seeks-funds-for-european-debt-crisis-as-u -s-stands-back.html.

8. Our GDP is equal to: Michael Heath, "RBA's Stevens Sees China's Share of Global GDP Nearing U.S.," Businessweek.com, April 13, 2011, http://www.busi nessweek.com/news/2011-04-13/rba-s-stevens-sees -china-s-share-of-global-gdp-nearing-u-s-.html.

9. one-third of the: "Gross Domestic Product 2010," WorldBank.org, July 1, 2011, http://siteresources .worldbank.org/DATASTATISTICS/Resources/GDP .pdf.

10. GDPs of G20 Nations: Ibid.

11. France and Germany's combined GDP: Ibid.

12. Europe is pushing . . . into line: Bob Davis and Stephen Fidler, "Nations Ready Big Changes to Global Economic Policy," *Wall Street Journal* September 22, 2009, htto://online.wsj.com/article/ SB125348959155226421.html.

13. "Europeans [are] emboldened . . . it's finished": Steve Hargreaves, "G-20 Shaping a New World Order," CNN.com, November 14, 2008, http//money .cnn.com/2008/11/14/news/economy/g20_powerplay/ index.htm.

14. "greater oversight . . . US banks": Ibid.

15. "as a kind of": Davis and Fidler, "Nations Ready Big Changes to Global Economic Policy."

16. "to define ways . . . the US": Ibid.
17. "third rank students": Ngaire Woods, *The Globalizers: The IMF, the World Bank, and Their Borrowers* (Ithaca: Cornell University Press, 2006), p. 2.
18. Members of the European: "Salaries and Allowances," EuroParl.Europa.eu, http://www.europarl.europa.eu/parliament/expert/staticDisplay.do?id=39&language=en&pageRank=2.
19. "The wisdom of the few": "Balanced Government," The Founder's Constitution, 1656, http://press-pubs.uchicago.edu/founders/documents/v1ch11s2.html.
20. "a basket of currencies": Elizabeth Delaney, "Move to Replace Dollar as World Reserve Currency Hastening, IMF Suggests SDR," Examiner.com, February 11, 2011, http://www.examiner.com/christianity-politics-in-national/move-to-replace-dollar-as-world-reserve-currency-hastening.
21. "a potential claim": "What is an SDR (Special Drawing Right)?" *International Business Times*, April 2, 2009, http://www.ibtimes.com/articles/20090402/what-is-an-sdr.htm.
22. CNN reported that: Ben Rooney, "IMF Calls for Dollar Alternative," CNN.com, February 10, 2011, http://money.cnn.com/2011/02/10/markets/dollar/index.htm.
23. help correct global: Ibid.
24. "over time, there may": Ibid.
25. "goal is to have": Ibid.
26. "the IMF also proposed": Ibid.

27. "the rulers of . . . more money": James Ridgeway, "The Rulers of the Exchange of Mankind's Goods Have Failed . . ." MotherJones.com, September 30, 2008, http://motherjones.com/mojo/2008/09/rulers -exchange-mankinds-goods-have-failed.

PART TWO

1. "[b]ecause of the Supremacy Clause": Joseph Abrams, "Boxer Seeks to Ratify U.N. Treaty That May Erode U.S. Rights," FoxNews.com, February 25, 2009, http://www.foxnews.com/politics/2009/02/25/boxer -seeks-ratify-treaty-erode-rights.
2. "In November 2009 . . . US citizens": Smith, "An Inconvenient Founding: America's Principles Applied to the ICC."
3. "shall satisfy itself": Ibid.
4. "the use of armed force": "Delivering on the Promise of a Fair, Effective and Independent Court > The Crime of Aggression," ICCNow.org, http://www .iccnow.org/?mod=aggression.
5. "this scenario . . . highlights": Smith, "An Inconvenient Founding: America's Principles Applied to the ICC."
6. "Fundamentally, the Rome Statute": Simon Jennings and Blake Evans-Pritchard, "US Takes Cautious Step Towards ICC," globalpolicy.org, May 6, 2010, http://www.globalpolicy.org/empire/us-un-and -international-law-8-24/us-opposition-to-the-icc-8 -29/49067.html.
7. "[i]n 2009, ICC Chief": Smith, "An Inconvenient Founding: America's Principles Applied to the ICC."

8. "due to the . . . the country": "Bush Cancels Visit to Switzerland Due to Threat of Torture Prosecution, Rights Groups Say," HuffingtonPost.com, February 5, 2011, http://www.huffing tonpost.com/2011/02/05/bush-switzerland-torture_n_819175.html.

9. "several African . . . HIV/AIDS": Corbett B. Daly, "Amnesty International Calls for Arrest of George W. Bush," CBSNews.com, December 2, 2011, http://www.cbsnews.com/8301-503544_162-57335679-503544/amnesty-international-calls-for-arrest-of-george-w-bush/.

10. "carried away by the": Smith, "An Inconvenient Founding: America's Principles Applied to the ICC."

11. "the United States has no": Ibid.

12. "the American government": Jennings and Evans-Pritchard, "US Takes Cautious Steps Towards ICC."

13. "since assuming the": Ibid.

14. "during the Review": "Review Conference of the Rome Statute," ICCNow.org, http://www.iccnow.org/?mod=review.

15. "the US must": Marion Smith, "Of Red-Coats and Black-Robes: The ICC Threatens American Justice," Heritage.org, June 3, 2010, http://www.heritage.org/research/commentary/2010/06/of-red-coats-and-black-robes-the-icc-threatens-american-justice.

16. FOX News describes how: "U.N. Floats Global 'Climate Court' to Enforce Emissions Rules," FoxNews.com, December 10, 2011, http://www.foxnews.com/politics/2011/12/10/un-floats-global-climate-court-to-enforce-emissions-rules/.

17. "the draft document": Ibid.
18. guarantee the compliance: Ibid.
19. "'finance, technology and'": Ibid.
20. "money from productive": Doug Bandow, "Washington's Night of the Living Dead: The Law of the Sea Treaty Stirs," Forbes.com, September 12, 2011, http://www.forbes.com/sites/dougbandow/2011/09/12/washingtons-night-of-the-living-dead-the-law-of-the-sea-treaty-stirs/.
21. to the horror: Ibid.
22. "Unfortunately, treaties attract": Ibid.
23. "if the Senate": Dan Blumenthal and John Bolton, "Time to Kill the Law of the Sea Treaty—Again," *Wall Street Journal*, September 29, 2011, http://online.wsj.com/article/SB10001424053111904836104576560934029786322.htm.
24. "to enhance international": Ibid.
25. "endless legal maneuvering": Ibid.
26. "China is exploiting": Ibid.
27. "China simply . . . peripheral seas": Ibid.
28. "the navigational rights": Bandow, "Washington's Night of the Living Dead: The Law of the Sea Treaty Stirs."
29. "the evidence indicates": Ibid.
30. "have generally adhered": Ibid.
31. "many billions, if not": Steven Groves, "Law of Sea Treaty Could Cost U.S. Trillions," Heritage.org, July 6, 2011, http://www.heritage.org/research/commentary/2011/07/law-of-sea-treaty-could-cost-us-trillions.

32. "about half of the": Ibid.
33. "thirteen of the": Ibid.
34. "promote and encourage . . . relevant technology": Bandow, "Washington's Night of the Living Dead: The Law of the Sea Treaty Stirs."
35. "if the Enterprise": Ibid.
36. "may prove to be": Ibid.
37. "the potential impacts": Ibid.
38. In *Medillin v. Texas* 552 . . . our courts: Ibid.
39. "The administration is trying to act as though": John Bolton to the NRANews: http://www.factcheck .org/2009/12/international-gun-ban-treaty/.
40. "regulate international weapons sales": Maxim Lott, "Proposed U.N. Treaty to Regulate Global Firearms Trade Raising Concern for U.S. Gun Makers," FoxNews.com, August 5, 2011, http://www .foxnews.com/world/2011/08/05/proposed-un-treaty -to-regulate-global-firearms-trade-raising-concerns -for-us/.
41. "every country to submit": Ibid.
42. "countries to set up": Ibid.
43. "Parties shall take": Ibid.
44. "leaves room for the [UN] to declare": Ibid.
45. "Acknowledging also the right of States": UN General Assembly Resolution A/C.1/64/ L.38/Rev.1, October 28, 29, http://www.factcheck.org/2009/12/ international-gun-ban-treaty/.
46. "the United States would support": Arshad Mohammed, "US reverses stance on treaty to regulate arms trade," Reuters.com, October 14, 2009, http://www

.reuters.com/article/2009/10/15/us-arms-usa-treaty-id
USTRE59E0Q920091015.

47. NASA estimates: Mike Wall, "US Joins Effort to Create Code of Conduct for Space," SPACE.com, January
17, 2012, http://www.space.com/14271-space-code
-conduct-space-debris.html

48. "the long-term sustainability": Mohammed, "US
reverses stance on treaty to regulate arms trade."

49. "It's been clear": Wall, "US Joins Effort to Create
Code of Conduct for Space."

50. "for peaceful purposes": "US joins EU effort to
develop space 'code of conduct'" *The Telegraph*,
February 9, 2012, http://www.telegraph.co.uk/
science/space/9021800/US-joins-EU-effort-to-develop
-space-code-of-conduct.html.

51. "prevent harmful interference": Ibid.

52. "the best interests of children": "FACT SHEET:
A summary of rights under the Convention of the
Rights of the Child," http://www.unicef.org/crc/files/
Rights_overview.pdf.

53. "when countries ratify the Convention": Ibid.

54. "Atkinson pointed out that children's rights":
Randeep Ramesh, "Welfare payments cap poses
'real risks to children's rights,'" Guardian.co.uk,
January 11, 2012, http://www.guardian.co.uk/poli
tics/2012/jan/11/welfare-payments-cap-children
-rights.

55. "when adults are making decisions": UNICEF,
"FACT SHEET: A summary of rights under the
Convention of the Rights of the Child."

56. "Whether you ground your kids": Abrams, "Boxer Seeks to Ratify U.N. Treaty That May Erode U.S. Rights."

57. "Children have the right": UNICEF, "FACT SHEET: A summary of rights under the Convention of the Rights of the Child."

58. "any form of discipline": Ibid.

59. "help from the government": Ibid.

60. "help families and guardians": Ibid.

61. "governments must ensure": Ibid.

62. "Children should not be put": Ibid.

63. "children deserve basic human rights": Abrams, "Boxer Seeks to Ratify U.N. Treaty That May Erode U.S. Rights"

64. "when acceding to the convention": Ibid.

65. " 'When it comes to signatories' ": Ibid.

66. "a comprehensive plan": Wendell Cox, Brett Schaefer, and Ronald Utt, Ph.D., "Focus on Agenda 21 Should Not Divert Attention from Homegrown Anti-Growth Policies," RightSideNews.com, December 6, 2011, http://www.rightsidenews.com/2011120615098/life-and-science/energy-and-environment/focus-on-agenda-21-should-not-divert-attention-from-home grown-anti-growth-policies.html.

67. "hundreds of specific goals": Mike Brownfield, "Morning Bell: Agenda 21 and the Threat in Your Backyard," Heritage.org, December 5, 2011, http://blog.heritage.org/2011/12/05/morning-bell-agenda-21-and-the-threat-in-your-backyard/.

68. "voluntary plan": Ibid.

538 • Notes

69. "rethink economic development": Ibid.
70. "Ready to trade in": Brownfield, "Morning Bell: Agenda 21 and the Threat in Your Backyard."
71. "[e]ven though the U.S.": Jim Acosta, "What's with Newt Gingrich and Agenda 21?" CNN .com, November 18, 2011, http://politicalticker .blogs.cnn.com/2011/11/18/whats-with-newt-gingrich -and-agenda-21/?hpt=hp_bn3.
72. "translates into restrictive": Brownfield, "Morning Bell: Agenda 21 and the Threat in Your Backyard."
73. "impose land use": Cox, Schaefer, and Utt, "Focus on Agenda 21 Should Not Divert Attention from Home-grown Anti-Growth Policies."
74. "a massive . . . and condominiums": Richard Rothschild and Scott Strzelczyk, "UN Agenda 21—Coming to a Neighborhood Near You," Ameri canThinker.com, October 28, 2009, http://www .americanthinker.com/2009/10/un_agenda_21_coming _to_a_neigh.html.
75. "Smart growth . . . right to left": Ibid.
76. "rezoning of . . . (subsidies)": Ibid.
77. "Carroll County, Maryland": Ibid.
78. "which forced . . . the world": Cox, Schaefer, and Utt, "Focus on Agenda 21 Should Not Divert Atten-tion from Homegrown Anti-Growth Policies."
79. "Growth control efforts": Ibid.
80. "will destroy . . . state funding": "Battle Against Agenda 21 Heating Up," DeWeeseReport. com, December 18, 2011, http://deweesereport .com/2011/12/.

81. "some churches in South": Ibid.
82. "enable[s] municipalities to": Rothschild and Strzelczyk, "UN Agenda 21: Coming to a Neighborhood Near You."
83. "to begin taking": Mike Opelka, "Does the New White House Rural Council=UN's Agenda 21?" TheBlaze.com, June 21, 2011, http://www.theblaze.com/stories/does-the-new-white-house-rural-council-uns-agenda-21/.
84. "Sixteen percent of the": Ibid.
85. "on streamlining and leveraging": Ibid.
86. "a hint . . . that": Ibid.
87. "I would adopt a very": Acosta, "What's with Newt Gingrich and Agenda 21?"
88. "Everywhere I go": Ibid.
89. "a United Nations": Ibid.
90. "between 2007 and 2011": Lester Brown, "U.S. Carbon Emissions Down as Renewable Energy Keeps Growing," Grist.org, November 2, 2011, http://www.grist.org/fossil-fuels/2011-11-02-u.s.-carbon-emission-down-7-percent-in-four-years-even-bigger.
91. "And . . . this is only": Ibid.
92. "We are now looking": Ibid.
93. U.S. Energy-Related Carbon Dioxide Emissions: Ibid.
94. Cumulative Installed Wind Power Capacity: Ibid.
95. "the fuel efficiency": Ibid.
96. Brown writes that: Ibid.
97. natural gas, which releases: "Natural Gas and the Environment," NaturalGas.org, http://www.naturalgas.org/environment/naturalgas.asp.

98. "it's a simple theory": Barack Obama, "Obama Delivers Remarks on the Economy in Osawatomie, Kansas," WashingtonPost.com, December 6, 2011, http://proj ects.washingtonpost.com/obama-speeches/speech/891/.

99. "it's not surprising": Maria Gavrilovic, "Obama Comments Put Him on the Defensive," CBSNews.com, April 12, 2008, http://www.cbsnews.com/8301 -502443_162-4011169-502443.html.

PART THREE

1. That quiet diplomacy: Associated Press, "Congress Tackles Chinese Currency Manipulation," FoxNews .com, October 1, 2011, http://www.foxnews.com/politics/2011/10/01/congress-tackles-chinese-currency -manipulation/#ixzz1gSOxupgh.

2. "top-secret design": David Wise, "China's Spies are Catching Up," *New York Times*, December 10, 2011, http://www.nytimes.com/2011/12/11/opinion/sunday/ chinas-spies-are-catching-up.html.

3. "a cheaper renminbi": Associated Press, "U.S. Declines to Say China Manipulates It's Currency," *New York Times*, December 27, 2011, http://www .nytimes.com/2011/12/28/business/global/china-isnt -manipulating-currency-us-says.html.

4. The department based: Ibid.

5. "I'm disappointed that": Ibid.

6. "The Chinese government": Sewell Chan, "China Says it Will Not Adjust Exchange Rate," *New York Times*, March 24, 2010, http://www.nytimes .com/2010/03/25/business/global/25yuan.html.

7. Instead of using: Rajashri Chakrabarti, Donghoon Lee, Wilbert Van Der Klaauw and Basit Zafar, "Household Debt and Saving During the 2007 Recession," NewYorkFed.org, Staff Report no. 482, January 2011, http://www.newyorkfed.org/research/staff_reports/sr482.pdf.

8. "oil and Chinese": Peter Morici, "Trade Deficit Blocks Jobs Creation and Growth," November 8, 2011, https://mail.google.com/mail/?shva=1#search/Peter+Morici/13383268f03f209a.

9. "the trade . . . American jobs": Ibid.

10. China already holds: Wes Goodman and Monami Yui, "Treasuries Rise on European Debt Crisis; Gross Sees Low Rates," Bloomberg.com, November 15, 2011, http://www.bloomberg.com/news/2011-11-15/treasuries-hold-gain-on-italy-debt-losses-gross-sees-low-rates.html.

11. $40 billion more: "IRBD Statement of Loans—By Country," WorldBank.org, https://finances.world bank.org/Loan-and-Credit-Administration/IBRD-Statement-of-Loans-By-Country/akb9-rbcs.

12. Twenty years ago: Wayne M. Morrison, "China-U.S. Trade Issues," Congressional Research Service, September 30, 2011, http://www.fas.org/sgp/crs/row/RL33536.pdf.

13. "prior to China's": Nick Carey and James B. Kelleher, "Special Report: Does Corporate America Kowtow to China?" Reuters.com, April 27, 2011, http://www.reuters.com/article/2011/04/27/us-special-report-china-idUSTRE73Q10X20110427.

14. "The level playing field": William McQuillen, "Chinese Distorting Policies Causing Trade Friction, U.S. Says," Bloomberg.com, December 13, 2011, http://www.bloomberg.com/news/2011-12-13/chinese -distorting-policies-causing-trade-friction-u-s-says .html.
15. Since China joined: Carey and Kelleher, "Special Report: Does Corporate America Kowtow to China?"
16. "while [all our economic]": Ibid.
17. "opening China's markets": Ibid.
18. "Membership in the WTO": Peter Ford, "How WTO membership made China the workshop of the world," *Christian Science Monitor*, December 14, 2011, http://www.csmonitor.com/World/Asia -Pacific/2011/1214/How-WTO-membership-made -China-the-workshop-of-the-world.
19. "a raft of . . . in response": Ibid.
20. "We're in the middle": Ibid.
21. "The river . . . to notice": Gordon G. Chang, "China's "Red" Revival: Implications for Business," Forbes .com, October 9, 2011, http://www.forbes.com/sites/ gordonchang/2011/10/09/chinas-red-revival-impli cations-for-business/.
22. "Hu Jintao": Ibid.
23. Chang warns that: Ibid.
24. He notes that Hu: Ibid.
25. "a system in which": Ian Bremmer, "State Capitalism Comes of Age," ForeignAffairs.com, May/June 2009, http://www.panzertruppen.org/2010/economia/ mh002.pdf.

26. "The state's stimulus": Chang, "China's "Red" Revival: Implications for Business."

27. "Now that the": Ibid.

28. "China is raping": Jeff Zeleny, "On Trail, Trump Basks in Spotlight," *New York Times*, April 27, 2011, http://www.nytimes.com/2011/04/28/us/politics/28 trump.html.

29. While the United States: Carey and Kelleher, "Special Report: Does Corporate America Kowtow to China?"

30. "technological advances": "Technology Transfer to China," Bureau of Industry and Security, U.S. Department of Commerce, bis.doc.gov, http://www. bis.doc.gov/defenseindustrialbaseprograms/osies/de fmarketresearchrpts/techtransfer2prc.html.

31. "the remaining power": Carey and Kelleher, "Special Report: Does Corporate America Kowtow to China?"

32. "The patents Cathay": David Barboza, "Entrepreneur's Rival in China: The State," *New York Times*, December 7, 2011, http://www.nytimes .com/2011/12/08/business/an-entrepeneurs-rival-in -china-the-state.html?pagewanted=all.

33. "According to Cathay": Ibid.

34. "with the help of": Ibid.

35. the Chinese government has sided: Ibid.

36. dominant economic force: Ibid.

37. Profits in state owned: Geoff Dyer, "State Capitalism: China's 'Market-Leninism' Has Yet to Face Biggest Test," FT.com, September 13, 2010, http://

www.ft.com/intl/cms/s/0/439ccee0-bec6-11df-a755-00
144feab49a,dwp_uuid=9bee261a-bec7-11df-a755-0014
4feab49a,s01=1.html#axzz1g8j6rkbl.

38. "Bolstered by the": Lolita Baldor, "Pentagon: China
Military Growing Rapidly," Yahoo.com, August 24,
2011, http://news.yahoo.com/pentagon-china-military
-growing-rapidly-180951838.html.
39. "Beijing has closed": Ibid.
40. "all with an eye": Ibid.
41. "The pace and scope": Ibid.
42. As Congresswomen Michele: "Bachmann: The
Greater Our Debt, the Less Money for Our Military
and More Power for China," FoxNews.com, November 23, 2011, http://nation.foxnews.com/michele
-bachmann/2011/11/23/bachmann-greater-our
-debt-less-money-our-military-and-more-power
-china.
43. In fact, our interest: "The Debt to the Penny and Who
Holds It," TreasuryDirect.gov, http://www.treasury
direct.gov/NP/BPDLogin?application=np; "Interest
Expense on the Debt Outstanding," TreasuryDirect
.gov, http://www.treasurydirect.gov/govt/reports/
ir/ir_expense.htm; "October," TreasuryDirect
.gov, http://www.treasurydirect.gov/govt/rates/pd/
avg/2011/2011_10.htm; "Major Foreign Holders of
Treasury Securities," Treasury.gov, http://www
.treasury.gov/resource-center/data-chart-center/tic/
Documents/mfh.txt.
44. "the communist-controlled": Alex Newman, "China's Growing Spy Threat," The-Diplomat.com, Sep-

tember 19, 2011, http://the-diplomat.com/2011/09/19/
chinas-growing-spy-threat/.

45. "In early November": Siobhan Gorman, "U.S. Homes
In on China Spying," *Wall Street Journal*, December
13, 2011, http://online.wsj.com/article/SB1000142405
29702043361045770946908935528130.html.

46. Since 2008, fifty-eight: Newman, "China's Growing
Spy Threat."

47. "There is a lower": Ed Oswald, "US blasts China, Russia Over 'Extensive' Cyberspying," betanews.com,
November 3, 2011, http://betanews.com/2011/11/04/
us-blasts-china-russia-over-extensive-cyberspying/.

48. "Thousands of Chinese": Joe McDonald, "Cyber
Attacks on Chemical Companies Traced to China,"
USA Today, November 1, 2011, http://www.usatoday
.com/money/industries/technol ogy/story/2011-11-01/
China-hackers/51024936/1.

49. "Cyber attacks traced": Ibid.

50. "make advanced materials": Ibid.

51. "the purpose of the": Ibid.

52. The hackers sent: Ibid.

53. "security consultants say": Ibid.

54. "against more than": Ibid.

55. McAfee found hackers: Ibid.

56. "implicated in numerous": "Hackers Used 'Poison
Ivy' Malware to Steal Chemical, Defense Secrets,"
TechCentral.ie, November 2, 2011, http://www.tech
central.ie/article.aspx?id=17710.

57. Military contractors in the: Somini Sengupta,
"Guardians of Internet Security Are Targets," *New*

York Times, August 4, 2011, http://www.nytimes
.com/2011/08/05/technology/guardians-of-internet
-security-are-targets.html.

58. "updates to . . . systems": "Hackers Used 'Poison
Ivy' Malware to Steal Chemical, Defense Secrets."

59. Google has charged: Richard Clarke, "China's Cyberassault on America," *Wall Street Journal*, June 15,
2011, http://online.wsj.com/article/SB1000142405270
2304259304576373391101828876.html.

60. Symantec says that: "Hackers Used 'Poison Ivy' Malware to Steal Chemical, Defense Secrets."

61. In March 2011: Sengupta, "Guardians of Internet
Security Are Targets."

62. In all, the director: Jason Ryan, "US Official Singles
Out China, Russia on Cyber-spying," ABCNews
.com, November 3, 2011, http://abcnews.go.com/
blogs/politics/2011/11/u-s-takes-hard-line-on-chinese
-economic-cyberspying/.

63. "business information" Ibid.

64. "the governments of": Scott Canon, "Foreign Cyber
Thieves Stealing U.S. Trade Secrets, Agency Warns,"
Kansas City Star, November 3, 2011, http://www
.kansascity.com/2011/11/03/3247030/foreign-cyber
-thieves-stealing.html.

65. The government report: Ibid.

66. "Representative Mike Rogers": Eric Engleman,
"China is World's Biggest Cyber Thief: U.S. Report,"
Bloomberg.com, November 3, 2011, http://mobile
.bloomberg.com/news/2011-11-03/u-s-intelligence-re
port-calls-china-world-s-biggest-cyber-thief.

67. "Michael Hayden": Ellen Nakashima, "Lawmaker Calls for International Pressure to Stop China's Cyber-espionage," *Washington Post*, October 4, 2011, http://www.washingtonpost.com/world/national-security/lawmaker-calls-for-international-pressure-to-stop-chinas-cyber-espionage/2011/10/04/gIQAAR26LL_story.html.

68. "have been probed": Fahmida Y. Rashid, "Cyber-Attackers Already Targeting Critical Infrastructure: DHS," eweek.com, October 30, 2011, http://www.eweek.com/c/a/Security/CyberAttackers-Already-Targeting-Critical-Infrastructure-DHS-573564/.

69. "Cyber-attacks have": Ibid.

70. When asked, at a: Ibid.

71. "Wall Street, transportation": Ibid.

72. "in fiscal year": Ibid.

73. "in 2007, angry U.S.": Brett M. Decker and William C. Triplett II, *Bowing to Beijing: How Barack Obama Is Hastening America's Decline and Ushering a Century of Chinese Domination* (Washington, DC; Regnery, 2011), http://www.washingtontimes.com/news/2011/nov/11/ithe-following-is-an-excerpt-from-bowing-to-beijin/.

74. "We now know that": Ibid.

75. " 'terabytes of information' ": Ibid.

76. "Air Force Gen. . . . is admitting": Ibid.

77. The Senate Armed: Malcolm Moore, "US Weapons 'Full of Fake Chinese Parts,' " *Daily Telegraph*, November 8, 2011, http://www.telegraph.co.uk/news/worldnews/northamerica/usa/8876656/US-weapons-full-of-fake-Chinese-parts.html.

78. "it had found": Ibid.
79. Senator Carl Levin: Ibid.
80. The committee reported: Ibid.
81. "in Chinese bazaars": Ibid.
82. "We cannot tolerate": Ibid.
83. "Clinton administration to": Ibid.
84. "a major international": Bill Gertz, *The Failure Factory* (New York: Crown Forum, 2008).
85. "A report by": Congressional China Caucus, "Caucus Brief: Chinese Telecom Firm Tied to Spy Ministry," Forbes.House.gov, October 12, 2011, http://www.forbes.house.gov/ChinaCaucus/Blog/?post id=263993.
86. "despite U.S. government": Bill Gertz, "Chinese Telecom Firm Tied to Spy Ministry," *Washington Times*, October 11, 2011, http://www.washington times.com/news/2011/oct/11/chinese-telecom-firm-tied -to-spy-ministry/?page=all.
87. "big companies like": Ibid.
88. "two years ago": Ibid.
89. "a September 2009": Ibid.
90. "raid on an Iraqi": Gertz, *The Failure Factory*.
91. In 2003, Cisco: "Huawei Climbs 'Food Chain' in Cisco Enterprise Challenge," Bloomberg.com, May 9, 2011, http://www.bloomberg.com/news/2011-05-08/huawei-moves-up-the-food-chain -in-cisco-enterprise-challenge.html.
92. "found a ring": Gertz, *The Failure Factory*.
93. "in 2009, the": Clarke, "China's Cyberassault on America."

94. "left behind software": Newman, "China's Growing Spy Threat."

95. "there is no": Clarke, "China's Cyberassault on America."

96. "January 2003 until": Bill Singer, "Chinese Agricultural Researcher Charged Under Economic Espionage Act for Trade Secret Thefts at Dow and Cargill," Forbes.com, October 19, 2011, http://www.forbes.com/sites/billsinger/2011/10/19/chinese-agricultural-researcher-charged-under-economic-espionage-act-for-trade-secret-thefts-at-dow-and-cargilll/.

97. Huang published Dow's: Ibid.

98. A Chicago grand: "United States of America v. Hanjuan Jin," Justice.gov, February 2008, http://www.justice.gov/usao/iln/pr/chicago/2008/pr0402_01a.pdf.

99. "accused of stealing": Chuck Goudie, "Corporate Espionage Case Example of Growing Issue," ABClocal.go.com, November 3, 2011, http://abclocal.go.com/wls/story?section=news/iteam&id=8418090.

100. In March 2011: "Former Defense Contractor Employee Faces Additional Charges for Allegedly Exporting Military Technology to China," United States Attorney's Office, District of New Jersey, Justice.gov, September 7, 2011, http://www.justice.gov/usao/nj/Press/files/Liu,%20Sixing%20Superseding%20Indictment%20News%20Release.html.

101. "worked on navigation": Ibid.

102. On November 12 . . . the PRC: Ibid.

103. "As early as": Ibid.

104. "has been involved": James Vicini, "US Man Charged with Exporting Space Data to China," Reuters.com, September 24, 2008, http://www.reuters.com/article/2008/09/24/us-usa-space-chinareport-id USTRE48N8LF20080924.
105. "Specifically, Shu provided": "Virginia Physicist Sentenced to 51 Months in Prison for Illegally Exporting Space Launch Data to China and Offering Bribes to Chinese Officials," Justice.gov, April 7, 2009, http://www.justice.gov/opa/pr/2009/April/09-nsd-317.html.
106. "the number one . . . more readily": Jameson Berkow, "Careful in China," *Financial Post*, November 1, 2011, http://www.financialpost.com/entrepreneur/international-business/Careful+China/5636068/story.html.
107. "gaining access to": Leslie Hook, "AMSC to Sue Sinovel in Beijing Court," *Financial Times*, November 4, 2011, http://www.ft.com/intl/cms/s/0/b5e190c8-05db-11e1-a079-00144feabdc0.html#axzz1ekvyYYCx.
108. "was once AMSC's": Ibid.
109. "technology transfer[s] . . . are": "China's 'Technology Transfer' Draws Ire," NPR.org, November 22, 2010,http://www.npr.org/2010/11/22/131520776/china-s-technology-transfer-draws-ire.
110. "some key US": Carey and Kelleher, "Special Report: Does Corporate America Kowtow to China?"
111. "no one . . . China Inc.": Ibid.
112. "big American companies": Ibid.
113. "The Chinese . . . criticize it": Ibid.

114. "four foreign companies": "China's 'Technology Transfer' Draws Ire."
115. "the [Chinese] government": Carey and Kelleher, "Does Corporate America Kowtow to China?"
116. "While aware of the": Ibid.
117. "Now, Chinese companies": Ibid.
118. "We attained our": Norihiko Shirouzu, "Train Makers Rail Against China's High-Speed Designs," *Wall Street Journal*, November 17, 2010, http://online.wsj.com/article/SB10001424052748704814204575507353221141616.html.
119. "the transfer of": "Technology Transfer to China."
120. "the majority of": Ibid.
121. "China's is a": Ibid.
122. "one cannot not": Ibid.
123. "Under the rubric": Dyer, "State Capitalism: China's 'Market-Leninism' Has Yet to Face Biggest Test."
124. "most US and other": "Technology Transfer to China."
125. "limit investment by": Carey and Kelleher, "Does Corporate America Kowtow to China?"
126. "the establishment of": "US Commercial Technology Transfer to the People's Republic of China," FAS.org, http://www.fas.org/nuke/guide/china/doctrine/China1.pdf.
127. "unless significant changes": Ibid.
128. "in China . . . is": Carey and Kelleher, "Special Report: Does Corporate America Kowtow to China?"
129. "his equipment ends": Ibid.
130. "export control review": Ibid.

131. "although it is": Ibid.
132. "continued pressures on": Ibid.
133. "for the most": David Barboza, Christopher Drew, and Steve Lohr, "G.E. to Share Jet Technology with China in New Joint Venture," *New York Times*, January 17, 2011, http://www.nytimes.com/2011/01/18/business/global/18plane.html?pagewanted=all.
134. "no Western company": Ibid.
135. "supplies China's military": Ibid.
136. "the electronics for": Ibid.
137. "risk that Western": Ibid.
138. "were originally developed": John Reed, "Lawmaker Seeks Probe into GE's China Ties," Military.com, November 3, 2011, http://www.military.com/news/article/2011/lawmaker-seeks-probe-into-ges-china-ties.html.
139. "given [the technology's]": Ibid.
140. "be equipped with": Barboza, Drew, and Lohr, "G.E. to Share Jet Technology with China in New Joint Venture."
141. Anyone working in the: Ibid.
142. "partnerships between Western": Reed, "Lawmaker Seeks Probe into GE's China Ties."
143. "enough is left out": Ibid.
144. "foreign involvement in China's aviation": Carey and Kelleher, "Special Report: Does Corporate America Kowtow to China?"
145. "It's unclear . . . taken place": John Bussey, "China Venture Is Good for GE but Is It Good for U.S.?" *Wall Street Journal*, September 30, 2011, http://online.wsj

.com/article/SB100014240529702042262045766012 11
373125234.html.

146. "China's airplane . . . decade off": Howard Schneider, "GE 'all in' on Aviation Deal with China," *Washington Post*, August 22, 2011, http://www .washingtonpost.com/business/economy/ge-all-in-on -aviation-deal-with-china/2011/07/17/gIQAgPmTXJ _story.html.

147. GE added insult: "General Electric Paid No Taxes on $14 Billion with a 57,000 Page Tax Return," Catho lic.org, November 18, 2011, http://www.catholic.org/ business/story.php?id=43735.

148. Except for the: "General Electric," OpenSecrets .org, http://www.opensecrets.org/lobby/clientsum .php?id=D000000125&year=2011.

149. "GE moved its one": Rachel Layne, "GE Moves 115-Year-Old X-Ray Unit's Base to China to Tap Growth," Bloomberg.com, July 25, 2011, http://www .bloomberg.com/news/2011-07-25/ge-healthcare -moves-x-ray-base-to-china-no-job-cuts-planned .html.

150. As part of a commitment: "General Electric Plans to Invest $2 Billion in China," Bloomberg.com, November 9, 2010, http://www.bloomberg.com/news/2010 -11-09/general-electric-to-spend-2-billion-on-china -technology-finance-ventures.html.

151. In the last decade: David Wessel, "Big U.S. Firms Shift Hiring Abroad," *Wall Street Journal*, April 19, 2011, http://online.wsj.com/article/SB1000142405274 87048217045762707836118239 72.html.

152. "Westinghouse Electric": "Senator Webb Introduces Legislation to Stop 'Giving Away' Taxpayer-Funded Technologies to China," Webb.Senate.gov, October 4, 2001, http://webb.senate.gov/newsroom/pressreleases/2011-10-04-02.cfm?renderforprint=1.

153. "Ford Motor Company": Ibid.

154. "Dr. John Holdren": "Obama Science Czar Giving China U.S. Technology," LibertyNews.com, November 8, 2011, http://libertynews.com/2011/11/08/obama-science-czar-giving-china-u-s-technology/.

155. "the PLA is not": Ibid.

156. "apparent eagerness": Ibid.

157. "we should be . . . 40 years": Ibid.

158. "participate, collaborate": Ibid.

159. Largely due to: Kenneth Rapoza, "Romney Says China Is Cheating," Forbes.com, November 21, 2011, http://www.forbes.com/sites/kenrapoza/2011/11/21/romney-says-china-is-cheating/.

160. "28.5 percent": Jim Abrams, "Congress Set to Take Up Trade, Jobs Bill," MSNBC.com, October 10, 2011, http://www.msnbc.msn.com/id/44848290/ns/politics-capitol_hill/t/congress-set-take-trade-jobs-bills/#.TtCEw67sSEk.

161. "committed to gradual": Paul Eckert, "Senate Approves China Yuan Bill, House Fate Unclear," Reuters.com, October 11, 2011, http://www.reuters.com/article/2011/10/12/us-usa-china-idUSTRE79A5AO20111012.

162. 6 percent in the: Eric Lichtblau, "Senate Nears Approval of Measure to Punish China Over Cur-

rency Manipulation," *New York Times*, October 6, 2011, http://www.nytimes.com/2011/10/07/business/senate-nears-approval-of-measure-to-punish-china-over-currency-manipulation.html.

163. "stopped short of formally": Eckert, "Senate Approves China Yuan Bill, House Fate Unclear."

164. "Commerce Department": Ibid.

165. "Up to now": "Congress Tackles Chinese Currency Manipulation," FoxNews.com, October 1, 2011, http://www.foxnews.com/politics/2011/10/01/congress-tackles-chinese-currency-manipulation/.

166. "for specific industries": Ibid.

167. House Republican: Deirdre Walsh, "Boehner Calls China Currency Bill 'Dangerous,'" CNN.com, October 4, 2011, http://politicalticker.blogs.cnn.com/2011/10/04/boehner-calls-china-currency-bill-%E2%80%98dangerous%E2%80%99/.

168. Here's the list: "U.S. Senate Roll Call Votes 112th Congress—1st Session," Senate.gov, http://www.senate.gov/legislative/LIS/roll_call_lists/roll_call_vote_cfm.cfm?congress=112&session=1&vote=00159.

169. "recent comments in": "US Senate Passes Bill to Pressure China on Yuan," BBC.com, October 11, 2011, http://www.bbc.co.uk/news/business-15269123.

170. For the past . . . of Congress: Susan Cornwell and Tim Reid, "Exclusive: China Launches Lobbying Push on Currency Bill," Reuters.com, October 11, 2011, http://www.reuters.com/article/2011/10/11/us-usa-china-lobbying-idUSTRE79A76S20111011.

171. "if passed, the": John Lott, "The China Currency Bill Will Make Americans Poorer, Not Richer," FoxNews.com, October 6, 2011, http://www.foxnews.com/opinion/2011/10/06/china-currency-bill-will-make-americans-poorer-not-richer/.
172. "China's currency manipulation": Ibid.
173. "increasing the value": Ibid.
174. "lobbyists for General": Lichtblau, "Senate Nears Approval of Measure to Punish China Over Currency Manipulation."
175. "They are threatening . . . it on!": Interview with author, Dick Morris, in Detroit, Michigan, October 21, 2011.
176. Jonathan E. Sanford . . . nation's products: Jonathan E. Sanford, "Currency Manipulation: The IMF and WTO," Congressional Research Service, January 26, 2010, http://www.policyarchive.org/handle/10207/bitstreams/20107_Previous_Version_2010-01-26.pdf.
177. "shall cooperate . . . making": Ibid.
178. "it is . . . might transpire": Ibid.
179. "might provide that": Ibid.
180. The agreement between: Ibid.
181. "in an amount equal": Peter Morici, "Smith Faculty Opinion Article," RHSmith.edu, November 8, 2011, http://www.rhsmith.umd.edu/opinion/morici/2011/110811.aspx.
182. "a nationwide survey": Sengupta, "Guardians of Internet Security Are Targets."
183. Federal spending on: Ibid.

184. "the FBI has placed": Natasha Korecki, "Stopping Economic Espionage Becomes Top FBI Priority," *Chicago Sun-Times*, November 4, 2011, http://www.suntimes.com/news/metro/8615181-418/spy-ware.html.

185. "it's really good": Sengupta, "Guardians of Internet Security Are Targets."

186. "when you talk": Lee Ferran, "China Still Spies the Old Fashioned Way, Russia Says," ABCNews.com, October 6, 2011, http://abcnews.go.com/Blotter/china-espionage-spotlight/story?id=14674961.

187. "The weak grow strong": Henry Kissinger, *Years of Upheaval* (New York: Simon & Schuster Paperbacks, 1982).

188. "Beijing is waging": Ferran, "China Still Spies the Old Fashioned Way, Russia Says."

189. "Rogers said the": Ibid.

190. "We have to make it": Andrea Shalal-Esa, "U.S. Should Stand Up to China More: McCain," Reuters.com, November 8, 2011, http://www.reuters.com/article/2011/11/09/us-washington-summit-china-cyber-idUSTRE7A805K20111109.

191. "You could begin": Ferran, "China Still Spies the Old Fashioned Way, Russia Says."

192. "What would we do": Clarke, "China's Cyberassault on America."

193. "in the realm": Ibid.

194. "Three years ago": Ibid.

195. "an electronic Pearl": Decker and Triplett, *Bowing to Beijing*.

196. "a pilot program . . . desk chairs": Ibid.

197. "prompt legislative action": "Obama Officials, Senator Agree to Seek Cyber Deal," Reuters.com, October 20, 2011, http://www.reuters.com/article/2011/10/21/us-usa-cyber-senate-idUSTRE79K03H20111021.

198. "new rules to force": Ibid.

199. "companies incentives to": Ibid.

200. Senator Jim Webb: "Senator Webb Introduces Legislation to Stop 'Giving Away' Taxpayer-Funded Technologies to China," Webb.Senate.gov, October 4, 2011, http://webb.senate.gov/newsroom/pressreleases/2011-10-04-02.cfm?renderforprint=1.

201. "we have seen a": "Obama Thinks China is Acting Shady on Solar," SolarFeeds.com, November 10, 2011, http://www.solarfeeds.com/obama-thinks-china-is-acting-shady-on-solar/.

202. "diplomatic considerations may": Gorman, "U.S. Homes In on China Spying."

PART FOUR

1. The United States . . . Medicaid budget: Alan Kronstadt, "Direct Overt U.S. Aid and Military Reimbursements to Pakistan, FY2002-FY2011," Congressional Research Service, February 16, 2010, https://docs.google.com/viewer?a=v&q=cache:-US-1yKG-LMJ:www.fas.org/sgp/crs/row/pakaid.pdf+US+aid+pakistan&hl=en&gl=us&pid=bl&srcid=ADGEESjJY11eSIRcMprhw58E5XRAin7Ad9k-sYK2ESkttxic_b-TItYJrz-xT4Ka3lS3m0mjZivgXsJYkw5j5O6CtlWDIXYWRCh6IrITDVAMM

QQHq0YUw2wDWp7paevZpz63cSl94V0p&sig
=AHIEtbQ4MDI6szd6-Wtkm0zdAqBVlin12A
&pli=1.

2. A survey in June: Saeed Shah, "Anti-US Politicians on the Rise as Pakistan Ponders Elections," *Miami Herald*, November 6, 2011, http://www.miamiherald .com/2011/11/03/2485705/anti-us-politicians-on-the -rise.html.

3. "The Americans who deal": Bill Keller, "The Pakistanis Have A Point," *New York Times*, December 14, 2011, http://www.nytimes.com/2011/12/18/maga zine/bill-keller-pakistan.html?pagewanted=1&ref =swatvalley.

4. "Ramesh Chopra, a former": Issam Ahmed and Owais Todd, "Osama Bin Laden Killed Near Pakistan's West Point. Was He Really Hidden?" *Christian Science Monitor*, May 2, 2011, http://www.csmonitor .com/World/Asia-South-Central/2011/0502/Osama -bin-Laden-killed-near-Pakistan-s-West-Point.-Was -he-really-hidden.

5. "The idea that": "Did Pakistani Gov't Know Where Osama Bin Laden Was Hiding," Democ racy Now.org, May 2, 2011, http://www.democracy now.org/2011/5/2/did_pakistani_govt_know_where _osama.

6. "The news is that": Ibid.

7. Navy SEALs, apparently: Anna Fifield, "Pakistan Lets China See US Helicopter," *Financial Times*, August 14, 2011, http://www.ft.com/intl/cms/ s/0/09700746-c681-11e0-bb50-00144feabdc0.html.

8. The helicopter was designed: Mark Mazzetti, "U.S. Aides Believe China Examined Stealth Copter," *New York Times*, August 14, 2011, http://www.nytimes.com/2011/08/15/world/asia/15copter.html.

9. "the bin Laden attack": James P. Farwell, "The Pakistan Cauldron, An Exclusive Interview with Author, James P. Farwell," JamesPFarwell.com, http://jamespfarwell.com/AuthorInterview.html.

10. "phony vaccination scheme": Mazzetti, "U.S. Aides Believe China Examined Stealth Copter."

11. "the most deadly": Mark Mazzetti, Alissa J. Rubin, and Scott Shane, "Brutal 'Haqqani Crime Clan Bedevils U.S. in Afghanistan," *New York Times*, September 24, 2011, http://www.nytimes.com/2011/09/25/world/asia/brutal-haqqani-clan-bedevils-united-states-in-afghanistan.html?pagewanted=all.

12. "The Haqqani network": Mazzetti, "U.S. Aides Believe China Examined Stealth Copter."

13. "With ISI support . . . operations": Elisabeth Bumiller and Jane Perlez, "Pakistan's Spy Agency Is Tied to Attack on U.S. Embassy," *New York Times*, September 22, 2011, http://www.nytimes.com/2011/09/23/world/asia/mullen-asserts-pakistani-role-in-attack-on-us-embassy.html.

14. In 2008, American: Jack Healy and Alissa J. Rubin, "U.S. Blames Pakistan-Based Group for Attack on Embassy in Kabul," *New York Times*, September 14, 2011, http://www.nytimes.com/2011/09/15/world/asia/us-blames-kabul-assault-on-pakistan-based-group.html ?pagewanted=all.

15. "according to two": Mazzetti, Rubin, and Shane, "Brutal 'Haqqani Crime Clan Bedevils U.S. in Afghanistan."

16. "They may believe": Bumiller and Perlez, "Pakistan's Spy Agency Is Tied to Attack on U.S. Embassy."

17. "The fragile and troubled": Jackie Northam, "Fragile U.S.-Pakistan Relations on Downward Spiral," NPR.org, September 26, 2011, http://www.npr.org/2011/09/26/140791165/fragile-u-s-pakistan-relations-on-downward-spiral.

18. "'The attack . . . Haqqani network": CNN Wire Staff, "U.S. Ambassador Says Evidence Links Pakistan to Militant Group," CNN.com, September 17, 2011, http://articles.cnn.com/2011-09-17/world/afghanistan.pakistan.haqqani_1_haqqani-network-isi-pakistan-s-inter-services-intelligence?_s=PM:WORLD.

19. "media people coming": Northam, "Fragile U.S.-Pakistan Relations on Downward Spiral."

20. "Barno says Pakistan": Ibid.

21. "The implication is that": Ibid.

22. "Some fear that": Myra Adams, "Pakistan, National Security, and 2012: It's Complicated," PJMedia.com, November 20, 2011, http://pjmedia.com/blog/pakistan-national-security-and-2012-its-complicated/.

23. Pakistan feels that: Ibid.

24. "you could see": Adams, "Pakistan, National Security, and 2012: It's Complicated."

25. "Pakistani soldiers ambushed": Chidanand Rajghatta, "Facing US Fury, Pakistan Woos India,"

TimesofIndia.com, September 28, 2011, http://
articles.timesofindia.indiatimes.com/2011-09-28/us/
30212547_1_pakistani-village-pakistani-soldiers-paki
stani-fan.
26. "The suspicion is that": Arnaud de Borchgrave,
"Black Swans Galore," UPI.com, December 2,
2011, http://www.upi.com/Top_News/Analysis/de
-Borchgrave/2011/12/02/Commentary-Black-swans
-galore/UPI-32481322824349/.
27. "closing two NATO": Ibid.
28. This year, the Obama: Eric Schmitt, "U.S. Pre-
pares for a Curtailed Relationship with Pakistan,"
New York Times, December 25, 2011, http://www
.nytimes.com/2011/12/26/world/asia/us-preparing
-for-pakistan-to-restrict-support-for-afghan-war
.html?_r=1&scp=1&sq=US%20prepares%20for
%20a%20curtailed&st=cse.
29. "With the United States": Ibid.
30. "The United States will": Ibid.
31. "We've closed the chapter": Ibid.
32. "arguably the world's": Borchgrave, "Black Swans
Galore."
33. Last year, we gave: Claire Provost, "Sixty Years
of US Aid to Pakistan: Get the Data," *Guardian*,
July 11, 2011, http://www.guardian.co.uk/global
-development/poverty-matters/2011/jul/11/us-aid-to
-pakistan.
34. total military budget: Raja Muhammad Khan,
"Inside Military Budget," PakObserver.net, http://
pakobserver.net/detailnews.asp?id=96060.

35. "(America's) tax dollars": Carey Schofield, "Exposing Pakistan Army," November 19, 2011, Daily Pioneer .com, http://www.dailypioneer.com/sunday-edition/ sundayagenda/books-reviews/21654-exposing-pakistan -army.html.

36. Thirty-eight percent . . . last year: Syed Fazl-e-Haider, "Pakistan Defense Budget Surges 12%," *Asia Times*, June 9, 2011, http://www.atimes.com/atimes/ South_Asia/MF09Df02.html.

37. Defense eats up: Ibid.

38. This year, the Pakistani: Ibid.

39. We give it another: Kronstadt, "Direct Overt U.S. Aid and Military Reimbursements to Pakistan, FY2002-FY2011."

40. "despite bin Laden's": Adams, "Pakistan, National Security, and 2012: It's Complicated."

41. "a culture of . . . dismissed": Farwell, "The Pakistan Cauldron, An Exclusive Interview with Author, James P. Farwell."

42. "Because tribal loyalty": Ibid.

43. "charismatic former cricket": Shah, "Anti-US Politicians on the Rise as Pakistan Ponders Elections."

44. "Our leaders owned": Ibid.

45. "Pakistan's alliance with": Sebastian Abbot and Asif Shahzad, "Pakistani Cricket Legend Imran Khan and Supporters Rally Against U.S.-Pakistan Alliance," HuffingtonPost.com, October 30, 2011, http://www .huffingtonpost.com/2011/10/30/imran-khan-rally _n_1066173.html.

46. "another critic of": Shah, "Anti-U.S. Politicians on the Rise as Pakistan Ponders Elections."

47. "stopped accepting U.S.": Ibid.

48. "government of President": Ibid.

49. "During its initial": Schofield, "Exposing Pakistan Army."

50. An American businessman: Tom Hussain, "Tensions Rise Between Pakistan's Civilian Leader and its Military," McClatchyDC.com, December 26, 2011, http://www.mcclatchydc.com/2011/12/26/134129/tensions-rise-between-pakistans.html?story_link=email_msg.

51. "[ISI] provided the Taliban": Greg Bruno and Jayshree Bajoria, Council on Foreign Relations, CRF.org, June 26, 2008, http://www.cfr.org/pakistan/us-pakistan-military-cooperation/p16644.

52. When al-Qaeda used: Ibid.

53. "Washington considers Afghan": "Ups & Downs in Pak-US Ties Likely to Continue," Nation.com, November 15, 2011, http://nation.com.pk/pakistan-news-newspaper-daily-english-online/Regional/Lahore/15-Nov-2011/Ups—downs-in-Pak US-ties-likely-to-continue?utm_source=feedburner&utm_medium=feed&utm_campaign=Feed%3A+pakistan-news-newspaper-daily-english-online%2Flahore+%28The+Nation+%3A+Lahore+News%29.

54. "Pakistani intelligence has long": "An Unhappy Alliance," Los Angeles Times, May 7, 2011, http://articles.latimes.com/2011/may/07/opinion/la-ed-pakistan-20110507.

55. US Military and Economic: Provost, "Sixty Years of US Aid to Pakistan: Get the Data."

56. Since World War: Ibid.

57. "the withheld aid": Ibid.

58. The *Guardian* recounts: Declan Walsh, "UP to 70% of US Aid to Pakistan 'Misspent,'" *Guardian*, February 27, 2008, http://www.guardian.co.uk/world/2008/feb/27/pakistan.usa.

59. "American officials . . . this money": Ibid.

60. At least half: Ibid.

61. "American military . . . ammunition apiece": Carlotta Gall, David Rohde, David E. Sanger, and Eric Schmitt, "U.S. Officials See Waste in Billions Sent to Pakistan," *New York Times*, December 24, 2007, http://www.nytimes.com/2007/12/24/world/asia/24military.html.

62. "[l]arge sums went": Brajesh Upadhyay, "US Aid 'Failing to Reach Target,'" BBC.co.uk, May 16, 2008, http://news.bbc.co.uk/2/hi/7405434.stm.

63. "[a] regular complaint": Ibid.

64. On October 29, 2008: "Pakistan Earthquake," USAID.gov, October 29, 2008, http://www.usaid.gov/locations/asia/countries/pakistan/eq/.

65. In August and September: "Pakistan Disaster Assistance at a Glance," USAID.gov, http://www.usaid.gov/our_work/humanitarian_assistance/disaster_assistance/countries/pakistan/template/index.html.

66. War has caused: Ibid.

67. In July 2010: Ibid

68. "bad marriage": "Ups & Downs in Pak-US Ties Likely to Continue."

69. Obama travelled . . . nuclear blast): Jayshree Bajoria, "A Closer U.S.-India Embrace," CFR.org, November 8, 2010, http://www.cfr.org/economics/closer-us -india-embrace/p23332.

70. "United States to": Ibid.

71. "terror machine is as": Ibid.

72. "conceded Pakistan's . . . Obama said": Ibid.

73. "Pakistan's view of": Howard B. Schaffer and Teresita C. Schaffer, "Dealing with India in the U.S.-Pakistan Relationship," TheHindu.com, June 13, 2011, http:// www.thehindu.com/opinion/lead/article2099122.ece.

74. "They feel that the": Ibid.

75. "Pakistan's spy agency": Associated Press, "Influence Game: India, Pakistan Vie for US Backing," FoxNews.com, July 25, 2011, http://www.foxnews .com/us/2011/07/25/influence-game-india-pakistan -vie-for-us-backing/.

76. "[m]ay have received": Ibid.

77. "Syed Ghulam Nabi": Ibid.

78. Pakistan has even hired: Ibid.

79. "There's little to show": Ibid.

80. "Pakistan expresses apprehension": Dr. Mohammed Samir Hussain, "Pakistan's Response to the Growing India-U.S. Strategic Relationship," ForeignPolicyJournal.com, October 14, 2011, http:// www.foreignpolicyjournal.com/2011/10/14/pakistans -response-to-the-growing-india-u-s-strategic-relatio nship/.

81. "bring down the": Ibid.

82. "the increasing number": Ibid.
83. "Washington regards India": Schaffer and Schaffer, "Dealing with India in the U.S.-Pakistan Relationship."
84. "As the Pakistanis": Ibid.
85. "have not stilled": Ibid.
86. As noted, the Pew: David Cohen, "The Problem of Pakistan, the Promise of India," DailyCaller.com, June 23, 2011, http://dailycaller.com/2011/06/23/the -problem-of-pakistan-the-promise-of-india/.
87. General Stanley A.: "Should the United States Withdraw from Afghanistan?" CATO.org, November/ December 2009, http://www.cato.org/pubs/policy _report/v31n6/cpr31n6-3.html.
88. "Well, if al": Ibid.
89. "[m]eeting [the people's]": Ibid.
90. "assumes that a foreign": Ibid.
91. "going after al": Ibid.
92. "What has happened": Ibid.
93. "We don't need": Ibid.
94. "We do not need": Ibid.
95. "we can develop": Ibid.
96. The *New York Times*: Helene Cooper, "Cost of Wars a Rising Issue as Obama Weighs Troop Levels," *New York Times*, June 21, 2011, http:// www.nytimes.com/2011/06/22/us/politics/22costs .html?pagewanted=all.

PART FIVE

1. One thousand, eight hundred: "Fatalities by Country," icasualties.org, http://icasualties.org/oef/.

2. Combat Deaths in Afghanistan: Ibid.
3. The United States gave: "Table 1297. U.S. Government Foreign Grants and Credits by Type and Country: 2000 to 2010," Census.gov, http://www.census.gov/compendia/statab/2012/tables/12s1297.pdf.
4. "Up to 30%": Justin Elliott, "Corruption in Afghanistan: Worse than You Thought," Salon.com, November 17, 2011, http://www.salon.com/2011/11/17/corruption_in_afghanistan_worse_than_you_thought/singleton/.
5. "Corruption takes many": Ibid.
6. It is tied for 176th place: "Corruption Perceptions Index 2010 Results," Transparency.org, http://www.transparency.org/policy_research/surveys_indices/cpi/2010/results.
7. "insulate them from": Mark Mazzetti and Rod Nordland, "U.S. Debates Karzai's Place in Graft Fight," New York Times, September 15, 2010, http://query.nytimes.com/gst/fullpage.html?res=9C0CE6DB163AF936A2575AC0A9669D8B63&scp=3&sq=Called%20%E2%80%98top-up%20raises,%E2%80%99%20they%20had%20been%20paid%20by%20the%20American%20government%20to%20keep%20&st=cse&pagewanted=1.
8. "the result of a": Rod Nordland and Alissa J. Rubin, "New Afghan Corruption Inquiries Frozen," New York Times, September 15, 2010, http://query.nytimes.com/gst/fullpage.html?res=9B0DE6D71E3BF936A2575AC0A9669D8B63&pagewanted=all.

9. "top official in": Ibid.

10. "part of . . . knitted together": James Risen, "Karzai's Kin Use Ties to Gain Power in Afghanistan," *New York Times*, October 5, 2010, http://www.nytimes.com/2010/10/06/world/asia/06karzai.html.

11. Taj Ayubi, who: Ibid.

12. Karzai's brother, Ahmed: Ibid.

13. His other brother: Ibid.

14. "One of President": Ibid.

15. "at least six": Ibid.

16. "American officials say": Ibid.

17. "Afghanistan's supply of": Nadia Prupis, "Opium Production in Afghanistan: Strong and Corrupt as Ever," RAWA.org, January 7, 2011, http://www.rawa.org/temp/runews/2011/01/07/opium-production-in-afghanistan-strong-and-corrupt-as-ever.html.

18. "to two individuals": Ibid.

19. "found an enormous . . . the truck": Risen, "Reports Link Karzai's Brother to Afghanistan Heroin Trade," *New York Times*, October 4, 2008, http://www.nytimes.com/2008/10/05/world/asia/05afghan.html?pagewanted=all.

20. "proved so valuable": Ibid.

21. "Narco-corruption": Ibid.

22. Afghan corruption briefly: Job Boone, "The Financial Scandal that Broke Afghanistan's Kabul Bank," Guardian.co.uk, June 16, 2011, http://www.guardian.co.uk/world/2011/jun/16/kabul-bank-afghanistan-financial-scandal.

23. "while some of that": Alissa Rubin, "Karzai Says Foreigners Are Responsible for Corruption," *New York Times*, December 11, 2011, http://www.nytimes.com/2011/12/12/world/asia/karzai-demands-us-hand-over-afghan-banker.html.
24. Neither of the: Ibid.
25. "When it comes": Dexter Filkins, "Bribes Corrode Afghans' Trust in Government," *New York Times*, January 1, 2009, http://www.nytimes.com/2009/01/02/world/asia/02kabul.html?scp=5&sq=the%20state%20built%20on%20the%20ruins%20of%20the&st=cse.
26. "Want to be . . . his release": Ibid.
27. "Kept afloat by billions": Ibid.
28. "There were irregularities": "Karzai Admits Election Fraud," *Washington Times*, October 14, 2009, http://www.washingtontimes.com/news/2009/oct/14/karzai-admits-election-fraud/.
29. "The United Nations": "White House Says Hamid Karzai's Election Fraud Outburst 'Troubling,'" Telegraph.co.uk, April 2, 2010, http://www.telegraph.co.uk/news/worldnews/northamerica/usa/7548085/White-House-says-Hamid-Karzais-election-fraud-outburst-troubling.html.

PART SIX

1. "The Saudi government bases": "2010 Human Rights Report: Saudi Arabia," State.gov, April 8, 2011, http://www.state.gov/g/drl/rls/hrrpt/2010/nea/154472.htm.

2. "Some interpretations are": "Fox News Brainroom: What is Sharia Law?" FoxNews.com, October 24, 2011, http://foxnewsinsider.com/2011/10/24/fox-news -brainroom-what-is-sharia-law/.

3. "Saudi Arabia had the": "Saudi Arabia," U.S. Department of State, State.gov, March 6, 2007, http://www .state.gov/g/drl/rls/hrrpt/2006/78862.htm.

4. "Judicially sanctioned corporal": "2010 Human Rights Report: Saudi Arabia."

5. "On July 10": Ibid.

6. "On September 28": Ibid.

7. "Rape is a punishable": Ibid.

8. "a 27 year old": Sarah N. Stern, ed., *Saudi Arabia and the Global Islamic Terrorist Network: America and the West's Fatal Embrace* (New York: Palgrave Macmillan, 2011).

9. "unlike in the": Ibid.

10. "In a Saudi Sharia": Ibid., page ix x.

11. The country has an: "Saudi Arabia," Wikipedia.org, http://en.wikipedia.org/wiki/Saudi_Arabia.

12. "[i]n August, 2010": Stern, *Saudi Arabia and the Global Islamic Terrorist Network*, page x.

13. "There is absolutely": Ibid.

14. On October 26: Ibid.

15. Two hundred and: "United States Military Casualties of War," Wikipedia.org, http://en.wikipedia.org/wiki/United_States_military_casualties_of_war.

16. "covered with . . . man-of-war": Colonel Bill Eddy, "An Earlier Envoy," Economist.com, November 6, 2008, http://www.economist.com/node/12551590.

17. "semi-literate desert": Thomas W. Lippman, "The Day FDR Met Saudi Arabia's Ibn Saud," *The Link*, Volume 38, Issue 2, April-May 2005, https://docs .google.com/a/culverad.com/viewer?url=http://www .hlinstruments.com/Worldpeace_Forum/Iraq-Moslems -War/AMEU-vol38_issue2_2005-FDR-KingSaud .pdf.

18. Saud's meeting . . . airborne: Ibid.

19. In the year after: Ibid.

20. U.S. troops comprised: "Gulf War," Wikipedia.org, http://en.wikipedia.org/wiki/Gulf_War.

21. "One-hundred twenty": "Bush's Brave New World Order," AirForce-Magazine.com, August 2007, http://www.airforce-magazine.com/MagazineAr chive/Pages/2007/August%202007/0807keeper.aspx.

22. $30 billion: Mark Landler and Steven Lee Myers, "With $30 Billion Arms Deal, U.S. Bolsters Saudi Ties," *New York Times*, December 29, 2011, http:// www.nytimes.com/2011/12/30/world/middleeast/with -30-billion-arms-deal-united-states-bolsters-ties-to -saudi-arabia.html.

23. "This sale will send": Ibid.

24. "Donors in Saudi": Eric Lichtblau and Eric Schmitt, "Cash Flow to Terrorists Evades U.S. Efforts," *New York Times*, April 2006, http://www.nytimes .com/2010/12/06/world/middleeast/06wikileaks-finan cing.html?pagewanted=all.

25. "Saudis [have] consistently": Rachel Ehrenfeld, "Their Oil Is Thicker than Our Blood," AC Democ racy.org, December 14, 2011, http://www.acde

mocracy.org/viewarticle.cfm?category=U.S.%20Po
licy&id=1223.

26. In 2007, the *New York Times*: Ibid.
27. "Abu Ahmed, one": Ibid.
28. "reported that millions": Ibid.
29. "Saudi Arabia has": Ibid.
30. "Saudi laxity in": Ibid.
31. "continuing to be": Ibid.
32. "raise millions of": Ibid.
33. "in May, 2010": Ibid.
34. "If I could": Ibid.
35. "Saudi Arabia today": Ibid.
36. "Pakistani police reported": Ibid.
37. "The Saudi-based": Ibid.
38. "the involvement of": Ibid.
39. "Saudi funding to": Ibid.
40. "Saudi Arabia is a": Ibid.
41. "Today's action targets": Ibid.
42. Indeed, in 2010: Stephen I. Landman, "Trial Exposes Charity Abuse," InvestigativeProject.org, September 8, 2010, http://www.investigativeproject.org/2170/trial-exposes-charity-abuse.
43. "Uneasy lies the": William Shakespeare, *Henry IV*, http://www.phrases.org.uk/meanings/396000.html.
44. Saudis have spent: "A Second Look at the Saudis," ASEcondLookattheSaudis.com, http://www.asecond lookatthesaudis.com/sitebuildercontent/sitebuilderfiles/asecondlookatthesaudisaglobalagenda.pdf.
45. "The mentality of each": "Not Much Joy at a Saudi Christmas," TomGrossMedia.com, December 24,

2002, http://www.tomgrossmedia.com/mideastdis
patches/archives/000750.html.

46. "along with other": Nina Shea, "Saudi Arabia: Fueling Religious Persecution and Extremism," Stone
gateInstitute.org, December 7, 2010, http://www
.stonegateinstitute.org/1717/saudi-arabia-religious-per
secution.

47. "The 'lesson goals' ": Ibid.

48. The Saudis have: Pierre Tristam, "A Warning to
Saudi Arabia from One of Its Own: Alwaleed bin
Talal," MiddleEast.about.com, February 25, 2011,
http://middleeast.about.com/b/2011/02/25/a-warning
-to-saudi-arabia-from-one-of-its-own-alwaleed-bin
-talal.htm.

49. "a dedicated . . . 'their ilk' ": Steven Stotsky, "Harvard's Middle East Outreach Center Headed by BDS
Supporter," CAMERA.org, December 13, 2011, http://
www.camera.org/index.asp?x_context=2&x_outlet
=118&x_article=2161.

50. "the town mayor": Ibid.

51. "pushed the controversial": Ibid.

52. "A 2008 report": Ibid.

53. Of the 1,300: Ehrenfeld, "Their Oil is Thicker than
Our Blood."

54. Frank Gaffney's Center: "Gaffney: 81% of US
Mosques Promote Jihad," TheRightScoop.com, June
12, 2011, http://www.therightscoop.com/gaffney-81
-of-us-mosques-promote-jihad/.

55. In Britain, for example: Ehrenfeld, "Their Oil Is
Thicker than our Blood."

56. "serves as a recruiting": Ibid.

57. "Saudi billionaire Prince": Ibid.

58. "lavishly funds Muslim": Ibid.

59. four of the top: Stern, *Saudi Arabia,* page 49.

60. "Their favored . . . terrorist financing": Ibid.

61. "A relatively . . . of Jihad": Stern, page 43.

62. Mufti Taqa . . ."of Islam": Ibid., page 42.

63. "I consider this": Ibid.

64. The Carter Center: Ibid.

65. "regularly published anti-Semitic": Ibid., page 94.

66. "orchestrated by the": Ibid., page 95.

67. "peace, health, and": Ibid.

68. Kyle Shideler and Ian Weinglass: Ibid.

69. In December . . . a year: Stern, *Saudi Arabia,* page 93.

70. "Loeffler might be": Allan P. Duncan, "So Who's Protecting the Saudis?" OpEdNews.com, July 17, 2003, http://www.opednews.com/Duncan_so_who.htm.

71. "to discuss the kingdom": Stern, *Saudi Arabia,* page 93.

72. "The cold fact": Ibid., page 94.

73. "If you have any": Ibid., page 4.

74. One-third of the: Dr. Majid Al-Moneef, "The Contribution of the Oil Sector to Arab Economic Development," OFID.org, September 2006, http://www.ofid.org/publications/PDF/ofid_pam34.pdf.

75. Oil accounts for: "Saudi Arabia," Encyclopedia.com, 2007, http://www.encyclopedia.com/topic/Saudi_Arabia.aspx.

76. Non-oil manufacturing: "Manufacturing Booms in Saudi Arabia," AMEinfo.com, October 31, 2007, http://www.ameinfo.com/136613.html.

77. North American oil: Tim Fowler, " Oil Output Could Top 40-Year-Old Peak," *Houston Chronicle*, September 28, 2011, http://www.chron.com/business/energy/article/N-American-oil-output-could-top-40-year-old-peak-2193837.php.
78. "US oil production": Ibid.
79. "The combination of horizontal": "Shale Oil—The Rush for Black Gold," EnergyNow.com, November 20, 2011, http://www.energynow.com/video/2011/11/18/shale-oil-rush-black-gold-11202011.
80. 1.5 to 2.6 trillion: "Oil Shale/Oil Sands," AltEnergy Sources.webs.com, http://altenergysources.webs.com/oilshaletarsands.htm.
81. In 2010, the US: "Hydraulic Fracturing 101," EarthWorksAction.org, http://www.earthworks action.org/issues/detail/hydraulic_fracturing_101.
82. "that the injection": "Evaluation of Impacts to Underground Sources of Drinking Water by Hydraulic Fracturing of Coalbed Methane Reservoirs; National Study Final Report," EPA.gov, http://www.epa.gov/ogwdw/uic/pdfs/cbmstudy_attach_uic_final_fact_sheet.pdf.
83. "I'm not aware": Thomas Lifson and Brian Schwarz, "EPA Administrator Confirms No Water Contamination from Fracking," AmericanThinker.com, May 26, 2011, http://www.americanthinker.com/blog/2011/05/epa_administrator_confirms_no.html.
84. "levels . . . standards": Katy Gresh, "DEP Announces Testing for Radioactivity of River Water Downstream of Marcellus Water Treatment Plants Shows Water is

Safe," Pennsylvania Department of Environmental Protection, portal.state.pa.us, March 7, 2011, http://www.portal.state.pa.us/portal/server.pt/community/newsroom/14287?id=16532&typeid=1.

85. "we could, in effect": "Energy's Myths," AlternativeEnergy.procon.org, July 3, 2008, http://alternativeenergy.procon.org/view.answers.php?questionID=1255.

86. But from 2002 to 2008: "Gulf of Mexico Oil and Gas Production Forecast: 2009–2018," http://www.gomr.boemre.gov/PDFs/2009/2009-012.pdf.

87. Petrobras, has contracted: Joe Carroll, "Petrobras Hires 80% of Deepwater Rigs, Inflates Rents (Update1)," Bloomberg.com, May 15, 2008, http://www.bloomberg.com/apps/news?pid=newsarchive&sid=a8V5CHwdycrk&refer=home.

88. 7.2 billion barrels: "An Assessment of the Undiscovered Hydrocarbon Potential of the Nation's Outer Continental Shelf," boemre.gov, http://www.boemre.gov/itd/pubs/1996/96-0034.pdf.

89. There are currently: Rick Jervis, William M. Welch, and Richard Wolf, "Worth the Risk? Debate on Offshore Drilling Heats Up," USAToday.com, July 14, 2008, http://www.usatoday.com/money/industries/energy/2008-07-13-offshore-drilling_N.htm.

90. They have produced: Ibid.

91. "only 852 barrels": Ibid.

92. "about 172 active rigs": Ibid.

93. 19.6 million barrels: "Oil Consumption in North America," Maps.UNOmaha.edu, http://maps.uno

maha.edu/peterson/funda/sidebar/oilconsumption
.html.

94. 18.7 million in 2009: "Energy Statistics, Oil, Consumption (most Recent) by Country," Nation Master
.com,http://www.nationmaster.com/graph/ene_oil_con
-energy-oil-consumption.

95. Gasoline consumption fell: "2010 Gasoline Consumption," AmericanFuels.blogspot.com, February 26,
2011,http://americanfuels.blogspot.com/2011/02/2010
-gasoline-consumption.html.

96. In the 1990s: "Energy in the United States," Wikipe
dia.org, http://en.wikipedia.org/wiki/Energy_in_the
_United_States.

97. "a small generator": Stern, *Saudi Arabia and the Global Islamic Terrorist Network*, page 6.

98. "G.M. Officials have said": Nick Bunkley and Bill Vlasic, "G.M. Re-examines Volt as Safety Concerns Rise," *New York Times*, December 7, 2011, http://
www.nytimes.com/2011/12/08/business/general-motors
-to-re-examine-volts-welded-parts.html.

99. "the shift in less than": David Welch, "GM Seeks Out Batteries Less Volatile than Volt's for Spark Model,"
Businessweek.com, December 9, 2011, http://www
.businessweek.com/news/2011-12-09/gm-seeks-out
-batteries-less-volatile-than-volt-s-for-spark-model
.html.

100. "mainstream U.S. companies": "Plug-In vehicles are Key Pillar in U.S. Energy Security Strategy,"
PRNewswire.com, December 8, 2011, http://www
.prnewswire.com/news-releases/plug-in-vehicles-are

-key-pillar-in-us-energy-security-strategy-1352552
28.html.

101. "in Europe . . . of cost": "Revenge of the Petrol-
heads," Economist.com, December 10, 2011, http://
www.economist.com/node/21541443.

102. "to meet a series": Ibid.

103. in 2008, natural gas: "Electricity Generation," Wiki
pedia.org, http://en.wikipedia.org/wiki/Electricity
_generation.

104. provides 24 percent: "What Is Natural Gas?" NWGA
.org, http://www.nwga.org/index.php?option=com
_content&view=article&id=119&Itemid=125.

105. 49 percent in 2008: "Coal," Wikipedia.org, http://
en.wikipedia.org/wiki/Coal.

106. "just three years ago": Ben Casselman, "Gas
Fields Go from Bust to Boom," *Wall Street Jour-
nal*, April 30, 2009, http://online.wsj.com/article/
SB124104549891270585.html.

107. Electricity Generation in the US: "Electric Power
Monthly," eia.gov, December 16, 2011, http://www
.eia.gov/electricity/monthly/index.cfm.

108. "Huge new . . . that size": Ibid.

109. In 2008 . . . for some time: "Natural Gas Year-in-
Review," eia.gov, December 9, 2011, http://www.eia
.gov/naturalgas/review/index.cfm.

110. "replace 75% of the": David Fessler, "My Plan for
Eliminating America's Dependence on Foreign Oil,"
InvestmentU.com, April 2, 2010, http://www.invest
mentu.com/2010/April/how-to-eliminate-americas
-dependence-on-foreign-oil.html.

111. "while electric cars might": Ibid.

112. "Converting heavy-duty trucks": "Pickens Encouraged by President Obama's Call for a More Secure American Energy Future," NotPetroleum.com, March 30, 2011, http://notpetroleum.com/2011/03/30/pickens-encouraged-by-president-obama%E2%80%99s-call-for-a-more-secure-american-energy-future/.

113. But a long-haul truck: Jim Snyder, "Pickens Losing to Koch in Natural-Gas Feud," Bloomberg.com, July 12, 2011, http://www.bloomberg.com/news/2011-07-12/pickens-losing-to-koch-in-billionaires-fight-over-natural-gas-subsidies.html.

114. At present . . . their pumps: Jim Motavalli, "A Bill for T. Boone Pickens: Doubling Natural Gas Car Subsidies," CBSNews.com, July 9, 2009, http://www.cbsnews.com/8301-505123_162-43140580/a-bill-for-t-boone-pickens-doubling-natural-gas-car-subsidies/.

115. "cost differential . . . diesel today": Howard S. Abramson, "Pickens Says Natural Gas Trucks Will Soon Cost the Same as Diesel," TTNews.com, September 22, 2011, http://www.ttnews.com/articles/basetemplate.aspx?storyid=27646.

116. In 1973 . . . barrels per day: David Murphy, "The True Value of Energy Is the Net Energy," TheOilDrum.com, June 12, 2010, http://netenergy.theoildrum.com/node/6545.

117. 10 percent of the cars: Barbara Powell, "U.S. Gasoline Demand at 14-Week High, MasterCard

Says," Bloomberg.com, December 6, 2011, http://
www.bloomberg.com/news/2011-12-06/u-s-gasoline
-demand-rises-to-14-week-high-mastercard-says
.html.

118. US Oil Imports by Country: "Crude Oil and Total
Petroleum Imports Top 15 Countries," eia.gov,
November 29, 2011, http://www.eia.gov/pub/oil_gas/
petroleum/data_publications/company_level_imports/
current/import.html.

119. 9 million barrels: "Registration of Crude Oil Imports
and Deliveries in the European Union," ex.europa
.eu, January-March 2011, http://ec.europa.eu/energy/
observatory/oil/doc/import/coi/eu-coi-from-extra-eu
-2011-01-03.pdf.

120. In September 2011: Isaac Arnsdorf, "U.S. Oil Independence Beckons as Exports Rise: Chart of the
Day," Bloomberg.com, December 12, 2011, http://
www.bloomberg.com/news/2011-12-13/u-s-oil-inde
pendence-beckons-as-exports-rise-chart-of-the-day
.html.

121. "The US is now": Timothy Taylor, "Conversable
Economist," ConversableEconomist.blogspot.com,
December 5, 2011, http://conversableeconomist
.blogspot.com/2011_11_06_archive.html.

122. "By the 2020s": Amy Myers Jaffe, "The Americas, Not the Middle East, Will Be the World Capital of Energy," ForeignPolicy.com, September/
October 2011, http://www.foreignpolicy.com/arti
cles/2011/08/15/the_americas_not_the_middle_east
_will_be_the_world_capital_of_energy.

PART SEVEN

1. "task force was established": George Russell, "ANALYSIS: Ban Ki-Moon's New Weapon in Battles Over U.N. Oversight," FoxNews.com, July 26, 2010, http://www.foxnews.com/world/2010/07/26/analysis-ban-ki-moons-new-weapon-battles-oversight/.
2. Ahlenius, angry at her: Ibid.
3. "I am often asked": Robert M. Appleton, "Chairman of the United Nations Procurement Task Force, to the United States House of Representatives, Committee on Foreign Affairs," For eignAffairs.house.gov, January 25, 2011, http://foreignaffairs.house.gov/112/app012511.pdf.
4. "the most disappointing": Ibid.
5. "the Oil-for-Food": Ibid.
6. "unquestionably reverted to": Ibid.
7. "the incentives in the": Ibid.
8. "pleaded guilty to federal": Claudia Rosett and George Russell, "The U.N.'s Spreading Bribery Scandal: Russian Ties and Global Reach," CFIF.org, September 8, 2005, http://www.cfif.org/htdocs/freedomline/un_monitor/guest_commentary/un-corruption-widespread.htm.
9. "noted in passing": Ibid.
10. "were convicted, after a": Appleton, "Chairman of the United Nations Procurement Task Force, to the United States House of Representatives, Committee on Foreign Affairs."
11. "significant sums of . . . this matter": Ibid.
12. Appleton also found: Ibid.

13. "the efforts of": Ibid.
14. "because the PTF": Ibid.
15. "prior to the": Ibid.
16. "the hostility to the": Ibid.
17. Up to the last: Ibid.
18. "including a report": Ibid.
19. "As far as I am": Ibid.
20. "a nondescript . . . the Organization": Ibid.
21. The Office of . . . financial support: Ibid.
22. "UN funding arrangements": Internal Oversight and Procurement Controls and Processes Need Strengthening," GAO.gov, April 27, 2006, http://www.gao.gov/products/GAO-06-701T.
23. "top UN officials": Russell, "ANALYSIS: Ban Ki-Moon's New Weapon in Battles Over U.N. Oversight."
24. "under a secretary": Ibid.
25. "Never before": Ibid.
26. "number of . . . as a mess": Ibid.
27. "a bigger say": Ibid.
28. "for the previous . . . the staff": Ibid.
29. "deliberately chosen from": George Russell, "U.N. Judges Charge Ban Ki-moon with Power Grab, Distortions of Their Rulings," FoxNews.com, November 11, 2011, http://www.foxnews.com/world/2011/11/11/un-judges-charge-ban-ki-moon-with-power-grab-distortions-their-rulings/.
30. "undermine the integrity": Ibid.
31. "the judges also . . . meaningless": Ibid.
32. "toothless, especially when": Ibid.

33. "produce a document": Ibid.
34. "hearing appeals from": Ibid.
35. "then whistleblowers will": Ibid.
36. This year, the United States: George Russell, "U.S. Diplomats Growing Frustrated at United Nations' Budget Games," FoxNews.com, October 7, 2011, http://www.foxnews.com/world/2011/10/07/us-diplomats-blow-whistle-on-united-nations-budget-games.
37. "The average total": Ibid.
38. Responding to global: George Russell, "Diplomats Growing Frustrated at United Nations Budget Games," FoxNews.com, October 7, 2011, http://www.foxnews.com/world/2011/10/07/us-diplomats-blow-whistle-on-united-nations-budget-games/.
39. "pursue the roll-back": Ibid.
40. "to be frank": "Testimony by Ambassador Bolton before the Senate Foreign Relations Committee," GlobalSecurity.org, May 25, 2006, http://www.globalsecurity.org/military/library/congress/2006_hr/060525-bolton.pdf.
41. "[a]t least two": George Russell, "U.N. Development Agencies Accumulate Billions—Keep Spending a Secret," FoxNews.com, December 12, 2011, http://www.foxnews.com/world/2011/12/12/un-development-agencies-accumulate-billions-and-keep-spending-secret/.
42. "contribute to . . . money goes": Ibid.
43. "grossly . . . recent staff costs": Ibid.
44. "implies that substantial": Ibid.

45. At UNFPA, the consultants: Ibid.

46. UNICEF, formerly one of: Ibid.

47. The United Nations Development: Ibid.

48. "culture of inaction": Randy Hall, "Bolton: US Reforms Challenging UN's 'Culture of Inaction,'" cnsnews.com, July 7, 2008, http://cnsnews.com/news/article/bolton-us-reforms-challenging-uns-culture-in action.

49. "changing that culture": "Challenges and Opportunities in Pushing Ahead on UN Reform," GlobalSe curity.org, May 25, 2006, http://www.globalsecurity .org/military/library/congress/2006_hr/060525-bol ton.pdf.

50. "in response to news": George Russell, "U.N.'s Botched Computer-System Overhaul: A Major 'Failure' of Ban Ki-Moon's Management," FoxNews .com, December 6, 2011, http://www.foxnews.com/world/2011/12/06/united-nations-failed-computer -system-highlights-bloat-that-defines-secretarys/.

51. "at the breaking point": Ibid.

52. Ban's office reports that: Ibid.

53. "not sufficiently supported": Eric Shawn, "Report Details Deficiencies in U.N. Procurement Department," FoxNews, December 6, 2005, http://www .foxnews.com/story/0,2933,177817,00.html.

54. "UN procurement employees": Ibid.

55. "There does not appear": Ibid.

56. "These countries have made": "Testimony by Ambassador Bolton before the Senate Foreign Relations Committee."

57. "There must be a": Appleton, "Chairman of the United Nations Procurement Task Force, to the United States House of Representatives, Committee on Foreign Affairs."
58. "The other structural": Ibid.
59. The United States pays: "US Contributions to UN Regular Budget," EYEontheUN.org, http://www.eyeontheun.org/facts.asp?pl=28&p=230.

PART EIGHT

1. "The state of Africa": Dambisa Moyo, *Dead Aid: Why Aid Is Not Working and How There Is a Better Way for Africa* (New York: Farrar, Straus, Giroux, 2009), introduction.
2. In May 2004: Moyo, page 52.
3. Take up the White Man's: "Rudyard Kipling, The White Man's Burden (1899)," public.wsu.edu, http://public.wsu.edu/~wldciv/world_civ_reader/world_civ_reader_2/kipling.html.
4. 41 percent to 25 percent: "International Poverty Comparisons," WorldBank.org, http://site resources.worldbank.org/INTPA/Resources/429966-12597748 05724/Poverty_Inequality_Handbook_Ch10.pdf.
5. But of the $525: "IRBD Statement of Loans—By Country."
6. 7 percent of the Bank's: Ibid.
7. "For the last eight": Brady Yauch, "More Money, More Problems: The World Bank's Way," Probe International.org, September 25, 2009, http://www

.probeinternational.org/odious-debts/more-money
-more-problems-world-banks-way.

8. "paints a much": Ibid.

9. "Because there is not": Ibid.

10. African GDP Growth: Ibid.

11. "Economic figures show that": Ibid.

12. "The World Bank's . . . markets": "The World Bank's
Real Problem," *Time*, May 3, 2007, http://www.time
.com/time/magazine/article/0,9171,1617526,00.html.

13. "Now we live in a": Ibid.

14. Sub-Saharan Africa gets: "List of Countries by FDI
Abroad," Wikipedia.org, http://en.wikipedia.org/
wiki/List_of_countries_by_FDI_abroad.

15. And, partially as . . . only 8 percent: "2011 World
Hunger and Poverty Facts and Statistics."

16. Comparison of Sub-Saharan: "2011 World Hunger
and Poverty Facts and Statistics," World Hunger
.com, http://www.worldhunger.org/articles/Learn/
world%20hunger%20facts%202002.htm.

17. Africa $313B: "List of Countries by Received FDI,"
CIA World Factbook, Wikipedia.org, http://en.wiki
pedia.org/wiki/List_of_countries_by_received_FDI.

18. Latin America $1,180B: Ibid.

19. Latin American Foreign: Ibid.

20. Sub-Saharan African: Ibid.

21. In 2010, the bank: "The World Bank Annual Report
2011," WorldBank.org, http://siteresources.world
bank.org/EXTANNREP2011/Resources/8070616-13
15496634380/WBAR11_YearInReview.pdf.

22. "lending and grantmaking": "The World Bank's Real Problem."
23. "aid means . . . aid money": Yauch, "More Money, More Problems: The World Bank's Way."
24. "in Africa particularly": Ibid.
25. "Has more than . . . developing world": Moyo, Introduction to *Dead Aid.*
26. "the most aid-dependent": Moyo, Preface to *Dead Aid.*
27. "The receipt of concessional": Ibid.
28. "is estimated to have: Ibid.
29. Nigerian President . . . to Nigeria: Moyo, *Dead Aid*, page 48.
30. In Uganda in the 1990s: Ibid., page 52.
31. Zambia's current president: Ibid., page 53.
32. In the midst of a: Ibid., page 55.
33. $1.5 billion was transferred: "Bank Scam Threatens Kenya Economy," BBC.co.uk, November 7, 2006, http://news.bbc.co.uk/2/hi/africa/6123832.stm.
34. "the provision of loans": Moyo, Preface to *Dead Aid.*
35. "In a cash-strapped": Moyo, *Dead Aid*, page 59.
36. "removing pressures to": Ibid., page 58.
37. Since 1995, Transparency: Ibid., page 51.
38. $1,000 decrease in personal: Ibid.
39. "around 500,000 people": Ibid., page 54.
40. From 1981 through 2005: Anup Shah, "Poverty Around the World," GlobalIssues.org, November 12, 2010, http://www.globalissues.org/article/4/poverty-around-the-world#WorldBanksPovertyEstimatesRevised.

41. Marvin J. Cetron, founder : "Reduction in Poverty," FutureIndia.org, http://www.futureindia.org/index .php/reduction-in-poverty.
42. "access the international": Moyo, Preface to *Dead Aid*.
43. "large-scale direct": Ibid.
44. "press for genuine": Ibid.
45. "They should encourage": Ibid.
46. "Foreign direct investment": Ibid.
47. "civil-society activists": Christopher Hitchens, "Sliming Wolfowitz," Slate.com, April 17, 2007, http:// www.slate.com/articles/news_and_politics/fighting _words/2007/04/sliming_wol fowitz.html.
48. "The in-house ethicists": "The World Bank's Real Problem."
49. "Mr. Wolfowitz was": "Zoellick's Clean-Up Duty," *Wall Street Journal*, May 31, 2007, http://forum.gon .com/showthread.php?t=117130.
50. "sources inside and outside": Ibid.
51. "despite fierce" . . . her responsibilities: Ibid.
52. Folsom's Institutional Integrity . . . to India: "The World Banks Tolerance for Corruption," September 4, 2007, http://prairiepundit.blogspot.com/2007/09/ world-banks-tolerance-for-corruption.html.
53. "Zoellick would . . . good ones": "World Bank Scorpions," *Wall Street Journal*, May 8, 2008, http://online.wsj.com/article/SB121020217031275183 .html.
54. "sufficient evidence . . . million grant": Ibid.
55. "shove-the-money": Ibid.

56. "For most developmental": Moyo, *Dead Aid*, page 54.
57. "Any non-distributed": Ibid.
58. "This circular logic": Ibid.
59. "Why does the bank": "Zoellick's Clean-Up Duty."
60. "The system by which": Ibid.
61. "dysfunctional institutional culture": Ibid.
62. Compensation of World Bank Staff: "The World Bank Annual Report 2009," WorldBank.org, http://siteresources.worldbank.org/EXTAR2009/Resources/6223977-1252950831873/AR09_Complete.pdf.
63. executive directors earn: Ibid.
64. The bank is the: Ibid.
65. "instead of . . . or commodities": Tom Barkley, "Zoellick Faults G-7, Calls for New Order," *Wall Street Journal*, October 7, 2008, http://online.wsj.com/article/SB122332497193908843.html.
66. "America's days . . . the dollar": Edmund L. Andrews, "World Bank Head Expects Dollar's Role to Diminish," *New York Times*, September 20, 2009, http://query.nytimes.com/gst/fullpage.html?res=9902E6D81E3EF93AA1575AC0A96F9C8B63&ref=robertbzoellick.http://query.nytimes.com/gst/fullpage.html?res=9902E6D81E3EF93AA1575AC0A96F9C8B63&ref=robert bzoellick.

PART NINE

1. increased our foreign aid: "Table 1297. U.S. Government Foreign Grants and Credits by Type and Country: 2000 to 2010."

2. The United States gave: Brian Wingfield, "Making Sense of U.S. Foreign Aid to Egypt and Elsewhere," Forbes.com, January 29, 2011, http://www.forbes.com/sites/brianwingfield/2011/01/29/making-sense-of-u-s-foreign-aid-to-egypt-and-elsewhere/.

3. Thirty-four billion: Grace Vuoto, "Time to Cut All Foreign Aid," *Reflections Magazine*, June–July 2011, http://www.ebireflections.com/printer.php?volume=2&number=7&file=Foreign%20aid.xhtml.

4. Lawmakers cut $6 billion: Susan Cornwell, "U.S. Foreign Aid Escapes Slashing Cuts in Fiscal 2012," Reuters.com, December 19, 2011, http://www.reuters.com/article/2011/12/19/us-usa-aid-id USTRE7BI1KO20111219.

5. Countries Getting More Than: "Table 1299. U.S. Foreign Economic and Military Aid by Major Recipient Country: 2001 to 2009," Census.gov, http://www.census.gov/compendia/statab/2012/tables/12s1299.pdf.

6. Why do we . . . Castro's Cuba: Wingfield, "Making Sense of U.S. Foreign Aid to Egypt and Elsewhere."

7. With Nigeria pumping 2.5: "Operators, Analysts Fault Nigeria's 2.48M B/D Oil Production Estimates for 2012," SweetCrudeReports.com, December 14, 2011, http://sweetcrudereports.com/2011/12/14/operators-analysts-fault-nigerias-2-48m-bd-oil-production-estimates-for-2012/.

8. The Congressional Research . . . Treasury debt): "U.S. Offers Foreign Aid to Countries Holding Billions in Treasury Securities," FoxNews.com, June 3, 2011, http://www.foxnews.com/politics/2011/06/02/

us-offers-foreign-aid-to-countries-holding-billions-in
-treasury-securities/.

9. "If countries can afford": Ibid.

10. "Two Thanksgiving Day Gentlemen": O. Henry, "Two Thanksgiving Day Gentlemen," Literature Collection.com, http://www.literaturecollection.com/ a/o_henry/211/.

11. The almost $60 billion: "Development Aid," Wiki pedia.org, http://en.wikipedia.org/wiki/Development _aid.

12. The only countries: Ibid.

13. In 2010, the United States: "U.S.-African Trade Pro- file," AGOA.gov, http://www.agoa.gov/resources/ US_African_Trade_Profile_2009.pdf.

14. The GDP of sub-Saharan: "List of African Countries by GDP," Wikipedia.org, http://en.wikipedia.org/ wiki/List_of_African_countries_by_GDP_(nominal).

15. "To those peoples": "Inaugural Addresses of the Presi- dents of the United States," Bartleby.com, January 20, 1961, http://www.bartleby.com/124/pres56.html.

16. According to the Heritage: Kim Schaefer, "How Do U.S. Foreign Aid Recipients Vote at the U.N.? Against the U.S."

17. of the top thirty: Ibid.

18. Foreign Aid and Support: Ibid.

19. In 2006 . . . unfavorable rating: "The Decline in America's Reputation: Why?" ForeignAffairs .house.gov, June 11, 2008, http://foreignaffairs.house .gov/110/42566.pdf.

20. An August 2011 survey: Jeffrey Fleishman and Paul Richter, "U.S. Pro-Democracy Effort Rubs Many in Egypt the Wrong Way," *Los Angeles Times*, August 10, 2011, http://articles.latimes.com/2011/aug/10/world/la-fg-us-egypt-20110811.

21. 15 percent of Jordanians: "Severed Head in the Freezer, Favorability Ratings in the Toilet," Com monDreams.org, December 12, 2011, http://lpintak .wordpress.com/2011/12/12/severed-head-in-the -freezer-favorability-ratings-in-the-toilet-common dreams-org/.

22. In Indonesia, America's: "The Decline in America's Reputation: Why?"

23. Latin Americans have: Ibid.

24. "There has really been": Ibid.

25. "certainly over this": Ibid.

26. "Despite the billions": Tawfik Hamid, "Anti-US Countries Should Not Receive Aid," News Max. com, August 18, 2011, http://www.newsmax.com/ TawfikHamid/muslim-egypt-aid/2011/08/18/id/ 407837.

27. "Japan and France": Ibid.

28. OPIC made $2.3: "Overseas Private Investment Corporation, 2010 Annual Report," OPIC.gov, http:// www.opic.gov/sites/default/files/docs/annualreport _2010.pdf.

29. OPIC has generated: Ibid.

30. "For US small businesses": Ibid.

31. OPIC financed . . . 328 units: Ibid.

PART TEN

1. "History repeats itself": "Karl Marx Quotes," ThinkExist.com, http://thinkexist.com/quotation/history_repeats_itself-first_as_tragedy-second_as/.

2. "When the western": Leah Soibel, "Iran in Our Own Backyard: Hezbollah Operatives Are Rampant in Remote Areas of Latin America," *New York Daily News*, December 22, 2011, http://www.nydailynews.com/opinion/iran-backyard-hezbollah-operatives-rampant-remote-areas-latin-america-article-1.995069?localLinksEnabled=false.

3. "Venezuela purchased 10": Martin Arostegui, "Iran Tries to Gain Sway in Latin America," *Wall Street Journal*, December 6, 2011, http://online.wsj.com/article/SB10001424052970203503204577040594039247890.html.

4. "an increased presence": Ibid.

5. "to strengthen its . . . Brazil": Soibel, "Iran in Our Own Backyard: Hezbollah Operatives Are Rampant in Remote Areas of Latin America."

6. "most important center": Ibid.

7. net $20 million: Ibid.

8. "the direct involvement": Jo Becker, "Beirut Bank Seen as a Hub of Hezbollah's Financing," *New York Times*, December 13, 2011, http://www.nytimes.com/2011/12/14/world/middleeast/beirut-bank-seen-as-a-hub-of-hezbollahs-financing.html?smid=tw-nytimes&seid=auto.

9. Venezuela did . . . return empty: Arostegui, "Iran Tries to Gain Sway in Latin America."

10. "various European newspaper": Ibid.
11. "of supplying uranium": Ibid.
12. In 2008, the Bush: Ibid.
13. Mr. Al Din was: Ibid.
14. Venezuela and Iran: Ibid.
15. "we worry about these": "Alarm Grows in Congress, U.S. Intelligence, Over Iran's Latin America Threat," TheDailyBeast.com, December 15, 2011, http://www .thedailybeast.com/articles/2011/12/15/alarm-grows-in -congress-u-s-intelligence-over-iran-s-latin-america -threat.html.
16. "Venezuela is the port": Ibid.
17. $2.5 billion in 2005: Christopher Swan, Chavez Exploits Oil to Lend in Latin America, Push- ing IMF Aside," Bloomberg.com, February 27, 2007, http://www.bloomberg.com/apps/news?pid =newsarchive&sid=atN8OPWGA4nE.
18. $800,000 in cash: Rory Carroll, "Suitcase Full of Cash Adds to Chavez Corruption Claims," Guard- ian, September 20, 2008, http://www.guardian.co.uk/ theobserver/2008/sep/21/usa.venezuela.
19. "They discussed a plot": Ryan Mauro, "Iran, Venezuela, Cuba and the Cyber Threat," Front PageMag.com, December 23, 2011, http://frontpagemag.com/2011/ 12/23/iran-venezuela-cuba-and-the-cyber-threat/.
20. "Like Ghadiri she was": Ibid.
21. "said he and other": Eli Lake, "Alarm Grows in Con- gress, U.S. Intelligence, Over Iran's Latin America Threat," AmericasForum.com, December 15, 2011, http://americasforum.com/content/alarm-grows-con

gress-us-intelligence-over-iran%E2%80%99s-latin
-america-threat.

22. "revealed . . . the involvement": Mauro, "Iran, Venezuela, Cuba and the Cyber Threat."

23. "The Venezuelan state": Mary Anastasia O'Grady, "Chavez May Be Violating Iran Sanctions," *Wall Street Journal*, March 7, 2011, http://online.wsj.com/article/SB10001424052748703867704576182591335200636.html.

24. CISADA has . . . of lading: Ibid.

25. "with hundreds . . . central Libya": Colum Lynch, Jeffrey Smith, and Jody Warrick, "Iran May Have Sent Libya Shells for Chemical Weapons," *Washington Post*, November 20, 2011, http://www.washingtonpost.com/world/national-security/iran-may-have-sent-libya-shells-for-chemical-weapons/2011/11/18/gIQA7RPifN_story.html.

26. 'We are pretty': Ibid.

27. "To get top dollar": O'Grady, "Chavez May Be Violating Iran Sanctions."

28. "actions, which have": Associated Press, "Obama Criticizes Venezuela's Ties to Iran, Cuba," SFGate.com, December 19, 2011, http://articles.sfgate.com/2011-12-19/world/30536706_1_venezuelan-people-venezuelan-president-hugo-chavez-venezuelan-newspaper.

29. "In Venezuela, we have": Ibid.

30. "It's unfortunate that": Ibid.

31. "I would argue": Ibid.

32. "Ultimately, it is . . . closely": Ibid.

PART ELEVEN

1. "130 countries spent": Knott, "Lobbying by Foreign Countries Decreases."

2. the Podesta Group: "Podesta Group," InfluenceEx plorer.com, http://influenceexplorer.com/organization/ podesta-group/e02f39d9e0c544a78f68d4fee249551b.

3. In July 2011, two: Kim Barker and Habiba Nosheen, "Man Behind Pakistan Spy Agency's Plot to Influence Washington," ProPublica.org, October 3, 2011, http://www.propublica.org/article/the-man-behind -pakistani-spy-agencys-plot-to-influence-washing ton/single.

4. over $40 million: James Hohmann, "Newt Collects $37+Million from Health Care Company," Politico .com, November 18, 2011, http://www.politico.com/ morningscore/1111/morningscore462.html.

5. $1.6 million to advise: "Did Newt Gingrich Play a Part in Freddie Mac's Fundraising Scandal?" The Atlantic .com, November 17, 2011, http://www.theatlantic .com/politics/archive/2011/11/did-newt-gingrich-play -a-part-in-freddie-macs-fundraising-scandal/248 617/.

6. "Lobbyists and . . . money's worth": "Minting Bank Lobbyists on Capitol Hill," New York Times, April 13, 2010, http://dealbook.nytimes.com/2010/04/13/ minting-bank-lobbyists-on-capitol-hill/.

7. $2,799,849 to Congressional: "Campaign Finance," InfluenceExplorer.com, http://influenceexplorer .com/organization/livingston-group/4326614fea87489 eaa1602e6b9c6c69f.

8. "Qaddafi established terrorist": Eben Kaplan, "How Libya Got Off the List," CRF.org, October 16, 2007, http://www.cfr.org/libya/libya-got-off-list/p10855.

9. $2.7 billion to: Jackie Northam, "Moammar Gadhafi Ruled Libya with an Iron Fist," NPR.org, October 20, 2011, http://www.npr.org/2011/10/20/134128567/moammar-gadhafi-ruled-libya-with-an-iron-fist.

10. Perle was hired: Laura Rozen, "Among Libya's Lobbyists," Politico.com, February 21, 2011, http://www.politico.com/blogs/laurarozen/0211/Among_Libyas_lobbyists.html.

11. "At a critical . . . the future": Ibid.

12. "Richard Perle": Ibid.

13. "Perle made two visits": Ibid.

14. "continue the cultivation": Ibid.

15. "proved problematic for": Paul Blumenthal, "U.S. Companies Lobbied to Keep Libyan Market Open for Business," SunlightFoundation.com, February 23, 2011, http://sunlightfoundation.com/blog/2011/02/23/u-s-companies-lobbied-to-keep-libyan-market-open-for-business-2/.

16. "cables show that": Ibid.

17. "For the large part": Ibid.

18. "ensure that the": "S Res 320 in Congressional Session 109," ThePoliticalGuide.com, http://www.thepoliticalguide.com/Legislation/Senate/109/S%20Res%20320/.

19. In 1915, there were: "Fact Sheet: Armenian Genocide," UMich.edu, http://www.umd.umich.edu/dept/armenian/facts/genocide.html.

20. "the Armenians . . . at sea": Ibid.
21. "A few years ago": "Dick Gephardt," Armeniapedia .org, http://www.armeniapedia.org/index.php?title =Dick_Gephardt.
22. "Gephardt attended a": Ibid.
23. "We implore . . . genocide": Ibid.
24. In 2007, Turkey retained: Ibid.
25. "These new Department": "Armenian National Committee of America," ANCA.org, June 5, 2007, http://www.anca.org/press_releases/press_releases.php ?prid=1199.
26. "Mr. Gephardt was a": "Hon. Richard Gephardt, President & CEO," GephardtGroup.com, http://www.gephardtgroup.com/pages/team.html.
27. "Congressman Dick Gephardt": Bryan M. Corbin, "The Uses and Effects of Negative Political Television Advertisements in the 1988 Presidential Election," CardinalScholar.bsu.edu, April 16, 1990, http://cardinalscholar.bsu.edu/bitstream/handle/189919/1/C677_1990CorbinBryanM.pdf.
28. "[t]here is nothing": Robert Shogan, "Presidential Campaign Skirmish Erupts," *Los Angeles Times*, May 28, 1997, http://articles.latimes.com/1997 -05-28/news/mn-63118_1_democratic-presidential -campaign.
29. "where the company": Loretta Chao, Farnaz Fassihi, and Steve Stecklow, "Huawei to Scale Back Business in Iran," *Wall Street Journal*, December 10, 2011, http://online.wsj.com/article/SB100014240529702043 19004577088001900708704.html.

30. "As the Republic": "Engagement of Patton Boggs LLP," FARA.gov, http://www.fara.gov/docs/2165 -Exhibit-AB-20100204-23.pdf.
31. "Nevertheless, as suggested": Ibid.
32. "cast a long shadow": Ibid.

CONCLUSION

1. "A Republic, madame, if you": "Respectfully Quoted: A Dictionary of Quotations," Bartleby.com, http:// www.bartleby.com/73/1593.html.

Acknowledgments

Our thanks and gratitude go out to our editor, Adam Bellow; to our agent and friend, Stan Pottinger; to our diligent researcher Morgan Buehler, whom we've worked with on five books; to our newest researcher, Christopher Liotta; and to our friend and illustrator Clayton Liotta, who did the cartoons and the cover design. Also, once more, many thanks to our talented staff—Tom, Irma, and Liam Gallagher and Maureen Maxwell. Thanks to Jim Duggan for his excellent editorial work on the manuscript. And thank you to Barry Elias, our economist friend, for his assistance in grappling with the complex economic issues.

About the Authors

Dick Morris served as Bill Clinton's political consultant for twenty years. A regular political commentator on Fox News, he is the author of ten *New York Times* bestsellers (all with Eileen McGann) and one *Washington Post* bestseller.

Eileen McGann is an attorney who, with her husband, Dick, writes columns for the *New York Post* and for their website, dickmorris.com. She has written extensively about the abuses of Congress and the need for reform.